8

POWERS OF THE
PRESIDENT
DURING CRISES

Da Capo Press Reprints in

AMERICAN CONSTITUTIONAL AND LEGAL HISTORY

GENERAL EDITOR: LEONARD W. LEVY

Claremont Graduate School

POWERS OF THE PRESIDENT DURING CRISES

By
J. Malcolm Smith
and
Cornelius P. Cotter

DA CAPO PRESS • NEW YORK • 1972

Library of Congress Cataloging in Publication Data

Smith, John Malcolm.
    Powers of the President during crises.

    (Da Capo Press reprints in American constitutional
and legal history)
    Bibliography: p.
    1. Executive power—U.S.   2. U.S.—Constitu-
tional history.   I. Cotter, Cornelius P., joint
author.   II. Title.
[JK516.S66 1972]   353'.032   71-39371
ISBN 0-306-70462-5

This Da Capo Press edition of *Powers of the President During
Crises* is an unabridged republication of the first edition published
in Washington, D.C., in 1960. It is reprinted by special arrangement with the Public Affairs Press.

Published by Da Capo Press, Inc.
A Subsidiary of Plenum Publishing Corporation
227 West 17th Street
New York, New York 10011

Manufactured in the United States of America

POWERS
OF THE
PRESIDENT
DURING
CRISES

POWERS
OF THE
PRESIDENT
DURING
CRISES

J. Malcolm Smith
and
Cornelius P. Cotter

PUBLIC AFFAIRS PRESS
WASHINGTON, D. C.

FOREWORD

The use of emergency power in a democracy raises many questions relative to the constitutional basis for its authorization and the manner of its exercise. If used too little and too late a democratic state might be destroyed when the proper use of the emergency power possibly could have saved it. If used arbitrarily and capriciously, its use could degenerate into the worst form of dictatorship.

As a boy I was the chauffeur for a country doctor. One day while driving to see a patient who was gravely ill, the doctor opened his medicine chest and pointed to a glass vial containing morphine. "That drug," he said, "is the most potent medicine in my chest but requires great skill in prescribing. Used properly it relieves pain and suffering. Used improperly it makes animals of men." Emergency power bears to government the same general relationship of morphine to man. Used properly in a democratic state it never supplants the constitution and the statutes but is restorative in nature. Used improperly it bceomes the very essence of tyranny.

By reference to particular statutes and specific instances this volume affords a graphic picture of the broad extent to which emergency power has been employed by the United States government in recent years. Many will view this development with alarm for the many instances of its use make a lengthy list. Military emergency today is but one type of national emergency. Catastrophies and economic emergencies may also require the exercise of this type of power. Indeed, its use in this day and time has been so frequent that the very term "emergency" is being "shorn of meaning."

In the present volume the authors describe and comment upon the use of emergency power in the United States since 1933. It is their contention that the use of emergency power was contemplated and provided for in the Constitution. The law also provides restraints upon its use. As Professor McIlwain has concluded, the proper test of constitutionalism is the existence of adequate processes for keeping government responsible. It is comforting to know that these processes exist within our government. The primary requirement of all Americans, then, is to keep government responsible and within these limitations, for only when this is done can emergency power be justified under the law of the land.

The always present danger is that emergency power may be used by an officer or an agency of the government in order to have its own way when constitutional or other legal restrictions might irritate or interfere. This danger can be lessened by the selection of good governmental personnel, but removed to a greater degree by the enforcement of these constitutional and statutory limitations which are made effective at times by resort to judicial review.

Readers will be indebted to the authors for this first exhaustive account of the actual use of emergency power by the United States government since 1933. The restraint on the freedom of the individual, the regulation of private enterprise, the control of communications are but some of the topics that receive minute and careful treatment. Some readers will be concerned with the frequency of the resort to emergency power and will view with uneasiness, as does this writer, the possible curtailment of individual rights. Yet the authors would be the first to agree with the statement that, "Freedom and civil liberties, far from being incompatible with security, are vital to our national strength." Security and rights are here made interdependent. Others will take satisfaction in the flexibility of the United States government that can maintain its democratic character and still have the means of preserving its existence under the tremendous pressure of a world war and periods of economic crises. Irrespective of attitude, the present volume is a telling account of the manner in which the government of the United States has been made adaptable under the Constitution to the problems and exigencies of the modern world.

ROBERT S. RANKIN

Washington, D. C.

PREFACE

A preface is a kind of last call to dinner, as it were, in which the authors suggest the purpose of their undertaking, chart the course they have chosen to pursue, and acknowledge the help they have received.

This study of the President's use of emergency powers grew out of research and discussions in Washington, D. C., and at Harvard, the University of California, and other institutions. In one sense, it is a sequel to Dr. Cotter's study of emergency powers in Great Britain, prepared under Harvard's Sheldon Travelling Fellowship during the academic year 1951-52.

In preparing a political science course at the University of California's Riverside campus, one of the most significant gaps in available sources and treatises about the Presidency concerned the vast range of power, generally called emergency powers, available to the Chief Executive should he choose to follow the prescription used by many predecessors, notably F.D.R.

Both authors have, of course, profited from the monumental work of Professor Edward S. Corwin, whose classic study, *The President: Office and Powers* remains the outstanding work in the field. Professor Robert S. Rankin's study, *When the Civil Law Fails*, contained valuable historical data of particular importance. Both authors have also had the inestimable privilege and opportunity of studying under Professor Charles Fairman, now at Harvard Law School. Professor Fairman's study, *The Law of Martial Rule*, was very helpful in providing the historical setting for government under military control. The authors were fortunate in having read Professor Fairman's paper delivered at the National War College, "A Post-Atomic Attack Situation," wherein it is clearly brought forth that a complete plan and pattern for dealing with a nuclear attack must be worked out that does envisage the restoration of civil government to the nation as quickly as circumstances permit, should the cold war ever turn into an all-out nuclear holocaust.

While the original work on the manuscript was completed before either of the authors came to Washington, both have benefitted from the experience of working in the Pentagon, the Commission on

vii

Civil Rights, the Republican National Committee and the U. S. Senate. One is apt to view the executive branch of government from a slightly different perspective, once having been associated with "the Hill." And, while the Congress may feel powerless to act against a determined Chief Executive, the power of the purse still provides the most effective of all the "checks and balances" in our national government, except in time of war.

The Fund for the Republic provided the authors with a grant-in-aid in 1955 to begin work on the book, although the Fund had no contact or association with the authors during the preparation of the manuscript.

Parts of some chapters have previously appeared as article in the *Western Political Quarterly* and *The Journal of Politics,* and the authors wish to acknowledge their appreciation at being able to reproduce all or parts of these articles.

Mr. Warren Campbell served as a helpful research assistant while a graduate student at Stanford and rendered invaluable aid. Dr. Norman Small of the American Law Division of the Library of Congress performed an essential editorial task in reading the entire manuscript and suggesting very useful changes.

The authors are both grateful to Mrs. Connie Smith, a patient wife, who spent long, dreary hours typing and re-typing the manuscript. And, last, but by no means least, the authors reserve a special vote of the very deepest appreciation to the Executive Director of Public Affairs Press, Mr. M. B. Schnapper whose patience, confidence and continued good humor made publication possible.

J. MALCOLM SMITH AND CORNELIUS P. COTTER

Washington, D. C.

CONTENTS

ABOUT THE AUTHORS

J. Malcolm Smith received his education at the U.S. Naval Academy, the University of Washington, and Stanford University. After three years as an officer in the Army during World War II, he received an A.B. degree from the University of Washington in 1946, and an M.A. (1948) and Ph.D. (1951) from Stanford University. He has combined academic and governmental service since he began his career as an instructor in political science at Stanford University in 1947. He has taught at Columbia University and the University of California. He organized the first World Affairs Council in Los Angeles, for the Foreign Policy Association and served as its first Executive Director from 1952-54.

Since coming to Washington, D. C., Mr. Smith served as a consultant to the Assistant Secretary of the Air Force (1957-58), and the President's Commission on Civil Rights (1958-59) before joining the staff of Senator Thomas H. Kuchel of California as Assistant to the Minority Whip of the U.S. Senate.

Cornelius P. Cotter began his academic career at Stanford University in 1946 following three years as a Navy Seabee in the Pacific during the Second World War. He received his A.B. in 1949 from Stanford, and an M.P.A. (1951) and Ph.D. in government (1953) from Harvard University. He was a Sheldon Travelling Fellow from Harvard University to the University of London from 1951-52. After serving as Instructor in Government at Columbia University 1952-53, he returned to his alma mater, Stanford, in 1953 as an Assistant Professor of Political Science. He is currently on leave as an Associate Professor from Stanford University to serve as a special assistant to the Chairman of the Republican National Committee, Senator Thruston B. Morton. From December 1958 to December 1959, he served as the Citizenship Clearinghouse Fellow to the Republican National Committee.

The authors have contributed to the Western Political Quarterly, Stanford Law Review, the Journal of Politics, and the Midwestern Political Science Review. Currently they are collaborating on a textbook in American Government.

This study of presidential emergency powers was initiated by the authors in 1955 while teaching at Stanford and the University of California; revision and expansion were undertaken in Washington, D. C., during 1959 and 1960.

CHAPTER I

INTRODUCTION

The general welfare, and military effectiveness of a modern industrial nation depend upon the harmonious interaction of a complex, interdependent network of production and transportation facilities. The interruption of this process at any of a myriad of critical points can disrupt the supply of essential civilian and military materials, possibly undermining the economic health or military security of the nation.[1] The urban concentration of population and the refinement of communication devices and techniques for manipulating public opinion make it increasingly possible to instill in the civilian population an hysteria and terror which could effectively thwart national mobilization.[2] Realization of the magnitude of the problem, and a pervasive fear of military assault, vitally influence the process of continuous redefinition of the balance between collective authority and individual liberty which is the essential task of democratic government in war as in peace. Emergency government has become the norm for twentieth century constitutional states.

An assessment of the adequacy with which democratic government has, in the recurrent economic and military emergencies since 1933, combined mobilization of "the ... power of every individual and of every material resource at its command"[3] toward the objective of national survival and well-being, with the protection of basic individual freedoms and the principle of responsible government which are the heart of democracy, must in substantial part rest upon an analysis of the contents of the statute books. That is the purpose of this study. Its classification of legislative delegations of emergency powers to the executive since 1933 should provide not only indication of the extent to which coercive powers over persons and property have been granted the executive in the name of emergency, but also a framework for the organization of a series of studies into the use of such powers by the executive branch, and the success of congressional and other efforts to maintain responsible administration in time of emergency.

There exists no dearth of recorded efforts to define the ultimate

1

scope of the constitutional emergency power of the American executive. Various justices of the Supreme Court have hypothesized, at one end of a continuum, inflexible constitutional restraints upon executive response to perceived emergency,[4] and at the other end an emergency power which is either unrestrained[5] or unrestrainable.[6] In this manner the Supreme Court has sought to resolve the conundrum, "How can a virtually unlimited emergency power and a systematic body of constitutional limitations upon government action logically coexist? How can constitutionalism be ought but an anachronism in the twentieth century unless constitutional governments are equipped with adequate legal authority to carry the body politic through economic and military emergencies of staggering dimensions?"

The considerable body of scholarly literature in this field is principally devoted to speculation on the breadth of the "inherent," "residual," "executive," or "war" power of the President, and description of occasions on which the nation's chief executives have considered it necessary to exercise a prerogative "power to act according to discretion for the public good, without the prescription of the law and sometimes even against it."[7] But despite such incidents as President Roosevelt's 1942 Labor Day speech admonishing the Congress that unless it repealed certain provisions of the Emergency Price Control Act by October 1st, he would consider them repealed,[8] emergency administration is overwhelmingly characterized by joint participation and cooperation of the varying branches of the federal government. American government in time of war does not degenerate to anything resembling dictatorship, and to focus attention upon the exceptions to executive-legislative cooperation in war administration is to study the pathology of emergency administration.

The statute books provide at any given time a more accurate indication of the breadth and limits of executive emergency power than do exegeses on the Constitution, or histories emphasizing executive action unsupported by Congress. For in theory[9] and in practice the President will resort to an "inherent" emergency power only to the extent to which Congress has failed to anticipate and prescribe remedial action for such an emergency. On the assumption that a detailed study of the emergency powers which have been delegated to the executive by Congress in the immediate past provides insight into the probable range of such powers which will be exercised by government in the future, the authors have undertaken to survey and classify such delegations in the period 1933 to 1955.[10]

It is believed that the accumulation in selected contexts of the instances of legislative delegation of emergency power will provide striking revelation of the scope and detail of control over individuals and groups which is practiced by constitutional governments in time of emergency. To this we now turn.

CHAPTER II

THE CONCEPT OF EMERGENCY IN DEMOCRATIC POLITICAL THOUGHT

When President Eisenhower on June 16, 1955 suspended the privilege of the writ of *habeas corpus* and declared a nationwide state of mock martial law, in response to simulated A-bomb and H-bomb attacks taking a toll of some 14 million civilian casualties, he acted on the premise that the ordinary processes of democratic and constitutional government do not suffice to protect the state in time of emergency and must surrender to a modified authoritarian regime.[1] This premise is deeply embedded in the teachings of democratic political theory, which in its traditional and contemporary expression have counseled the need to abandon the processes of democratic government as the first essential response to emergency conditions.

Thus, ironically, the Western democracies which today approach the close of three decades of economic and military emergency, and turn their faces to additional decades in the shadow-land between peace and war, are offered a guiding theory which regards emergency governance as an aberration, supplanting the relationships between the various branches of government, and between rulers and ruled which prevail in "normal" times. In theory the struggle to preserve limited and popularly responsible government has already been lost, for this is a luxury we are told we cannot afford.

In the United States we have been especially prone to accept the alleged need for transition from responsible to authoritarian government in time of emergency, for we have on the one hand accepted an interpretation of the Constitution whereunder the rigid restraints imposed thereby on governmental power are susceptible of contradiction in time of emergency, and on the other hand we have with considerable complacence assigned to the Supreme Court the function of protecting the essentials of constitutionalism and democracy through periods of emergency. These two attitudes combine to enhance the sense of need and lull the fear of supposedly temporary reversions to authoritarian government.

In the belief that it is increasingly essential that emergency action be sustained by a workable and empirically-based theory of democratic emergency governance, the authors have undertaken, in the present study, to survey the treatment of emergency by democratic political theorists; to review the work of the Supreme Court in assessing the validity of governmental exercises of emergency powers (placing special emphasis upon the implications of the 1952 "Steel Seizure" cases); and, in conclusion, to submit tentatively an approach to emergency which they consider related to the needs of today and the realities of recent experience.

Democratic political theorists traditionally have assumed the need in time of emergency to subvert the governmental processes prescribed for peacetime and to rely upon a generically different method of government, frequently designated "constitutional dictatorship." Many factors contribute to this tendency.

First, it must be recognized that a theory of democratic government so comprehensive as to traverse every vicissitude which might confront it cannot reasonably be demanded of political philosophers.

Second, a certain amount of inertia is inevitable in any phase of man's endeavors. Thus it is not surprising that political theorists to date have picked up the traditional interpretation of emergency in terms of the Roman dictatorship and fitted it to their schemes of constitutional government. It is a safely ambiguous doctrine with the respectability of age. It invests an aspect of the experience of constitutional democracies, about which very little in the way of cumulative knowledge has been attained, with an aura of reassuring and doctrinaire certainty.

A third factor influencing the casual reliance of democratic theorists on emergency dictatorship is the tendency to polarize the concept of "limited" government and the supposed need for "unlimited" emergency action. This is related to the tendency to exaggerate substantively limited (enumerated) powers, and compartmentalized powers as integral elements in the concept of constitutionalism.[*] In positing rigidly circumscribed and divided governmental powers, one posits a need contingent upon emergency to transcend such limitations. The doctrine of constitutional dictatorship fulfills this need.

DEMOCRATIC POLITICAL THEORISTS

John Locke, describing the architecture of civil government, called upon the English doctrine of prerogative to cope with the problem of emergency. In times of danger to the nation, positive law set down by the legislature might be inadequate or even a fatal obstacle to the promptness of action necessary to avert catastrophe. In these situations the Crown retained a prerogative "power to act according to discretion for the public good, without the prescription of the law and sometimes even against it."[1] The prerogative "can be nothing but the people's permitting their rulers to do several things of their own free choice where the law is silent, and sometimes too against the direct letter of the law, for the public good and their acquiescing in it when so done."[2]

Properly the prerogative was exercisable only for the public good. But Locke recognized that this moral restraint might not suffice to avoid abuse of prerogative powers. When one government has utilized prerogative powers for the public good, a successor may retain the habit or resort to such powers, utilizing them for a less worthy purpose.[3] Who shall judge the need for resorting to the prerogative, and how may its abuse be avoided? Here Locke, too, readily admits defeat, suggesting that "the people have no other remedy in this, as in all other cases where they have no judge on earth, but to appeal to Heaven."[4]

Rousseau also assumed the need for temporary suspension of democratic processes of government in time of emergency:

"The inflexibility of the laws, which prevents them from adapting themselves to circumstances, may, in certain cases, render them disastrous, and make them bring about, at a time of crisis, the ruin of the State . . .

"It is wrong therefore to wish to make political institutions so strong as to render it impossible to suspend their operation. Even Sparta allowed its laws to lapse.

". . . If . . . the peril is of such a kind that the paraphernalia of the laws are an obstacle to their preservation, the method is to nominate a supreme ruler, who shall silence all the laws and suspend for a moment the sovereign authority. In such a case, there is no doubt about the general will, and it is clear that the people's first intention is that the State shall not perish. Thus the suspension of the legislative authority is in no sense its abolition; the magistrate who silences it cannot make it speak; he dominates it, but cannot represent it. He can do anything, except make laws."[5]

Rousseau did not fear the abuse of the emergency dictatorship or "supreme magistracy" as he termed it. It would more likely be cheapened by "indiscreet use."[6]

He would rely upon a tenure of office of prescribed duration to avoid perpetuation of the dictatorship:

"However this important trust be conferred, it is important that its duration should be fixed at a very brief period, incapable of being ever prolonged. In the crises which lead to its adoption, the State is either soon lost, or soon saved; and, the present need passed, the dictatorship becomes either tyrannical or idle. At Rome, where dictators held office for six months only, most of them abdicated before their time was up. If their term had been longer, they might well have tried to prolong it still further, as the decemvirs did when chosen for a year. The dictator had only time to provide against the need that had caused him to be chosen; he had none to think of further projects."[7]

Rousseau was unwilling to rely upon an "appeal to Heaven."

John Stuart Mill concluded his ardent defense of representative government with a shattering aside: "I am far from condemning, in cases of extreme necessity, the assumption of absolute power in the form of a temporary dictatorship."[8] This is not a loose usage of the term "dictatorship," but a forthright support of a grant of "absolute power" to the dictator.

Just as in political theory the nineteenth century liberals neglected adequately to provide for the problems which war creates, so also in their economic theory they ignored the dislocations of a war period. In his study of war in the nineteenth century,[9] Edmund Silberner has shown how the liberals' repugnance to the destructiveness of war, their conviction of its immorality and stupidity, coupled with their faith that the economic and cultural bonds which would be created among nations by extensive free trade would prevent future wars, caused them to neglect adequate theoretical treatment of the problem of war in their economic thought. Silberner points out, for example, that in his chief work, *Elements of Political Economy* (1821), James Mill virtually does not deal at all with war.[10] And Mill's distinguished son is brief on the subject of war. John Stuart Mill, according to Silberner's interpretation, seemed to admit that virtually everything that can be said on this theme had already been expressed before him.[11]

Thus do democratic political theorists tacitly admit the existence of a fatal defect in any system of constitutional democracy: Its processes are inadequate to confront and overcome emergency.

MACHIAVELLI

Machiavelli's view of emergency powers as one element in the whole scheme of limited government furnishes an ironic contrast to the Lockean theory of prerogative. He recognized and attempted to bridge this chasm in democratic political theory:

"Now in a well-ordered republic it should never be necessary to resort to extra-constitutional measures; for although they may for the time be beneficial, yet the precedent is pernicious, for if the practice is once established of disregarding the laws for good objects, they will in a little while be disregarded under that pretext for evil purposes. Thus no republic will ever be perfect if she has not by law provided for everything, having a remedy for every emergency, and fixed rules for applying it."[1]

Machiavelli attempted, perhaps without complete success, but with greater caution than the later theorists, to design a system of constitutionalized emergency powers.

The incumbent executive authority, on finding that an emergency existed, could appoint a temporary "dictator"[2] on the Roman model. The constitution was not suspended, and the emergency executive did not enjoy absolute power. His narrow function was to cope with the emergency.[3] He operated under the surveillance of the regularly constituted legislators and government officials. A key element of Machiavelli's scheme was a short term of office—"and I call a year or more a long time."

Thus Machiavelli—in contrast to Locke, Rousseau and Mill—sought to incorporate into the constitution a regularized system of standby emergency powers to be invoked with suitable checks and controls in time of national danger. He attempted forthrightly to meet the problem of combining a capacious reserve of power and speed and vigor in its application in time of emergency, with effective constitutional restraints.

CONTEMPORARY THEORISTS

Contemporary political theorists, addressing themselves to the problem of response to emergency by constitutional democracies, have employed the doctrine of constitutional dictatorship. Criticism of their schemes for emergency governance is made difficult by the ambiguities latent in the terminology they adopt. An effort is made below to distinguish between those who mean dictatorship when they say dictatorship, and those who say dictatorship when they mean to refer to any effort by constitutional government to respond adequately to emergency conditions. However idiosyncratic the individual definitions of dictatorship, the theories of constitutional dictatorship explicit or implicitly posit a transition in time of emergency from the processes of constitutionalism to those of an outright or slightly modified authoritarian system.

Frederick M. Watkins, who is responsible for the classic study of the Weimar experience with emergency powers,[1] appears to have based his general discussion of emergency powers upon *a priori* reasoning rather than upon empirical research.[2] Provided it "serves to protect established institutions from the danger of permanent injury in a period of temporary emergency, and is followed by a prompt return to the previous forms of political life," Watkins can see "no reason why absolutism should not be used as a means for the defense of liberal institutions."[3] He recognized the two key elements of the problem of emergency governance, as well as all constitutional governance: increasing administrative powers of the executive while at the same time "imposing limitations upon that power."[4] He rejects legislative checks upon the exercise of executive emergency powers as an effective method of imposing such limitations, for "it is clearly unrealistic to rely on a government-controlled majority in the legislature to exercise effective supervision over that same government in its use of emergency powers."[5] On the other hand, judicial review of executive emergency action on its merits is regarded with admiration tempered only by regret at the delay inherent in judicial proceedings.[6]

Watkins places his real faith in a scheme of "constitutional dictatorship." These are the conditions of success of such a dictatorship: "The period of dictatorship must be relatively short . . . Dictatorship should always be strictly legitimate in character . . . Final authority to determine the need for dictatorship in any given case must never rest with the dictator himself . . ."[7] The objective of such an emergency dictatorship should be "strict political conservatism."

"Radical social and economic measures may, of course, be necessary as a means of preventing political change . . . Boldly inventive as it may be in other directions, however, a truly constitutional dictatorship must always aim at the maintenance of an existing *status quo* in the field of constitutional law. Deviations from the established norms of political action may be necessary for the time being. The function of a truly constitutional dictatorship is to provide such deviations and at the same time to make sure that they do not go any further than is actually necessary under the circumstances."[8]

Carl J. Friedrich casts his analysis in terms similar to those of Watkins.[9] It is a problem of concentrating power—in a government where power has consciously been divided—"to cope with . . . situations of unprecedented magnitude and gravity."[10] There must be a

broad grant of powers, subject to equally strong limitations as to who
shall exercise such powers, when, for how long, and to what end."[11]
Professor Friedrich, too, offers criteria for judging the adequacy of
any scheme of emergency powers. The emergency executive ("dictator") must be appointed by constitutional means—*i.e.*, he must
be legitimate; he should not himself enjoy power to determine the
existence of an emergency (and here, strangely enough, he finds the
United States and Great Britain conforming to the criterion); emergency powers should be exercised under a strict time limitation; and
last, the objective of emergency action must be the defense of the
constitutional order.[12]

Recognizing that "there are no ultimate institutional safeguards
available for insuring that emergency powers be used for the purpose
of preserving the constitution" excepting "the people's own determination to see them so used," Friedrich nonetheless sees some in-
definite but influential role which the courts, even though "help-
less in the face of a real emergency," may play to restrict the use
of emergency powers to legitimate goals. They may "act as a sort
of keeper of the President's and the people's conscience."[13]

Clinton L. Rossiter, after surveying the recent history of the employment of emergency powers in Great Britain, France, Weimar
Germany, and the United States, reverts to a description of a scheme
of "constitutional dictatorship" as solution to the vexing problems
presented by emergency.[14] Like Watkins and Friedrich, he is concerned to state, *a priori*, the conditions of success of the "constitutional dictatorship."

"1. No general regime or particular institution of constitutional
dictatorship should be initiated unless it is necessary or even indispensable to the preservation of the state and its constitutional
order . . .

"2. . . . the decision to institute a constitutional dictatorship should
never be in the hands of the man or men who will constitute the
dictator . . ."[15]

"3. No government should initiate a constitutional dictatorship
without making specific provision for its termination . . .

"4. . . . all uses of emergency powers and all readjustments in the
organization of the government should be effected in pursuit of constitutional or legal requirements . . .

"5. . . . no dictatorial institution should be adopted, no right invaded, no regular procedure altered any more than is absolutely
necessary for the conquest of the particular crisis . . .

"6. The measures adopted in the prosecution of a constitutional dictatorship should never be permanent in character or effect . . .

"7. The dictatorship should be carried on by persons representative of every part of the citizenry interested in the defense of the existing constitutional order . . .

"8. Ultimate responsibility should be maintained for every action taken under a constitutional dictatorship . . .

"9. The decision to terminate a constitutional dictatorship, like the decision to institute one, should never be in the hands of the man or men who constitute the dictator . . .

"10. No constitutional dictatorship should extend beyond the termination of the crisis for which it was instituted . . .

"11. . . . the termination of the crisis must be followed by as complete a return as possible to the political and governmental conditions existing prior to the initiation of the constitutional dictatorship . . ."[16]

Rossiter accords to the legislature (in the case of the United States, at any rate) a far greater role in the oversight of executive exercise of emergency powers than does Watkins. He would secure to Congress final responsibility for declaring the existence or termination of an emergency,[17] and he places great faith in the effectiveness of congressional investigating committees.[18] In this work he offers no clear statement of the proposed relationship of the judiciary to his scheme of "constitutional dictatorship." In a subsequent study, he concluded on the basis of a critical review of the Supreme Court that it was impotent "as overseer and interpreter of the war powers."[19]

CONTEMPORARY THEORIES IN THE LIGHT OF RECENT EXPERIENCE.

The suggestion that democracies surrender the control of government to an authoritarian ruler in time of grave danger to the nation is not based upon sound constitutional theory, or the experience of Great Britain or the United States in this century.

To appraise emergency powers—in spite of all experience to the contrary—in terms of the Procrustean mold of constitutional dictatorship serves merely to distort the problem and hinder realistic analysis. It matters not whether the term "dictator" is used in its normal sense (as applied to recent authoritarian rulers) or is employed as Friedrich makes explicit[1] and Rossiter implies, to embrace all chief executives administering emergency powers. However used, "constitutional dictatorship" cannot be divorced from the implication of suspension of the processes of constitutionalism. Suspension is required because constitutionalism is viewed as a system imposing and providing inflexible safeguards against evasion of these limitations.

A concept of constitutionalism which is less misleading in the analysis of problems of emergency powers, and which is consistent with the findings of this study, is that formulated by Charles H. McIlwain.[2] While it does not by any means necessarily exclude some indeterminate limitation upon the substantive powers of government, full emphasis is placed upon procedural limitations, and political responsibility. McIlwain clearly recognized the need to repose adequate power in government. And in discussing the meaning of constitutionalism he insisted that the historical and proper test of constitutionalism was the existence of adequate processes for keeping government responsible. He refused to equate constitutionalism with the enfeebling of government by an exaggerated emphasis upon separation of powers and substantive limitations on governmental power. He found that "the really effective checks on despotism have consisted not in the weakening of government, but rather in the limiting of it; between which there is a great and very significant difference."[3] In associating constitutionalism with "limited" as distinguished from "weak" government, McIlwain meant government limited to the orderly procedure of law as opposed to the processes of force.[4] "The two fundamental correlative elements of constitutionalism for which all lovers of liberty must yet fight are the legal limits to arbitrary power and a complete political responsibility of government to the governed."[5]

If such is the basic nature of constitutionalism, it does not wrap government in the steel bonds of a series of substantive limitations, or compartmentalize power in discrete units.[6] The true nature of the issue which emergency presents for constitutional governments may then be recognized: It is the two-pronged problem of determining the extent to which the objectives of human action shall be socially defined and achieved or self-determined by the individual or group;[7] and, correlatively, that of balancing, through adequate legislative, administrative and judicial checks, the increased discretionary powers of the executive which accompany expanded governmental functions. It is a matter of historical fact that modern constitutional democracies have not, upon the rise of emergency conditions, found it necessary to suspend constitutional processes, or to resort to the schemes for organization of power hypothesized by those who hitherto have written on the subject.

What the British, particularly, have come to recognize in the course of the last five decades is that emergency governance is one form of an acute and continuing problem in modern constitutional democracies: that of allotting increasing areas of discretionary powers to the executive, while insuring that such powers will be exercised with a sense of political responsibility and under effective limitations and checks.[8] In time of emergency, governmental action may vary in breadth and intensity from more normal times, yet it need not be less constitutional. In time of war as in peace government according to the orderly procedure of the law, and government responsible to the governed, has proven its ability to meet the needs imposed by the accelerated tempo and the growing complexity of the twentieth century.

Chapter III

THE CONCEPT OF EMERGENCY IN
AMERICAN LEGISLATION

Emergency, as a generic term applicable to individual and group situations as well as to the state, connotes the existence of conditions suddenly intensifying the degree of existing danger to life or well-being beyond that which is accepted as normal. (A standard dictionary definition mentions the element of surprise, which may be present but is by no means necessarily integral to the existence of an emergency. An intense threat to life or well-being is not necessarily lessened by anticipation.) An emergency requires extraordinary and prompt corrective action. A typical British recital of the proper objectives of emergency action inferrentially includes ". . . securing the public safety, the defense of the realm, the maintenance of public order and the efficient prosecution of any war in which His Majesty may be engaged, and . . . maintaining supplies and services essential to the life of the community."[1] Public disorder, war and threat of invasion, interruption of the production or flow of essential supplies and services—any of these may intensify danger to life or well-being beyond acceptable limits. A similarly broad definition is contained in the American Labor-Management Relations Act of 1947, the national emergency section of which permits the President to curb strike action which "if permitted to occur or to continue, [would] imperil the national health or safety."[2]

Implicit in these definitions are the elements of intensity, variety, and perception. Presumably when the point of normal tolerance of danger has been passed, it remains possible to measure the intensity of the danger according to some scale. Obviously there are varieties of emergency. A war emergency differs in some respects from an emergency caused by natural catastrophe or industrial unrest. Emergencies vary in their source or cause, and in their impact. Finally, before corrective action can be taken, someone in a position of authority must perceive the existence of the emergency.

It would be idle to conduct an analysis of the problem of emergency in the constitutional state without first determining the range of situations which have been recognized by democratic legislatures and executives to constitute emergencies—*i.e.*, to warrant exceptionally quick, vigorous, and possibly novel action. When the legislature enacts a standby statute, instead of itself proclaiming an emergency, to whom does it entrust the power to determine the existence of an emergency, and within what limits? What are the powers which democratic legislatures grant the executive branch, enabling it to so order individual and group behavior as, in the first instance, to avoid intensification of the threat to the life or well-being of community and state, and ultimately restore conditions to normal? Finally, what if any measures are prescribed for insuring responsible administration of such powers?

This chapter is addressed to the basic questions going to the nature of emergency—intensity, variety, perception. The remaining parts of this study respond to the other questions posed above.

EMERGENCIES VARY IN INTENSITY

The executive and the legislature certainly appear to think in terms of a scale of intensity when they declare emergencies. We might, perhaps, project our listing from the shadow land verging upon or falling just short of emergency. A Presidential Proclamation of 1934 speaks of regulations justified by the existence of "exceptional and exigent circumstances."[1] The Central Intelligence Agency Act of 1949 uses the terms extraordinary and emergency interchangeably, speaking of expenditure of unaudited funds "for objects of a confidential, extraordinary, or emergency nature."[2] The simple declaration "that a national emergency exists,"[3] contained in the President's September 8, 1939 Proclamation of a neutrality emergency, will serve as well as any other enactment as a characteristic example of the scale of intensity necessary to declare a national emergency.

Beyond this intensity of emergency, Congress has addressed itself to "distressed" emergencies,[4] "serious" emergencies,[5] "intensified" emergencies,[6] "unprecedented" emergencies,[7] "acute" emergencies,[8] and at the outer extreme, "unlimited" emergencies.[9]

VARIETIES OF EMERGENCY

Emergencies, as perceived by legislature or executive in the United States since 1933, have been occasioned by a wide range of situations, classifiable under three principal heads: a. economic, b. natural disaster, and c. national security.

ECONOMIC EMERGENCIES

Depression: President Roosevelt in declaring a bank holiday a few

days after taking office in 1933 proclaimed that "heavy and unwarranted withdrawals of gold and currency from . . . banking institutions for the purpose of hoarding; and . . . continuous and increasingly
extensive speculative activity abroad in foreign exchange" resulting
in "severe drains on the Nation's stocks of gold . . . have created a
national emergency," requiring his action.[1] The Bank Conservation
Act, passed a few days later gave the President plenary power in time
of war or during any other period of "national emergency" to control
transactions in foreign exchange, transfers of payment, and preven-
tion of hoarding. It also declared "that a serious emergency exists
and that it is imperatively necessary speedily to put into effect
remedies of uniform national application."[2] Later in March, in permitting Federal Reserve Bank loans to state banks and trust
companies, Congress made specific reference to the existing emergency
in banking.[3]

The Federal Emergency Relief Act of 1933 opened with a declaration that the economic depression created a serious emergency, due
to wide-spread unemployment and the inadequacy of State and local
relief funds, resulting in the existing or threatened deprivation of a
considerable number of families and individuals of the necessities of
life, and making it imperative that the Federal Government cooperate
more effectively with the several States and Territories and the
District of Columbia in furnishing relief to their needy and distressed
people.[4] Here then was an emergency created by the inadequacy
of previous effort to cope with abnormal threats to the well-being
of the population. The Municipal Bankruptcy Act of May 24, 1934
also described the emergency in terms which related it to the inability
of local government units to function properly. Congress declared
a national emergency existed, caused by the increasing financial
difficulties of many local governmental units, which rendered imperative "the further exercise of the bankruptcy powers of the
Congress."[5]

On the same day that he signed the Emergency Relief Act, the
President also signed an Act describing another facet of the emergency. The latter Act stated "the present acute economic emergency"
was in part the result of very low prices for farm products. The effect
of declining income for the American farmer had virtually destroyed
his purchasing power, thus undermining the agricultural assets
supporting the national credit structure.[6] The causal phenomena
for declarations of emergency were, according to the statutes, heavy

and unwarranted withdrawals of gold, severe drains on the Nation's stocks of gold, widespread unemployment, and a severe and increasing disparity between the prices of agricultural and other commodities. Efforts to meet the emergency situation were directed immediately to ameliorate the existing emergency conditions and ultimately so alter the causal phenomena as to eliminate the causes of the existing threat to national well-being. The Gold Reserve Act of 1934 made passing reference to "the existing emergency."[7] The President in January 1936 proclaimed that this emergency had not been terminated but, on the contrary, had been intensified in different ways by unsettled conditions in international commerce and finance and in foreign exchange.[8] As late as 1941 Congress continued certain of the powers delegated in the Gold Reserve Act until June 1943 "unless the President shall sooner declare the existing emergency ended."[9]

In 1953 Congress authorized the President to declare the existence of economic disaster in any area. Thereafter the Secretary of Agriculture, on finding that an economic disaster had created a need for agricultural credit that could not be met for a temporary period from commercial banks or other responsible sources, might authorize emergency loans to farmers.[10]

Some statutes, on the other hand, identify emergency with the causal phenomena instead of their product. The National Industrial Recovery Act, for example, simply declared that a national emergency existed. This emergency, according to the statute was productive of widespread unemployment and disorganization of industry, which burdened interstate and foreign commerce, affected the public welfare, and undermined the standards of living of the American people.[11]

The Securities Exchange Act of 1934 found that national emergencies, which produced widespread unemployment and the dislocation of trade, transportation, and industry, burdened interstate commerce and adversely affected the general welfare, were "precipitated, intensified, and prolonged by manipulation and sudden and unreasonable fluctuations of security prices and by excessive speculation on such exchanges and markets."[12] In these two statutes the term emergency is first used in a context associating it with causal agency, and secondly as something intermediate between the causal agents and the disagreeable ultimate effects.

While calling attention to the occasionally variable usage of the term emergency, we by no means intend to develop a metaphysics

of emergency in order to settle the question whether it is rightfully
applied to cause, effect, or something intermediate. We are satisfied
to accept the overwhelming legislative tendency to apply the term
to the undesired effects of events, attributing variant usages to
imprecise draftmanship.

At this point it is appropriate to indicate that many statutes
(some of which are described here; some of which, for sake of brevity
or avoiding the redundant, are not,) either declare the existence of,
or describe action to be taken in the event of the occurence of, a
situation which by other statutes has been termed an emergency.
Statutes in this category, describing the situation but refraining from
applying the term emergency to them, are illustrated by the following:
A Tariff Act amendment of June 1934 gives the President the power
to curtail imports if he finds that existing duties or other import
restrictions of the United States or any foreign country burden
and restrict the foreign trade of the United States.[13] The Securities
Exchange Act associates emergency, among other things, with the
burdening of interstate and foreign commerce.

Did Congress intend the Tariff Act Amendment as an emergency
statute? At that particular time, probably not. But later amendments to the Tariff Act specifically refer to emergency conditions
affecting the American fisheries industry. We do not believe it is
necessary to ferret out the precise Congressional intent in Acts which
do not explicitly use the term emergency or describe the object of
correcting legislation in terms which clearly reflect Congress' finding
that an emergency exists.

Inflation: We have included in the economic section some of the
statutes designed to prevent or alleviate wartime inflation. Enacted
within months after Japan's attack on Pearl Harbor, the Emergency
Price Control Act of 1942 was designed to prevent economic dislocations from endangering the national defense and security and
the effective prosecution of the war.[14] The factors contributing to
the national emergency included "speculative, unwarranted, and
abnormal increases in prices and rents; . . . profiteering, hoarding,
manipulation, speculation, and other disruptive practices." The war
effort would be aided through insuring that defense appropriations
were not dissipated by excessive prices; by protecting persons with
relatively fixed and limited incomes, consumers, wage earners, investors, and persons dependent on life insurance, annuities, and pensions,
from undue impairment of their standard of living through sky-

rocketing prices.   Colleges, local government units, and other institutions with relatively fixed incomes were also to be protected against the inflationary spiral.   The emergency price control measure was formulated in anticipation of a possible post emergency collapse of values and was aimed at the avoidance thereof.

The Proclamation of May 27, 1941, in which President Roosevelt declared the existence of an unlimited emergency caused by the supposed expanded war aims of the Axis powers, carefully translated the emergency into economic terms.   The President advised businessmen that in maximizing war production they would be protecting a world in which free enterprise could exist; and workingmen, in so doing, would protect a society in which labor and management could bargain on free and equal terms.   Benefits were also forecast for privately endowed institutions and local governmental units.[15]   The extension of price controls in 1946 was attributed to the continued existence "of abnormally excessive spending power in relation to the presently available supply of commodities."[16]   And the Renegotiation Act was addressed to meeting the emergency within an emergency created by the wartime disruption of competitive conditions in regard to the placing of defense contracts.[17]

Strikes: The Emergency Railroad Transportation Act of 1933 was designed to relieve obstructions and burdens on interstate commerce resulting from "the present acute economic emergency."[18]

The Railway Labor Act of 1934 thereupon sought, by imposing collective bargaining upon the railroads and through a National Mediation Board and *ad hoc* emergency boards appointed by the President (nothing new, of course, in railroad regulation), to avoid exacerbation of the emergency through rail strikes.[19] The War Labor Disputes Act permitted drastic presidential and War Labor Board regulation of labor-management relations to avoid impeding or delaying the war effort in consequence of strikes.[20]   The Labor Management Relations Act, better known as the Taft-Hartley Act, created special procedures for delaying strikes whenever in the opinion of the President a threatened strike or lock-out affecting an entire industry or substantial part thereof would imperil the national health or safety if the strike occurred or were allowed to continue.   This Act of course, grants the determining power to the President only where interstate commerce, in all its varieties, is involved.[21]

Housing: The Veterans' Emergency Housing Act of 1946 declared that the long-term housing shortage and the war combined to create an unprecedented emergency shortage of housing, particularly for veterans of World War II and their families.[22] President Truman promptly cited the building program provided for in the Act and the unprecedented emergency shortage of housing in exercising his authority under the Tariff Acts to remove the duty from articles certified by the Housing Expediter as timber, lumber, or lumber products suitable for the construction or completion of housing acco-modations.[23] The Housing and Rent Act of 1949 also was directed at this emergency.[24]

Agricultural Commodities: Congress occasionally has recognized the existence of an emergency with regard to a particular agricultural or other commodity. Without using the term emergency, Congress plainly was taking emergency action when it adopted a concurrent resolution in June 1934 directing the Federal Trade Commission to investigate conditions with respect to the sale and distribution of milk and other dairy products.[25] Decline in the price of milk to the farmer had produced severe hardships and suffering to milk producers throughout the United States and strikes and violence in many rural and metropolitan centers. The Resolution went on to say that the continuation of the practices then engaged in by milk distributors and certain leaders of milk cooperatives seriously endangered the efforts of the Agricultural Adjustment Administration and of the several States to alleviate and remedy the distress so widespread among dairy farmers in the United States at the time. If this distress were permitted to continue the result would be the destruction of the already sorely pressed agricultural industry. Congress clearly noted the inability of the states to cope with an emergency situation and proceeded to initiate its own action.

In like manner the Tobacco Control Act of 1934 was aimed at improving conditions in the tobacco-growing industry by placing it on a sound financial and economic basis and by eliminating unfair competition and practices in the production and marketing of tobacco entering into the channels of interstate and foreign commerce. More-over the Act was in general designed to "relieve the present emergency with respect to tobacco."[26] The Sugar Act of 1937 permitted the President to suspend certain of its provisions upon a finding that a national economic or other emergency exists with respect to sugar or liquid sugar.[27] The President found conditions sufficiently severe in the sugar industry to declare a sugar emergency in 1939, 1942, and 1947.[28]

A 1942 Presidential Proclamation noted that codfish constituted

one of the basic staples in the diet of the low-income groups in Puerto Rico. Unfortunately, the war imposed severe limitations on this import from Canada, Newfoundland and Labrador, thereby vitally affecting Puerto Ricans dependent on this basic food in their diet.[29] The President sought a quick remedy by invoking the emergency provisions of the Tariff Act of 1930[30] to authorize the duty-free importation of "jerked beef . . . a satisfactory substitute for codfish," at least according to the proclamation. Invoking the same statute, the President, again in April 1942, authorized the duty-free importation of food, clothes, and medical, surgical, and other supplies by or directly for the account of The American National Red Cross for use by that agency in emergency relief work in connection with the "war emergency."[31]

EMERGENCIES OCCASIONED BY NATURAL CATASTROPHIES

Drought: Two statutes and one Presidential Proclamation in this category attribute emergency conditions to drought. In February 1934 Congress authorized the Farm Credit Administration to make loans for feed for livestock in drought- and storm-stricken areas.[1] The Emergency Appropriation Act for fiscal 1935 appropriated funds to meet the emergency and necessity for relief in stricken agricultural areas and in another section referred to "the present drought emergency."[22] The Presidential Proclamation noting that an unusual lack of rain in several western and mid-western states had caused an acute shortage of feed for livestock,[3] declared an emergency under the suitable provision of the 1930 Tariff Act and authorized suspension of duties on livestock feeds. Only livestock owners in the affected area were eligible to benefit from duty free livestock feeds.[4]

The Communications Act of 1934[5] and its 1951 amendment[6] grant the President certain powers in time "of public peril or disaster." The other statutes provide for existing or anticipated emergencies attributable to earthquake, flood, tornado, cyclone, hurricane, conflagration and landslides.[7]

Agricultural Pests: A joint resolution of April 1937 made "funds available for the control of incipient or emergency outbreaks of insect pests or plant diseases, including grasshoppers, Mormon crickets, and chinch bugs."[8] Funds were appropriated on this authorization later that month.[9]

Famine: The India Emergency Food Aid Act of 1951 provided for emergency shipments of food to India to meet famine conditions then ravaging the great Asian sub-continent.[10] In August 1953

Congress enacted general enabling legislation to permit the President
to furnish emergency assistance on behalf of the people of the United
States to friendly peoples in meeting famine or other urgent relief
requirements.[1] Thus the American Congress has sometimes defined
emergency in terms of occurrences in other countries.

NATIONAL SECURITY EMERGENCIES

These may be cataloged under the heads of (1) Neutrality, (2)
Defense, (3) Civil Defense, (4) Hostilities or War.

Neutrality Emergencies: For a nation which, at least during the
1930s raised to the topmost position on its list of twentieth century
mistakes its involvement in the First World War, and which during
the same period embraced the policy of non-involvement in future
wars, the chief problem of national security was not so much to be
prepared for war or to avoid the occurrence of war, as it was, rather,
to stay out of other people's wars, all wars being other people's. The
existence of a war elsewhere in the world, especially one involving a
major power, creates the need for emergency action designed to avoid
the greatest of all emergencies, participation in a war. This is the
meaning of the Neutrality Act of 1935 and its successors. The import
thereof is embodied in the Presidential Proclamations which, under
the Neutrality Acts, proclaimed the existence of wars between states
or factions within states; but also the more important Proclamation
of September 8, 1939 which, without citing the acts, declared the
existence of a national emergency "to the extent necessary for proper
observance, safeguarding, and enforcing of the neutrality of the
United States and the strengthening of our national defense within
the limits of peacetime authorizations."[1] Neutrality doctrine, oriented
as this was, contained the seeds of a more aggressive policy, and it was
appropriate that the President should phrase his May 27, 1941 declaration of an unlimited national emergency as an enlargement upon the
earlier Proclamation. The President declared that an unlimited
national emergency confronting the country required that its military, naval, air and civilian defenses be placed in a condition of
readiness to repel any and all acts or threats of aggression directed
toward any part of the Western Hemisphere.[2] The need was now for
adequate preparation rather than insulation. President Roosevelt's
forthright statement of the Nation's security requirements left
little doubt that we had passed from neutrality to all-out preparedness
as a national policy. For the security of this Nation and Hemisphere,
we should pass from peacetime authorizations of military strength

to whatever basis was needed to protect this entire hemisphere against invasion, encirclement or penetration by foreign agents.[3] The concept of neutrality dominant for a few years had been superseded by events.

Defense: Many of the statutes directed at meeting the threat to national survival posed by war are phrased in terms of the existence of war or threat of war. Thus it is not rigidly possible to assign separate pigeon-holes to those statutes which explicitly or by inference define emergency in terms of the need for defense preparedness, and those which define emergency in terms of the need for response to existing hostilities. The 1951 amendments to the Universal Military Training and Service, like the 1940 Act,[4] by inference suggest that military emergency is not related solely to the existence of hostilities. The President is authorized under the statute "from time to time, whether or not a state of war exists, to select and induct for training in the National Security Training Corps . . . such number of persons as may be required . . . "[5] The Interior Department Appropriation Act for fiscal 1948 included provision for cases of emergency caused by fire, flood, storm, act of God, or sabotage.[6] One cannot draw too sharp a distinction between war and peace; an act of sabotage is as likely as fire, flood, storm, or act of God. An Act of November 1940 launches upon an extensive list of national-defense material and national-defense premises — so comprehensive as to include anything whatsoever associated with defense production or transportation, including public utilities — and lists punishments for the willful injury or destruction of war material, or of war premises.[7] And following the war, it must be made clear that the emergency and the need for emergency action continue. The war emergency has reverted to a defense emergency. And so we turn to the First War Powers Act of 1941 and revise it "by striking out the words 'the prosecution of the war effort' and 'the prosecution of the war' and inserting the words 'the national defense'."[8]

Civil Defense: By Proclamation, on October 22, 1941, having in the spring of that year created an Office of Civilian Defense, President Roosevelt indicated that among the facets of a war emergency might be the endangering of civilian lives and property, and he invited all persons throughout the nation to give thought to their duties and responsibilities in the defense of this country, and to become better informed of the many vital phases of the civilian defense program.[9] The Federal Civil Defense Act of 1950 contemplated an attack or series of attacks by an enemy of the United States which conceivably would cause substantial damage or injury to civilian property or persons in the United States by any one of several means: sabotage, the use of bombs, shellfire, or atomic, radiological, chemical, bacteriological, or biological means or other weapons or processes.[10]   Such an occurrence would cause a "National Emergency for Civil Defense Purposes," or "a state of civil defense emergency," during the term which the Civil Defense Administrator would have recource to extraordinary powers outlined in the Act.[11]   Powers and relationships set up to effectuate response to a preparedness or civil defense emergency are shortly seen to be convenient for application to any garden-variety emergency which happens along, and so it is not surprising to observe that arrangements created in anticipation of military emergency are soon applied to natural catastrophes. The New York-New Jersey Civil Defense Compact supplies an illustration in this context for emergency cooperation. " 'Emergency' as used in this compact shall mean and include invasion or other hostile action, disaster, insurrection or imminent danger thereof . . ."[12]

Hostilities or War: The Tariff Act of 1930[13] which has already been cited a number of times in this chapter, permitted certain action by the President whenever an emergency exists by reason of a state of war, or otherwise. The Communications Act of 1934 and its 1951 amendment grant exceptional powers when there exists war or a threat of war.[14]   The 1940 National Defense Act amendments extended enlistments in the Army in time of war or other emergency.[15]   The May 1945 extension of the Selective Training and Service Act continued it in effect for the duration of hostilities in the present war.[16] And the threat seems the more intimate when the emergency is defined in terms of enemies who have entered upon the territory of the United States as part of an invasion or predatory incursion, . . . to commit sabotage, espionage or other hostile or warlike acts.[17]   The 1950 Emergency Detention Act[18] permits the President to declare the existence of an Internal Security Emergency, upon the occurrence of invasion, declaration of war by Congress, or insurrection within the United States.

PERCEIVING THE EXISTENCE OF AN EMERGENCY

Congress is more than likely to delegate to the President power to determine an emergency's existence, sometimes providing him with connotative definitions — such as "by reason of flood, earthquake, or drought" — for guidance. It is particularly inclined to permit the President to declare the termination of an emergency, frequently hinging the life of an emergency statute to such a Presidential declaration or to the continuance of emergency previously proclaimed by the President. But there is a growing tendency for the Congress to grant contingent powers which may be exercised in the event of a declaration of emergency either by Congress or the President, and sometimes by Congress alone. We discuss elsewhere the growing trend toward reservation to the Congress of power to terminate an emergency through adoption of a concurrent resolution (which does not require the President's signature). The Emergency Detention Act provision for declaration of an Internal Security Emergency, mentioned above, hinges the presidential declaration, among other things, to a prior Congressional declaration of war. Thus when Congress has declared a war emergency to exist, the President, at his discretion may declare the existence of an Internal Security Emergency caused by the prospect of internal subversion. Congress, perhaps, forecast the future trend of legislative-executive relations in this field and in the adaptation of emergency action when in the First Decontrol Act of 1947 it declared "in each . . . limited instance [that it is necessary to continue emergency controls in effect] the authority for such emergency controls and war powers should not be exercised by the grant of broad, general war powers but should be granted by restrictive, specific legislation."[1]

CONCLUSION

It may be seen that a varied assortment of situations threatening the economic interests of groups, the life and limb of the populace, or the physical integrity of the nation itself, have been defined as emergencies in the United States. The spread lies between a liquid sugar or codfish emergency and an emergency caused by the global military and ideological activities of the communist movement. The citizen of the democratic state, having weathered depression, natural disaster, agricultural, defense and war emergencies, and recognizing that by popular consensus he lives in a time of cold war emergency which may turn into a war emergency, or if lessened, may create an emergency by virtue of the threat to continued prosperity resulting from curbed defense orders, is entitled to be apprehensive.

The variety is so great, the invocation of emergency so ready that one must ask whether the term is not becoming shorn of meaning — a shibboleth for the legitimization of ordinarily suspect governmental action desired by influential groups. Shibboleth or not, the individual citizen, as we shall see subsequently, finds that its incantation is associated with increasing constrictions upon his freedom of action.

CHAPTER IV

EMERGENCY POWERS OVER PERSONS

Constitutional democracies as well as authoritarian states are confronted in time of military crisis with the need for a maximum productive and military effort directed at national survival. Totalitarian nations in their practice of total absorption of the materials and energies of conquered nations, and the Western democracies in their insistence upon "unconditional surrender" have contributed to the transformation of modern war from a struggle for limited objectives to a struggle for survival.

The initial response of Great Britain in the First World War indicated an assumption that war imposed upon a nation the necessity to adapt the machinery of the government, and especially its military arm, to the attainment of victory. Twentieth century wars, like those of the Nineteenth century, were to be fought by the military. In terms of the total national energies, war represented a temporary, localized diversion. Democracies continue to manifest a not necessarily unhealthy predisposition. even in the atomic age, to treat war as a subsidiary effort which should not unduly ripple the accustomed habits and interests of the major segment of the population and economy. War is fought by governments, not by peoples. True, perhaps, in regard to police actions which constitute occasional escape valves for aggressive energies which might otherwise erupt in world war, this aphorism which is maintained as a fiction in time of major war, is a residue of an earlier and simpler age.

However tentative their initial response to World War II, the Western democracies soon came to regard it as imposing the need not simply to adapt governmental structure to the major purpose of victory, but to maintain consistency between the political and economic activities of individuals and this overriding goal. Exercising a frankly coercive power, governments in the Second World War conscripted the energies of individuals. Great Britain imposed a labor draft as well as a military draft. The United States, resisting nationwide demands for conscription of labor, satisfied itself with commanding the military services of individuals. Both countries identified individuals whom, it seemed, could best be integrated in the war effort by being integrated *out* of it — *i.e.,* potential saboteurs, espionage agents, and the like. However adequate or inadequate the techniques for measuring individual and group loyalty, the measurement was undertaken and thousands found themselves immobilized behind barbed wires.

A person naive in political and human relations or a government facing nascent revolution would resort solely to the technique of command and coercion to secure the adjustment of individual goals and efforts to those of the nation. Thus in the United States many war programs depended upon the offering of incentives or simple exhortation and appeal to individual loyalty for their effectiveness. And, in a democracy it remains true in time of war as in peacetime, that the essential nature of the political process is "the translation of conflict among interest groups into authoritative decision."[1]

These are the conditions under which statutes and presidential proclamations relating to the mobilization of the human resources of the nation will be discussed.

Positive Integration

Civilian Labor Force: Notwithstanding the failure of the United States to adopt a form of outright labor conscription in the last war, a number of statutory provisions did attempt to integrate segments of the labor force more closely in the war effort. Those which were primarily repressive in nature — i.e., which principally concerned the imposition of penalties or the prohibition of specified activities — are treated in the second section of this chapter.

In June 1939, Congress set up a program for the training of civil aircraft pilots.[1] The Navy Department Appropriations Act for fiscal 1941[2] included an emergency fund to enable the President, among other things, to procure and train civilian personnel necessary in connection with the production of critical and essential items of equipment and material and the use or operation of such equipment and material. A month later, Congress authorized the Secretary of War, during the period of any national emergency declared by the President, to employ laborers and mechanics in excess of forty hours per week, at time and one-half for overtime.[3] Another 1940 law suspended during the national emergency statutory provisions imposing the eight hour day for Maritime Commission contractors.[4]

Section 801 of the Second War Powers Act of 1942 authorized the

President to direct the assignment of Civilian Conservation Corps manpower to protect the munitions, aircraft, and other war industries, municipal water supply, power, and other utilities, and to protect resources subject to the hazards of forest fires.[5]

Emergency conditions may lead to relaxation of the traditional American rule, based upon the assumption that public employment is a privilege and upon security grounds, that aliens are ineligible for governmental positions — especially positions in the military establishments. In 1946 Congress suspended statutory provisions prohibiting the employment of aliens.[6] Thus the Secretary of the Navy could authorize the Navy Department to employ non-citizens whose special technical or scientific knowledge or experience would be of benefit to the military services of the United States. The wisdom of this legislation may be more readily appreciated when it is remembered that German rocket experts like Dr. Werner von Braun were able to serve in the United States rather than behind the Iron Curtain. Similarly, as illustrated by the Selective Service Act of 1948,[7] effective mobilization of the labor force requires exemption of some specially skilled persons from military conscription. This Act authorized the President to provide for the deferment from training and service certain categories of individuals in many different fields as found to be necessary to the maintenance of the national health, safety, or interest.

Work stoppages are the nemesis of any defense production program. The wartime efforts to prevent or speedily terminate such stoppages are reported in the next section, on the theory that they were primarily coercive in nature. The Defense Production Act of 1950,[8] however, clearly reflects the statutory trend in the United States against the outlawing of strikes in time of emergency. Section 502 of the Act emphasizes that national policy is to place primary reliance upon the parties to any labor dispute to settle their differences through negotiation and collective bargaining, making full use of available mediation and conciliation facilities. All settlements should be made in the national interest. The President is to initiate strike settlement conferences, with representatives of the public present, but no action inconsistent with the Labor-Management Relations Act of 1947 may be taken.[9]

Current information on the availability of essential skills must be maintained. The National Science Foundation Act of 1950 included among the functions of the agency that of maintaining a register of scientific and technical personnel and providing a central clearinghouse for information covering all scientific and technical personnel in the United States.[10]

The Military Services: Maintenance on active duty or in reserve status of armed forces components adequate to the defense of the United States is of continuing concern to the government. It is not alone in time of war that attention is given to the adequacy of the military services. Thus the 1930's witnessed a series of amendments to the 1916 National Defense Act designed to improve the status of the reserve components of the Army. In June 1933, during the famous first hundred days of the Roosevelt administration, it was not too preoccupied with depression legislation to secure legislation introducing changes into procedures for establishing National Guard policy. All policies and regulations affecting the organization, training and distribution of the National Guard were to be prepared by committees of appropriate branches or divisions of the War Department General Staff.

The Guard would be entitled to equal representation with the Regular Army in formulating Guard policies, but the paramount fact was that of federal supervision and integration of the National Guard.[11] Further, the President was empowered to determine the number of reserve officers in the various grades to be appointed to the Officers' Reserve Corps, and to make such appointments, subject to Senatorial approval for ranks above Colonel.[12] This is a characteristic extension of the president's power as Commander-in-Chief.

Two years later, in June 1935, a further amendment to the 1916 statute gave the President authority in an emergency at any time to order officers of the National Guard to active duty for the duration of the emergency, with the proviso, however, that no officer could be employed on active duty for more than fifteen days in any calendar year without his own consent.[13] Later that year the President was authorized to call annually one thousand Reserve Officers (mostly R.O.T.C. graduates) for a year's active duty with the Regular Army in the grade of second lieutenant. Only those who applied and who had been screened by the War Department were eligible.[14]

Continuing to elaborate amendments to the National Defense Act, Congress, in April 1938, established the requirement that line officers should not be detailed to or remain as members of the General Staff Corps unless two of their immediately preceding six years had been served in actual command of or on duty other than General Staff duty, with troops of one or more of the combatant arms or as instructor with the National Guard, Organized Reserves, or Reserve Officers' Training Corps.[15] Two days later in another amendment to the basic act, Congress provided for establishment of a Regular Army Reserve, membership in which was restricted to persons under 36 years of age who had served in the Regular Army and from which an honorable discharge had been received.[16] The Regular Army Reserve was subject to call to active duty by the President in case of emergency declared by him. Within six months after the termination of an emergency declared by the President, the Reserve forces were to be placed in an inactive status or discharged, whichever was the more appropriate.[17]

In June 1938 the 1916 statute was amended to increase the allowed strength of enlisted men in the Army Air Corps from 16,000 to 21,500.[18] That same month an earlier Naval Reserve statute (Act of February 28, 1925) was superseded and a Naval Reserve to consist of the Fleet Reserve, the Organized Reserve, the Merchant Marine Reserve, and the Volunteer Reserve was created. All were to constitute a component part of the Navy.[19] The same Act also provided for a Marine Corps Reserve.[20] The reserve units were to be composed of persons transferred, enlisted, or appointed to them.[21]

But it is in 1940 that the statute books commence to reflect administration and congressional anticipation of American participation in the War and the attendant necessity to compel individuals to give military service. On May 14, 1940 provision was made for the extension of all enlistments in the active military service for the duration, plus six months in the event of war or other emergncy declared by Congress.[22] The Secretary of the Navy was given power, six days following Pearl Harbor, to extend for the duration of the war plus six months all enlistments in the Navy, Marine Corps, and Coast Guard.[23] Another enactment of that date permitted the similar extension of Army service.[24] This Act also eliminated all territorial restrictions on the use of units and members of the Army.[25]

Congress, having made provision for the extension of regular service enlistments for the duration in the event of emergency, then granted the President authority to call the reserve to active duty. This was accomplished in August 1940 when Congress delegated to the President power until June 30, 1942 to order into the active military service for a twelve month period any or all members and units of any or all reserve components of the Army of the United States, and retired personnel of the Regular Army, with or without their consent, in any manner the President deemed necessary for the strengthening of the national defense.[26] The August statute having empowered the President to order the National Guard, as well as other reserve units, into active duty, it seemed desirable to equip the States with authority to set up military units for home duty in the absence of the Guard.

An October 1940 statute accomplished this purpose by authorizing the states, while any part of the National Guard of the state concerned was in active federal service, to organize and maintain whatever military forces other than National Guard were believed necessary by the state.[27] These forces were subject to the Secretary of War's regulation on matters of discipline and training. They were not subject to federal call, but neither were individual members exempt by reason of service in such units from military service under any federal law. In September 1950, three months after outbreak of the Korean War, Congress authorized the President to call up reserve forces and retired personnel from all military branches, with or without the consent of those called.[28] And, as in the Second World War, state authorities were again empowered to set up military units to substitute for the National Guard as long as any part of the National Guard was in active federal service.[29]

Meanwhile the gradual inclusion of compulsory service provisions in statutes was carried to its ultimate conclusion in the Selective Training and Service Act of 1940.[30] The Act required the registration of all male citizens of the United States and male alien residents between the ages of 21 and 36.[31] The President was authorized from time to time, whether or not a state of war existed, to select and induct into the land and naval forces of the United States for training and service whatever number of men in his judgment might be required for such forces in the national interest.[32] A peacetime ceiling of 900,000 inductees was established, and provision made for a twelve months' maximum training period subject to extension whenever the Congress declared that the national interest was imperiled.[33] The remaining powers granted to the President in the Act, and the limitations which circumscribed his exercise of them, will be discussed in other contexts.

By proclamation that day, and on October 1, 8, and November 12, the President established registration days in the United States proper, Hawaii, Puerto Rico, and Alaska.[34] A second registration day was proclaimed in May 1941, and a third on January 5, 1942.[35] The Conscription Act was continued in effect for the duration of the war.

A post-war, or "cold war", conscription program was set up in June 1948.[36] The new statute provided for the registration of male citizens and alien residents between the ages of 18 and 26, and made those between 19 and 26 subject to induction into the armed forces at th᠂ discretion of the President.[37] He was empowered to induct a sufficient number of persons to maintain the personnel strengths of the armed forces at three million men.[38] The maximum term of service was two years, and the Act's duration was set at two years. A September 1950 amendment to the Act allowed the President to require special registration of medical, dental, and allied specialties, drafting persons below the age of 50 from the lists to fill requisitions submitted by the Department of Defense and approved by the President.[39] An eleventh hour enactment of June 23, 1950 deferred expiration of the Selective Service Act for fifteen days,[40] and seven days later July 9, 1951 was substituted for the July 9, 1950 expiration date.[41]

The next year saw systematic amendment of the 1948 statute, including a change of title to the Universal Military Training and Service Act.[42] The maximum of two years' service was continued, and the minimum age for both registration and induction set at 18½ years. A 1953 amendment to the Act provided for the special registration, classification, and induction of medical, dental, and allied specialist personnel.[43] A method for gaining release from military service, anachronistic in the age of universal military service and the citizen army, was removed when in July 1953 Congress repealed provisions of 1890 and 1893 statutes which permitted enlisted men to purchase discharge from the armed services.[44]

A series of non-coercive statutes from 1939 on were designed to augment the armed services. In June 1939 Congress established a Coast Guard Reserve, composed of owners of motorboats and yachts.[45] In March 1941 the President was empowered to appoint within the Navy 100 acting assistant surgeons above previous quotas, and the Secretary of the Navy given power in time of war or national emergency declared by the President to appoint for temporary service, such acting assistant surgeons as the exigencies of the service required.[46]

A June 1942 statute suspended all limitations on personnel strength in the military services.[47] Upon emergence of the "Cold War" Congress again authorized increases in military strength. In April 1946 the Navy and Marine Corps were permitted to increase the number of commissioned officers on the active list, and to maintain enlisted strength at 500,000 for the Regular Navy, and at 200,000 for the Marine Corps.[48] A Civil Air Patrol, to serve as a volunteer civilian auxiliary to the Air Force, was established in May 1948.[49] The Air Force was to establish, maintain, supply, and equip liaison offices with the CAP, and to detail Air Force military and civilian personnel to assist in training CAP members. Not dissimilar to the provision establishing the CAP as a civilian adjunct to the Air Force was a 1953 statute authorizing the President to employ the American National Red Cross under the Armed Forces whenever the President found it necessary to order such employment.[50]

The Women's Armed Services Integration Act of June 1948 integrated the women's services as Regular units within the Army, Navy, Marine Corps, and Air Force.[51] Four years later Congress authorized the appointment of qualified women as physicians and specialists in the medical services of the Army, Navy, and Air Force.[52] In 1950 provision was made for the five year enlistment in the Regular Army of 2,500 qualified unmarried male aliens.[53] Alien enlistees were integrated into established units with citizen soldiers and not segregated into separate organizations for aliens.

NEGATIVE INTEGRATION

It has become an axiom of democratic government that in time of emergency threatening the health or safety of the community or the territorial integrity of the nation, the objective of communal survival takes precedence over the desires and conveniences of the individual. The energies, wealth, talents of individuals may be conscripted in the national interest. Democratic governments also have asserted the right to constrict the range of permissible activities of individuals whose freedom, if unlimited, is calculated to exacerbate the emergency. Such limitations may apply to the population generally or to defined segments of it. The intensity of such limitations may be measured on a continuum ranging from precautionary detention to the relatively mild requirement that persons in defined categories register with the government.

Preventive Detention: At an early date Congress, with judicial approval, exercised the power to apprehend and detain all enemy aliens. On December 7, 1941, President Roosevelt issued the first of ten wartime proclamations founded upon Congressional enactments of 1798 and 1918, imposing limitations upon the activities of enemy aliens, and specifically announcing that "All aliens shall be liable to restraint, or to give security,"[1] and that dangerous aliens might be subjected to arrest and confinement. In two statutes enacted in 1952, Congress reiterated its desire that illegal entrants be apprehended and detained pending deportation. These statutes provided for the search of vessels and arrest of persons seeking to enter the United States illegally,[2] and authorized the establishment of necessary detention facilities to hold those arrested.[3]

It is well known that in World War II persons of Japanese ancestry, including even those possessed of American citizenship, were subjected to preventive detention.[4] Presidential exercise of this form of restraint is now sanctioned on a standby basis. Title II of the Internal Security Act of 1950 empowers the President in time of "Internal Security Emergency" to order the apprehension and detention of persons "as to whom there is reasonable ground to believe that," if free, they "will engage in, or probably will conspire with others to engage in, acts of espionage or of sabotage."[5] The President may declare a state of internal security emergency upon the invasion of the United States or any of its territories or possessions, the declaration of war by Congress, or insurrection within the United States in aid of a foreign enemy.

Access to the U.S. and U.S. Citizenship: Closely related to the detention of enemy aliens or others whose liberty is perceived to endanger the security of the state is the control of access to the United States and the acquisition of United States citizenship. By Act of June 20, 1941[6] Congress instructed American diplomatic and consular officers to refuse visas or entry permits to aliens believed seeking entry into the United States for the purpose of engaging in activities which would endanger the public safety. The following day Congress granted the President power during the existing national emergency to place restrictions and prohibitions in addition to those already provided by law upon the departure of persons from and their entry into the United States.[7] In proclamations of July and September 1945 and April 1946, President Truman ordered the deportation of enemy aliens resident in the United States without admission under the immigration laws, or enemy aliens deemed dangerous to the public peace and safety of the United States.[8]

In an earlier statute Congress excluded from admission to the United States persons who have departed from the jurisdiction of the United States for the purpose of evading or avoiding training or service in the armed forces of the United States during time of war or during a period declared by the President to be a period of national emergency. Among the myriad restrictions of the Internal Security

Act of 1950 are to be found additional categories of aliens ineligible for entry into the United States, principally aliens who at any time have been members of the Communist or other totalitarian party of any state of the United States, of any foreign state, or of any political or geographical subdivision of any foreign state, and aliens who advocate the economic, international, and governmental doctrines of world communism or of any form of totalitarianism.[9]

Naturalization is refused or citizenship withdrawn from persons falling into classifications created by a security-conscious Congress. The Nationality Act of 1940[10] restricted the eligibility of alien enemies for nationalization to those whose declaration of intention was made not less than two years prior to the beginning of the state of war and specified that enemy aliens were eligible for apprehension and removal at any time previous to actual naturalization. Section 25 of the Internal Security Act amends the Nationality Act of 1940 to make ineligible for naturalization persons subscribing to or giving evidence of subscribing to anarchist, communist, or any totalitarian movement or body of sentiment. Those who within the ten years next preceding the filing of naturalization petitions, or in the period between such filing and the time of taking the final oath of citizenship, have been members of, or affiliated with, communist-front organizations registered under the Subversive Activities Control Act of 1950, must rebut a presumption that they are persons not attached to the principles of the Constitution and thus ineligible for citizenship.[11]

Congress has devised appropriate means for handling the cases of persons seeking to renounce American citizenship. To facilitate the surrender of United States citizenship by persons of Japanese ancestry, Congress in July, 1944, specified that with the permission of the Attorney General, and when the United States is at war, citizens may accomplish expatriation by the simple act of making in the United States a formal written renunciation of nationality in such form as may be prescribed by, and before an officer designated by the Attorney General.[12] The assumption that persons departing from or remaining outside of the jurisdiction of the United States in time of war for the purpose of evading or avoiding military service renounce their American citizenship was created by an Act of Congress in September, 1944.[13]

President Roosevelt by proclamation of July 1941 provided for establishment of "The Proclaimed List of Certain Blocked Nationals" to be published in the Federal Register. The list was to contain the names of those persons deemed to be, or to have been, acting on

behalf of the interests of Germany and Italy. Any material or article
exported from the United States through the efforts of German and
Italian "blocked nationals" was declared to be detrimental to the
interest of national defense in the United States.[14] The Secretary
of State, acting in conjunction with the Secretary of the Treasury,
the Attorney General, the Secretary of Commerce, the Administrator
of Export Control, and the Coordinator of Commercial and Cultural
Relations between the American Republics was required to prepare
the list.[15]

Persons naturalized after January 1, 1951 created a *prima facie*
case that they were not attached to the principles of the Constitution
of the United States at the time of naturalization, if within five years
after naturalization they joined as a member or affiliated with any
organization, attachment to which would have precluded or hindered
naturalization in the first place. The unwary risked cancellation of
his citizenship for fraud if found to be connected with an organization
whose goals and objectives were directed against the United States.
This is one of the Internal Security Act provisions[16] designed to
exclude communists from naturalization. The Expatriation Act of
1954 provides for the loss of nationality of persons (whether natural
born or naturalized citizens) convicted by a court or court martial
of committing treason against the United States, or engaging in a
conspiracy to overthrow, put down, or to destroy by force the Government of the United States, or to levy war against them.[17]

Circumscribing Movement of Persons: The area of permissible
mobility is narrowd for all persons in time of war or emergency. The
population generally is excluded from specified security areas. By
Act of January, 1938,[18] Congress authorized the President to define
certain vital military and naval installations or equipment and made
it unlawful to photograph or sketch such installations without proper
authority. This obviously limits access to and activity in areas ad-
jacent to such equipment. A 1950 amendment to the Civil Aeronautics Act, for example, empowered the Secretary of Commerce,
after consultation with the Department of Defense and the Civil
Aeronautics Board, to define zones or areas in the airspace above
the United States, its Territories, and possessions as he may find
necessary in the interests of national security. The Secretary is also
given authority to prohibit or restrict flights of aircraft which he
cannot effectively identify, locate, and control in those areas.[19]
Selected groups of persons, generally enemy aliens, may be prohibited
from entering or remaining in certain areas of the country. Pro-

clamation No. 2525, December 7, 1941,[20] forbade the presence of alien Japanese in the Canal Zone, and restricted their entry into, or departure from, Hawaii, the Philippine Islands, and the United States, and provided for their exclusion from designated areas. Of maximum severity were limitations on mobility beyond the limits of a community, or confinement in a camp or cell. The movement to restrict travel by Americans dates from the 1935 endeavor of the American Congress to avoid American involvement in any future conflict. Section 6 of the Neutrality Act of 1935[21] empowered the President to prohibit or regulate travel by American citizens as passengers on the vessels of any belligerents in a war in which the United States was a neutral. Individuals travelling in violation of orders did so at their own risk.

Two months after passage of the Neutrality Act, in October 1935, President Roosevelt issued Proclamation No. 2142, applying Section 6 to the Ethiopian conflict, and ordering American citizens to refrain from traveling as passengers on vessels of either belligerent. The May 1937 amendments to the Neutrality Act[22] strengthened this provision by making it unlawful for any United States citizen to travel on belligerent vessels in contravention of the President's prohibition or regulation of such travel. In 1939 these provisions were broadened to include any American travelling on such a vessel as a member of its crew,[23] and to prohibit American ships from carrying goods or passengers to belligerent ports[24] or combat areas.

President Roosevelt's Neutrality Proclamation of September 5, 1939, among other things, prohibited Americans from accepting commissions with belligerents, or enlisting in the service of a belligerent. Hiring persons to enlist, or going beyond the jurisdiction of the United States with the intent to join belligerent forces, were also prohibited.[25]

By Act of March 28, 1940,[26] Congress extended application of an earlier prohibition[27] on unauthorized entry on military reservations to the outlying possessions of the United States. A year later it granted the Secretaries of War and Navy, jointly or singly, power to define areas within such reasonable distance of any military or naval camp or station in which prostitution would be prohibited by federal law.

By Proclamation of December 27, 1941 President Roosevelt established the Hawaiian Maritime Control Area, and regulated entry, radio calls, visual communications, and traffic in that area. Naval authorities were granted power to establish supplementary regulation.[28] Subsequently, the President established Maritime

Control Areas for Cristobal and the Gulf of Panama,[29] Boston,[30] San Francisco, Columbia River, Puget Sound, Southeastern Alaska, and other areas.[31] On May 20, 1942, invoking his powers as Commander-in-Chief, the President established the Padre Island Sea Range Area, and imposed regulations controlling entry to an activity in that area. The next day he signed into law an enactment providing a maximum penalty of $5,000 fine and one year imprisonment for knowingly violating restrictions established by the President, the Secretary of War, or military commanders designated by him, on entering, remaining in, leaving, or committing proscribed acts in military areas or zones.[32]

The areas thus far described were defined principally for exclusionary purposes. It is not unusual to define areas with a view to confining therein specific persons or categories of persons. Invoking a 1909 statute, the President on September 5, 1939 made it illegal for interned members of the armed forces of belligerent nations to leave the jurisdiction of the United States, or the limits of their internment, without permission.[33] In a later proclamation the President stipulated that no alien would be permitted to depart from the United States if the Secretary of State were satisfied that the alien's departure would be prejudicial to the interests of the United States.[34]

Section 6 of the Internal Security Act of 1950 makes it illegal for members of an organization which has registered under the Act as a communist organization or has been ordered to do so by the Subversive Activities Control Board, to apply for a passport, or to use or attempt to use a passport. It is also an offense for a federal officer knowingly to issue a passport to such a person. The Immigration and Nationality Act also empowers the President, in time of war or national emergency, to impose restrictions and prohibitions upon the departure of persons from the United States.[35]

Registration: The requirement that specified categories of individuals register, in consequence of their backgrounds, associations, or activities, or as a result of possession of certain articles, becomes increasingly familiar in the United States. Legislative motivation in requiring such registration may be varied and complex. The registration provision invariably provides the basis for defining new crimes and therefore opportunity to prosecute persons whose backgrounds, activities and beliefs are anathema to powerful groups in the nation. Combined with periodic reporting, registration may act as a deterrent to the commission of certain acts considered socially or politically undesirable. It may simply facilitate the informative function of government, enabling authorities to become aware of and continuously check upon the activities of selected groups of persons affecting the public interest. Or, registration may serve as a mild, yet nonetheless effective, restraint upon the freedom of individuals. Certainly, for example, it is an essential prerequisite to parolling enemy aliens in time of war, although its usefulness is not limited to wartime only.

The decade prior to the Second World War is popularly, and accurately, perceived as one of sustained economic emergency. During the second half of this decade the Congress frequently was preoccupied with the need for legislation designed to protect the United States from involvement in another world war. The Neutrality Act of 1935[36] referred to above contained a registration feature. Under the terms of that Act, every person engaged in the business of manufacturing, exporting, or importing any arms, ammunition, and implements of war was required to register within ninety days of entering such a business. Such individuals or firms had to provide the Secretary of State with a $500 registration fee, and information including personal or business name, principal place of business, places of business in the United States, and a list of the arms, ammunition and other implements of war which they handled. They were also required to inform the Secretary of State of any changes, and had to keep permanent records of business transactions which were subject to the scrutiny of the National Munitions Control Board.[37] The registration provision was retained in the May 1937 amendment to the Neutrality Act with very little change.[38]

In June 1938 Congress chose to compel registration of persons employed by agencies to disseminate propaganda in the United States.[39] Every person then acting as an agent for a foreign principal was given thirty days after the Act went into effect to register with the Secretary of State. His registration statement, under oath, required the agent's name and address, the name and address of his principal, and a copy of the contract or oral agreement covering the agent's services, including compensation. The agent was also to file a copy of the charter as well as a statement of the objectives of the organization employing him.[40] The term "agent of a foreign principal" was rather broad and included any person who acted or engaged or agreed to act as a public-relations counsel or publicity agent for a foreign principal or for any domestic organization subsidized directly or indirectly in whole or in part by a foreign principal.[41] New information statements were to be filed each six months. Failure to file and the making of false statements were punishable by a maximum of $1,000 fine and two years' imprisonment.[42]

Six months prior to Pearl Harbor, Congress enacted the Alien Registration Act, requiring all aliens fourteen years of age or older and remaining in the United States for thirty days or more, to apply for registration and be fingerprinted at post offices and other places to be designated by the Commissioner of Immigration and Naturalization. Parents must register for aliens under fourteen.[43] Alien registrants who were residents of the United States were required to notify the Commissioner in writing of each change of residence and new address within five days from the date of such change. All others were to notify him of their addresses at the expiration of each three months' period of residence in the United States.[44] And by Proclamation No. 2537, January 14, 1942,[45] the President ordered all alien enemies within the continental United States, Puerto Rico, and the Virgin Islands to apply for and acquire certificates of identification.

In the Spring of 1942 the Foreign Agents Registration Act was adapted to changed conditions. Congress announced its purpose to protect the national defense, internal security, and foreign relations of the United States by requiring public disclosure by persons engaging in propaganda activities and other activities. Anyone acting for or on behalf of a foreign government, foreign political party or other foreign principal would be identified and the Government and the American people would be in a better position to appraise their statements and actions in the light of their associations and activities.[46] In addition to elaborating the definition of a foreign principal, the Act specified numerous exemptions from its registration provisions. Agents whose foreign principals were governments, the defense of which was deemed by the President to be vital to the defense of the United States, were not required to register provided their activities were not intended to conflict with any of the domestic or foreign policies of the Government of the United States.[47]

A related statute of October, 1940 also compelled certain groups to register with the Attorney General.[48] Four categories of organizations were required to register: (1) Organizations subject to foreign control and engaging in political activity, (2) Organizations engaging both in civilian-military activity and in political activity, (3) Those subject to foreign control and engaging in civilian-military activity, and (4) Any organization one of whose aims was the overthrow of a government or subdivision thereof by force or violence.[49] By political activity Congress had reference to activity aimed at the control by force or overthrow of the Government of the United States or any of its subdivisions.[50] An organization, according to the statute, was engaged in civilian-military activity if it gave or received instruction in the use of firearms or other weapons, or participated, with or without arms, in military maneuvers, drills or parades of a miltary or naval character. And an organization was deemed subject to foreign control if its financial support was derived directly or indirectly from a foreign government, or if its policy was determined by, or at the suggestion of, or in collaboration with, a foreign government.[51]

The registration statements were to contain the name and address of the organization, the names of officers and contributors, the qualifications for membership, organizational aims, assets, income, and activities. Violation of the Act might entail a fine of $10,000 and five years' imprisonment.

The Internal Security Act of 1950 contains provisions similar to the older wartime law. Briefly stated, the Act defines "communist-action" and "communist-front" organizations, which together comprise a class of communist organizations.[52] Such organizations are compelled to register with the Attorney General, filing, in the case of communist-front organizations, a list of officers at time of registration and in the preceding twelve months; and, in the case of communist-action organizations, a list of officers and members for the preceeding twelve months.[53] A complete financial accounting is required and current information must be supplied in annual reports.

In July 1954 Congress amended the reporting provision to require a listing, in such form and detail as the Attorney General might prescribe, of all printing presses and machines used or intended to be used by a communist-action or communist-front organization. The statute went so far as to require registration of any printing machine used by an organization in which the communists or affiliates had an interest.[54] Adequate procedural protection and provision for judicial review is afforded those charged with failure to register.[55]

The Communist Control Act of 1954 amplified the Internal Security Act. It purports to be an Act to outlaw the Communist Party and to prohibit members of communist organizations from serving in certain representative capacities, and for other purposes. Despite its title, the Act does not outlaw the Communist Party in the sense of making membership in it illegal and proscribing its existence. It simply deprives the Communist Party of certain rights, privileges and immunities attendant upon legal bodies created under the jurisdiction of the laws of the United States or any political subdivision thereof.[56] The Act then defines a new species within the genus communist organization.[57] In effect it amends the Internal Security Act by setting up the trilogy; communist-action, communist-front, and communist-infiltrated organizations. And communist-infiltrated organizations—a euphemism for communist dominated trade unions must register.[58] Such organizations are ineligible to act as collective bargaining representatives and are deprived of access to the National Labor Relations Board.[59]

The Act makes it illegal for any member of a communist organization, which either has registered with the Attorney General or been ordered to register by the Subversive Activities Control Board, "to hold office or employment with any labor organization, . . . or to represent any employer in any matter proceeding arising or pending under the National Labor Relations Act."[60]

Freedom of Association: The Communist Control Act of 1954 and the registration provisions of the Internal Security Act might well have been subsumed under the classification freedom of association. Both have grave implications for the freedom of individuals to associate at will and according to conscience with political and economic groups. And similarly far-reaching in implication for this traditional freedom are those provisions which, going one step further than stipulating disqualifications for office-holding in representative associations, prohibit the creation of an employer-employee relationship, or facilitate the disruption of such relationships where they already exist.

The wheel has taken a full turn since the American Congress in 1937 repealed a District of Columbia Appropriation Act provision that no part of any appropriation for the public schools would be available for the payment of the salary of any person teaching or advocating communism.[61] Today, of course, the trend is toward maximizing the political disqualifications for public and private employment. This trend can be traced from the pre-war efforts of the Congress to prevent penetration of defense industries and government agencies by subversives.

We look first to legal efforts to exclude persons conceived to be subversive from private employment, and then survey the statutes governing public employment. The Defense Production Act of June 21, 1940,[62] for example, imposed the rule that aliens working for a defense contractor whose contract involved access to classified information were ineligible to work for the contractor. If, however, the head of the government agency for whom secret work was being performed gave the contractor written consent to use aliens, the contractor was free to do so.

Attempting to insure that employment opportunities created by the induction of young men into the service did not accrue to members of groups then opposing the American defense effort, Congress, in enacting the Selective Training and Service Act of 1940, stipulated that whenever a vacancy was caused in the employment rolls of any business or industry by reason of an employee's induction into the Armed Services of the United States, the vacancy could not be filled by any person then a member of the Communist Party or the German-American Bund.[63] Ten days after Pearl Harbor, restraints were placed on the liberty of maritime employers to hire radio operators for service on American flag vessels. For the duration of war emergency it became unlawful to employ any person to serve as radio operator aboard any vessel (other than a vessel of foreign registry) if the Secretary of the Navy (1) had disapproved such employment for any specified voyage, route, or area of operation, and (2) had notified the master of the vessl of such disapproval prior to the vessel's departure.[64]

Since the war, no less significant prohibitions have been placed on public or private employment of members of communist organizations. The effect thereof will be determined by the success of the Subversive Activities Control Board in compelling the registration of such groups. Section 5 of the Internal Security Act of 1950 makes it illegal for members of registered communist organizations to conceal or fail to disclose such membership in seeking or accepting any employment in any defense facility, as defined and listed by the Secretary of Defense. This provision was extended to make illegal defense employment for members of registered "Communist action" groups.[65]

It may be noted that the Butler Bill of April 1955 would have empowered the President to establish procedures for screening any person in defense employment "as to whom there is reasonable cause to believe may engage in sabotage, espionage, or other subversive acts." This process of screening also would be applied to firms seeking or holding defense contracts. Thus, increasingly access of private firms to government contracts as well as access of individuals to jobs under such contracts, which today may be the staff of life, is being restricted. Contributing to this trend is the provision in the Rubber Producing Facilities Disposal Act of 1953 that purchase proposals shall not be accepted from any person who has not identified his principal, or is not financially responsible, or is a poor security risk.[66]

Freedom of employees to strike defense industries or to engage in so-called emergency strikes has on occasion been severly limited. The War Labor Disputes Act of 1943 required that the government be given notice of labor disputes, and that production continue for a period of thirty days after notice of intention to strike. A secret ballot of employees had to be conducted prior to calling a strike.[67] The President was granted ultimate power to seize plants if necessary to avoid interruption of war production occasioned by labor disputes, and interference with government operation of such plants was made illegal.[68] The plants were to be operated under the terms and conditions of employment which were in effect at the time possession was taken by the government.[69]

In the post-war Labor-Management Relations Act a national emergency strike is defined as one imperiling "the national health or safety."[70] When, in the opinion of the President, a threatened or existing strike or lockout affecting an entire industry or a substantial part thereof imperils the national health or safety, he may appoint a board of inquiry to inquire into the issues involved in the dispute and to make a written report to him within such time as he shall prescribe.[71] When the President has received a report from a board of inquiry, he may direct the Attorney General to petition any district court of the United States having jurisdiction of the parties to enjoin such strike or lockout or its continuance, and if the court finds that a threatened or actual strike or lockout (1) affects an entire industry or a substantial part thereof engaged in trade, commerce, transportation, transmission, or engaged in the production of goods for commerce; and (2) if permitted to occur or to continue, will imperil the national health or safety, it shall have jurisdiction to enjoin any such strike or lockout.[72]

The President will be advised of such a strike or lockout sufficiently in advance of its occurence because Section 8 (d) of the Act requires 60 days' written notice of termination or modification of a collective bargaining contract, and notification of the Federal Mediation and Conciliation Service and equivalent state or territorial services within thirty days after such notice of the existence of a dispute.[73]

Looking to restrictions upon federal employment, it is convenient to begin with 1940, the year in which, in an effort to expedite the strengthening of the national defense, Congress gave the Secretary of War limited power to remove army civil service employees for security reasons. The Secretary might remove from the classified civil service of the United States any employee of the Military Establishment forthwith if he found that such person had been guilty of conduct inimical to the public interest in the defense program of the United States, and if the person terminated had received notice of the charges.[74] Discharged employees were given the opportunity within thirty days of removal to answer charges in writing and to submit affidavits in support of written answers.[75]

Great discretion was permitted the civilian heads of the armed services in promoting or demoting regular officers during wartime, and as early as July 29, 1941 the President signed a Joint Resolution giving the Secretary of War power during the time of the national emergency to remove any officer from the active list of the Regular Army. The only restriction on the exercise of this power was that a comparison of the officer's performance-of-duty record with those of his fellow officers would be made. But retention in or dismissal from the active list, of any officer, ultimately could be determined by the Secretary,[76] even though affected officers were guaranteed a hearing before a board of not less than five general officers prior to separation.[77] Supplementing this was the provision that no payment could be made from money appropriated in the Act to any officer on the retired list of the Army who, for himself or for others, was engaged in the selling or the sale of any war materials or supplies either to the Army or the War Department.[78]

Since 1950 it has become common practice for the Congress to attach to appropriation bills the provision that no salary or wages will be paid from any appropriation to an individual who either asserts the right to strike against the Government or belongs to an employees' organization asserting this right. And no monies will be paid to an individual who advocates or is a member of an organization that advocates the overthrow of the Government of the United States.[79] The Defense Production Act of 1950 contained this type of provision.[80] It further provided that an affidavit shall be *prima facie* evidence that the person making it has acted contrary to the statute.[81] Agencies also have been delegated broad power to suspend employees deemed security risks. An August, 1950 statute permitted the heads of the State, Commerce, Defense, Justice, and Treasury Departments, the Secretaries of the Army, Navy and Air Force, and others, in their absolute discretion and when deemed necessary in the interest of the national security, to suspend, without pay, any civilian official or employee.[82] Following notice and an opportunity to the suspended employee to submit statements and affidavits, and after investigation and review by the employing agency, his employment might be terminated as necessary or advisable in the interest of the national security. Since the employee is informed of the reasons for his suspension only to the extent that such agency head determines that the interests of the national security permit, he may encounter difficulty in formulating his defense.

Interestingly enough while miltary emergency may be assigned as justifiable for banning or terminating employment of persons on the basis of their political affiliations, Congress has recognized that other kinds of emergency may require temporary suspension of such disqualifications to federal employment. The Department of Interior Appropriation Act of 1948 provided that in cases of emergency, caused by fire, flood, storm, act of God, or sabotage, persons might be employed for periods of not more than thirty days and be paid salaries and wages without the necessity of inquiring into their membership in any organization.

Traditional Procedural Rights of Individuals: Whether justifiable or not, in time of crisis encroachment upon the traditional rights and privileges of indivduals invariably has been recorded. The Compulsory Testimony Act of August, 1954[83] may be an example of such legislation. It enables Congressional Committees in a limited number of instances to solicit the courts in compelling testimony from recalcitrant witnesses who have invoked their constitutional privilege against self-incrimination. Suspension of this constitutional safeguard is achieved by the immunity from prosecution accorded the witness under the terms of this measure. As to the scope of the immunity therein afforded, it is not in excess of that granted in laws previously enacted, notably the following: Interstate Commerce Act, Sherman Anti-Trust Act, Securities Exchange Act, Communications Act, National Labor Relations Act, Motor Carrier Act, Federal Power Act, Public Utility Holding Company Act, Industrial Alcohol Act, Merchant Marine Act, Bituminous Coal Act, Natural Gas Act, Civil Aeronautics Act, Fair Labor Standards Act, Railroad Unemployment Insurance Act, Social Security Act, Investment Company Act, Investment Advisers Act, Second War Powers Act, and Emergency Price Control Act, 1942. See a more extended listing in *Shapiro* v. *U.S.*[84]

Emergency entails restraints upon the freedom of indivduals to manipulate their property and to act as they please. Not only does the government, as has been noted, seize factories and mines, but can compel acceptance of government orders.

CHAPTER V

GOVERNMENTAL ACQUISITION OF PROPERTY

In recent years the federal government has set up programs for the acquisition or disposition of productive facilities and natural resources. These programs have had various objectives, as for example the acquisition in conjunction with its parity payments policy of surplus agricultural commodities. Later acquisition programs, justified in terms of national defense, include the following: stockpiling of strategic raw materials; acquisition of land and equipment for military sites and for federally-owned productive facilities; the lending or leasing of federally-owned productive equipment to private producers; and the acquisition of plants and raw and finished materials incidental to enforcement of emergency control programs.

STOCKPILING

The Government may acquire natural resources in an effort to stockpile for defense purposes, in the course of expanding the military establishments or governmentally owned productive facilities, or it may acquire such resources to facilitate a privately financed defense project. This last purpose sometimes leads the Government to lend its power of eminent domain to private business concerns.

In June 1939 Congress assigned to the Secretary of the Interior and the Army and Navy Munitions Board the task of determining which materials are strategic and critical to American defense, and provided for acquisition of stocks of these materials.[1] Congress also encouraged the development of mineral resources within the United States. Two months later Congress approved the exchange of surplus agricultural commodities held by the Commodity Credit Corporation for stocks of strategic and critical materials produced abroad.[2] Under the fiscal 1941 Appropriations Act, the Navy Department obtained funds for procurement of strategic and critical materials in accordance with the Act of June 7, 1939.[3] In this statute, and in a July 1940 Act to expedite the strengthening of the national defense, the President also was authorized to expend large sums on acquisition of such materials.[4]

The Defense Production Act of 1950 empowers the President to make provision either for purchases of, or commitments to purchase metals and other raw materials, including liquid fuels. The government may use the acquired items or offer them for resale. The same Act also empowers the President to encourage the exploration, development, and mining of critical and strategic minerals and metals.[5] The Mutual Security Act of 1951 also provides sustenance for the stockpiling program. The Director for Mutual Security is authorized to initiate projects designed to increase production and help in obtaining raw materials in which deficiencies exist among the United States' free world allies. The purpose of aiding recipients of American aid to develop their own stockpiling program of critical materials is to reduce the steady drain on United States resources.[6] The power of condemnation was added to the power of requisitioning granted in the 1950 Defense Production Act when Congress in a 1951 amendment empowered the President in the interest of national defense, and when deemed necessary by him, to acquire materials needed by the government. Acquisition may be by transfer, donation, purchase, or, if needed, properly instituted judicial proceedings.[7]

The Domestic Minerals Program Extension Act of 1953 sought to reduce American dependence on overseas sources of supply for strategic or critical minerals and metals during periods of threatening world conflict.[8] This was to be accomplished through a united effort on the part of each department and agency of the government having responsibility for the discovery, development, production, and acquisition of strategic or critical minerals and metals in order to decrease further and to eliminate where possible the dependency of the United States on overseas sources of supply of each such material.[9] The Act extended for an additional two years the termination dates of all purchase programs designed to stimulate the domestic production of tungsten, manganese, chromite, mica, asbestos, beryl, and columbium-tantalum-bearing ores and concentrates and established by regulations issued pursuant to the Defense Production Act of 1950.[10]

MILITARY SITES AND PRODUCTIVE FACILITIES

Scattered through the statute books, of course, are numerous authorizations to defense agencies to acquire land for specific projects. For example, a July 1939 statute authorized the Secretary of War to acquire fourteen described plots,[1] and a May 1949 statute authorized the Secretary of the Air Force to establish a joint long-range proving ground for guided missiles and other weapons and to acquire lands and rights necessary to set up the project.[2] An Act of 1951 authorized the Secretary of the Navy to enlarge existing water-supply facilities for the San Diego, California area for the purpose of insuring the existence of an adequate water supply for naval installations and defense production plants in that area.[3] Of equal, if not greater significance than the scope of the delegation contained therein are the provisions for extention of Congressional control set-out in these authorizations for acquisition of specific items.

In the Second War Powers Act, breadth of Congressional delegation rather than intensity of control is the dominant fact. For example, the President was authorized to permit the Secretaries of War and Navy, or any other officer, board or commission, to acquire real property by any means necessary, including condemnation, to insure its use by the Government when needed.[4] Immediate possession might be taken after filing of a condemnation petition.[5] Among the many powers granted to the Federal Civil Defense Administrator in the 1951 statute creating the FCDA was that of procuring by condemnation or otherwise, constructing, or leasing materials and facilities.[6]

Because they are extremely scarce or non-existent in their natural state in the United States, a few elements or other commodities have been the object of intensive government efforts to either directly produce them on a full scale, or to encourage private production by acquiring and transferring to private firms certain of the assets requisite to production. These are nitrogen, helium gas, fuels, rubber, synthetic liquid and abaca (a plant the fiber of which is used in making hemp).[7] Thus the Board of Directors of the Tennessee Valley Authority were given power to exercise the right of eminent domain[8] and to make and sell fixed nitrogen and fertilizers with the specific injunction that it maintain in stand-by condition suitable facilities for the production of explosives in the event of war or a national mergency.[9] The plant might be used for the fixation of nitrogen for agricultural purposes or leased, as long as conversion to war production could be made quickly. The TVA of course was authorized to produce and sell electric power,[10] but the government reserved the right in case of war or national emergency declared by Congress to preempt TVA-produced electricity as well as nitrogen.[11] The Helium Gas Conservation Act of 1937 authorized the Secretary of the Interior, through the Bureau of Mines, to acquire lands, and acquire or construct such plants as were necessary to establish a federal monopoly of helium.

In 1942 the Secretary of Agriculture was authorized to construct or operate factories for the growth and processing of guayule and

other rubber-bearing plants.[12]   In 1947 Congress proclaimed the
continued existence of a short supply of rubber, a highly strategic
and critical material needed for the common defense and which
cannot, in its natural state, be grown in the United States. It re-
affirmed the policy that there shall be maintained at all times in the
interest of the national security and common defense, in addition
to stock piles of natural rubber, a technologically advanced and
rapidly expandible domestic rubber-producing industry. To this end,
the powers of the United States to manufacture and sell synthetic
rubber were to continue in force and the government would retain
at least the minimum copolymer plant capacity to produce "not less
than six hundred thousand long tons per year."[13] A year later, in
March 1948, a policy of reliance upon the development of a free,
competitive synthetic-rubber industry and the termination of government production was enunciated, the President to exercise certain
powers of control to insure the existence of an extensive government
demand for domestic synthetic-rubber.[14]

The synthetic liquid fuels program was established in 1944. The
Secretary of the Interior, acting through the Bureau of Mines, was
authorized to develop and maintain one or more demonstration
plants to produce synthetic liquid fuels from coal, oil shale, and
other substances, and one or more demonstration plants to produce
liquid fuels from agricultural and forestry products. The Bureau
of Mines would also develop all facilities and accessories for the manufacture, purification, storage, and distribution of the products.[15]
Unlike the other plans for production of esssential defense elements
or commodities, this program was not designed directly to meet a
major portion of defense needs for the commodity produced. Rather,
the plants were to be of the minimum size which would allow the
government to furnish industry with the necessary cost and engineer-
ing data for the development of a synthetic liquid-fuel industry.[16]

In the Abaca Production Act of 1950, Congress declared that abaca,
a hard fiber used in the making of marine and other cordage, is a highly
strategic and critical material which cannot be produced in commercial
quantities in the continental United States, and of which an adequate
supply is vital to the industrial and military requirements for the
common defense of the United States.[17] The federal government was
therefore to continue the program for the production and sale of abaca
in which it was engaged at the termination of hostilities and to encourage abaca production throughout the world. The total acreage
produced by the government was not to exceed fifty thousand,

fluctuating below that upper limit at the discretion of the President.[18]

The year of Dunkirk witnessed a number of Congressional authorizations to the Executive to acquire and either directly utilize, or pass on to private enterprise, material of war, or productive equipment and facilities. In mid-1940 the President was given power to authorize the Secretary of War to manufacture in factories and arsenals under his jurisdiction, or otherwise procure, coast-defense and anti-aircraft material, including ammunition therefor, on behalf of any American Republic. He might also establish repair facilities for such equipment.[19] This was shortly extended to manufacturing for the government of any country whose defense the President deemed vital to the defense of the United States.[20] Later in 1940 he was authorized to requisition and take over for use of the United States any military or naval equipment or munitions which had been ordered for export, but which then could no longer be exported. Certain items of a military nature could not, for example, be sent to France once the Germans had occupied that country. The President could dispose of such material to a private corporation or individual if such action was deemed to be in the public interest.[21] The June 30, 1942 termination date was moved forward to June 30, 1944, and the President's power enlarged to requisition in the interest of national defense or prosecution of war in July 1942.[22]

In June 1940 the Secretary of the Navy was authorized to provide necessary construction facilities or manufacturing plants on federal land or elsewhere, and to man them with federal employees or otherwise whenever he found it imposible to make contracts or to secure facilities for procurement or construction of items authorized in connection with national defense.[23] By October 1941 this authority had grown to a general authorization to the President, that if he found that the use of any military or naval equipment, supplies, or munitions, or machinery, tools, or materials necessary for the manufacture, servicing and operation of such equipment, were needed for the defense of the United States the President could requisition such property. Only two conditions prevailed: first, that the need was immediate and impending, and second, that just compensation was paid to the owners. The original expiration date of June 30, 1943 was later changed to June 30, 1944.[24] But long before the Second World War, Congress gave the President authority to requisition merchant vessels. In Section 902 (a) of the Merchant Marine Act of 1936 the government reserved the right to requisition any vessel documented under the laws of the United States, during any national emergency

declared by proclamation of the President.[25] In authorizing the
President to utilize the power of eminent domain to acquire land
needed for pipe-line construction by private firms, Congress provided
that in the event it was impracticable for any private person promptly
and satisfactorily to construct such lines, the President could provide
for the construction by such department as he might designate.[26]
The government thus was privileged to go into the pipe-line business,
constructing and operating defense needed pipe-lines. Among the
prerogatives which Congress made available to the Secretary of the
Navy for purposes of insuring adequacy of maritime salvage operations
during the war, was that of acquiring such vessels and equipment as
he might deem necessary therefor.[27] The Secretary also was empowered to transfer, by charter or otherwise, such equipment for
operation by private salvage companies.

The Defense Production Act of 1950 gave the President powers virtually equal to those granted by Congress to the President in
1941. Again the President was empowered to requisition needed
materials for the defense of the United States.[28] And in July 1953
the three armed service secretaries were empowered to acquire, construct, establish, expand, rehabilitate or convert industrial plants,
either publicly or privately owned, as might be needed for the defense
of the United States. The statutory language followed the familiar
prescription that acquisition could be by purchase, donation, lease,
condemnation or otherwise as necessary.[29]

FACILITATING ACQUISITION BY PRIVATE ENTERPRISES

In July 1941 Congress used the power of eminent domain to facilitate the construction of public utilities for defense purposes.[1] Upon
finding that the construction of any pipe-line for the transportation
and/ or distribution of petroleum or petrol products moving in
interstate commerce was or might be necessary for national-defense
purposes, the President was permitted to acquire such land or interest
in land, including rights-of-way or easements, by the exercise of the
right of eminent domain, as, in his opinion might be necessary.[2] The
President invoked this Act on a number of occasions.[3]

The Second War Powers Act earlier mentioned not only authorized
the acquisition of real property by the Secretaries of War and Navy
or their agents, but permitted them to dispose of such property or
interest therein by sale, lease or otherwise.[4] The Small Business
Concerns Mobilization Act of June 1942 empowered the Smaller
War Plants Corporation, established under the Act,[5] to purchase or

lease land, to purchase, lease, build, or expand plants, and to purchase or produce equipment, facilities, machinery, materials, or supplies, as might be needed to enable the Corporation to provide small business concerns with the means and facilities to engage in the production of war materials.[6] The Corporation could also enter into contracts with the United States government and any department, agency, or officer of the government having procurement powers and obligate the Corporation to furnish articles, equipment, supplies, or materials to the government.

AVAILABILITY OF FEDERALLY OWNED PROPERTY TO PRIVATE ENTERPRISE

Actually no clean demarcation can be made between this and the preceding section. A graduation can be established. moving from statutes lending the power of eminent domain to private enterprise, to those emphasizing government acquisition and lending or leasing. and ultimately to those principally concerned with providing government-owned equipment to private enterprise—the equipment presumably already in the hands of the government or subject to acquisition under other statues.

One of the very first Acts to provide for placing educational production of munitions of war stipulated that initial orders placed with any person, firm, or corporation for supplying such munitions, accessories, or parts, could include a complete set of such gages, dies, jigs, tools, fixtures, and other special aids and appliances, including drawings as needed for the production of munitions in quantity in the event of emergency.[1] The title to all such facilities was to remain in the government of the United States. The fiscal 1941 Navy Department Appropriations Act granted the Navy funds to furnish Government-owned facilities at privately owned plants,[2] and a July 1940 Act to expedite the strengthening of the national defense accorded like authority to the President.[3] Section 303 (a) (d) of the Defense Production Act of 1950 gave the President a general power to purchase raw materials including liquid fuels for government use or for resale, and when in his judgment it would aid the national defense, to install government-owned equipment in plants, factories, and other industrial facilities owned by private persons.[4]

ACQUISITIONS INCIDENTAL TO ENFORCEMENT OF A CONTROL PROGRAM.

Of the acquisition statutes hitherto discussed, most required that an effort be made to negotiate a fair price with the individual or concern whose property was acquired and, failing that, recourse

might be had to eminent domain proceedings. By the terms of the
latter, private entrepreneurs or investors in effect are confronted with
the option of utilizing their property in conformity with the Government's mobilization program or, in lieu thereof, of relinquishing it
to the Government. The statutes now to be considered sanction
acquisition of private property in those cases in which the owners or
operators are not managing it to the Government's satisfaction.

A June 1940 Act to expedite national defense empowered the
Secretary of the Navy, under the general direction of the President,
whenever he deemed any existing manufacturing plant or facility
necessary for the national defense, and whenever he was unable to
arrive at an agreement with the owner of any such plant or facility
for its use or operation, to take over and operate such plant or facility
either by Government personnel or by contract with private firms.[1]
The Selective Training and Service Act of 1940 authorized the President, acting through the Secretaries of War or Navy, to take immediate possession of any plant or plants which in the opinion of the
Secretary of War or the Secretary of the Navy were capable of
being readily geared to war production. This drastic action came
only when the owners refused to give to the United States preference
in the matter of the execution of orders, or refused to manufacture
the kind, quantity, or quality of arms or ammunition, or who refused
to furnish the materials demanded at a reasonable price.[2]

The War Labor Disputes Act gave the President a similar power
to seize struck industries. It might be exercised with respect to
any plant, mine, or facility equipped for the manufacture, production,
or mining of any articles or materials which might be required for the
war effort, or which might be useful in connection therewith. But a
presidential finding was necessary first, that there was an interruption
of the operation of the plant, mine, or facility as a result of a strike
or other labor disturbance, and that the war effort would be unduly
impeded or delayed by the interruption, and that the exercise of such
power and authority was necessary to insure operation in the interest
of the war effort.[3]

Not, perhaps, punitive in its object, but nonetheless related to
enforcement of a control program, was the provision of the Emergency
Price Control Act of 1942, permitting the Price Administrator to buy
or sell commodities and goods or grant subsidies to assure necessary
production.[4]

CHAPTER VI

REGULATION OF PROPERTY

We have seen that the effort to rationalize the national economy in time of economic or war emergency may lead democratic governments to assert a power to acquire the raw materials of production and productive facilities. This power of acquisition may be designed or exercised as a sanction for the coercion of "co-operation" upon the part of the private units of the economy, or it may express the finding that particular stockpiling or production functions can only, or most efficiently be conducted by public agencies.

Significant as may be the readiness of democratic governments in time of critical economic or crucial war emergency to enter the market place or to produce, either to the exclusion of private enterprises or in competition with them, these are exceptional circumstances; rationalization of the economy is principally achieved by coercing private owners and producers to act consistently with a governmental definition of the public interest. It is such examples of direct governmental control of private entrepreneurs, producers, and distributors that are to be examined in this chapter.

CONTROL OF GOODS AND MATERIALS

In surveying the possible alternatives of a nation aware of a threatened or existing shortage of strategic raw materials or finished products it is appropriate to review first negative and general controls and thereafter to consider those which become increasingly particular and positive. An initial precautionary move in such circumstances is to prevent the escape of scarce materials from the country. Also relevant thereto is the conservation of domestic supplies. Beyond conservation, implementing these safeguards are affirmative programs encouraging increased domestic production of such materials as well as their importation from abroad. Such programs have been reviewed under the heading of government acquisition. It will be recalled that in addition to stockpiling strategic materials, the government created and operated new productive facilities in an effort to insure adequate supply. However, in addition to these measures the govern-

ment generally has been unable to escape the necessity of establishing
priorities and allocations systems to insure that whatever supply is
available is utilized for successful prosecution of the war or to combat
effectively any other domestic emergency.

Restrictions on Export: Congress, in the Tennessee Valley Authority Act of 1933, stipulated that no products of the Corporation could
be sold for use outside of the United States, its Territories and possessions, except to the United States government for the use of its Army
and Navy, or to its allies in case of war.[1]

In a series of enactments, commencing with a joint resolution of
May 1934, Congress sought to insulate the United States from the
danger of involvement in foreign wars by embargoing the shipment
of arms to foreign belligerents.   The resolution mentioned enabled
the President after consultation with the governments of other
American Republics to proclaim that the prohibition of the sale of
arms and munitions of war in the United States to those countries
then engaged in armed conflict in the Chaco might contribute to the
reestablishment of peace between those countries, after which it would
become illegal to sell such material to the disputants or their agents.[2]
On the same day that he signed the Chaco resolution, President
Roosevelt issued the proclamation contemplated by the Act.[3]   In
August 1935 the embargo method was imposed uniformly without
limitation as to area.   The Neutrality Act of that year provided that
if war broke out between two or more foreign states, the President
should proclaim this fact, and thereafter it would be unlawful to
export arms, ammunition or implements of war from any place in
the United States, or its possessions to the belligerents, or to any
neutral area for eventual trans-shipment to a belligerent country.[4]
In addition, the Act placed a blanket prohibition upon the export or
import of arms, except insofar as authorized under license procured
from the National Munitions Control Board established by the Act.[5]
When he had cause to believe a given ship was about to carry material
to a belligerent, but the evidence was not deemed sufficient to justify
forbidding the departure, the President could require the owner or
commander to give a bond to the United States, with sufficient sureties, that the vessel would not deliver the men, or the cargo, or any
part thereof to a belligerent.[6]

Congress maintained a vigilant oversight over enforcement of its
neutrality policy.   Since the embargo authorized by the 1935 Act
could be applied only on the occurrence of war between, or among,
two or more foreign states, it could not be invoked in the Spanish

Civil War. This situation Congress immediately rectified upon assembling in January 1937. Public Resolution No. 1, which became law on January 8, 1937, specifically prohibited the export of war material for use of either of the opposing forces in Spain.[7] Thereafter it amended the 1935 statute, retaining its provisions virtually intact, but directing it at instances of internecine as well as international war.[8] The same day that the President signed this law, he issued a proclamation finding that a state of civil strife unhappily existed in Spain and prohibited the direct or indirect export of material of war to either of the opposing armies.[9]

A series of proclamations were issued under this and other contingent emergency statutes in September 1939.[10] The prohibition on export of war material was narrowed to a prohibition on the export of such material until title had unconditionally passed to the foreign purchaser—the cash and carry system.[11] A number of Presidential proclamations effected application of the new statute.[12]

Presidential proclamations also reflect the change in emphasis of statutory prohibitions of the export of war materials. In September 1939, the President issued a clearly neutrality-oriented proclamation prohibiting enlistment in, or recruitment for, belligerent armed forces, provisioning of belligerent ships,[13] and subsequent proclamations of 1940 and 1941 were equally clearly concerned with preserving adequate domestic stocks of strategic materials.[14]

Upon amendment of the July 1940[15] Act in June 1942, the President was authorized to prohibit or curtail the exportation of any articles. technical data, materials, or supplies, except under such rules and regulations as he might prescribe.[16] Unless the President otherwise directed, the functions and duties of the President under this section of the Act were to be performed by the Board of Economic Warfare.[17] The Export Control Act of 1949 empowered the President to prohibit or curtail the exportation from th United States, its Territories and possessions, of any articles, materials, or supplies, including technical data but excluding agricultural commodities in excess of domestic requirements.[18] The purpose here was to protect the United States from the excessive drain of scarce materials.[19] The Atomic Energy Act also prohibited the export from or import into the United States or curtail the exportation from the United States, its Territories and as authorized by the Atomic Energy Commission upon a determination by the President that the common defense and security would not be adversely affected thereby.[20]

Obviously embraced within the power to embargo is the power conditionally to permit exports. Thus, in December 1941 following Pearl Harbor, Congress permitted the President, whenever he deemed it to be in the interest of national defense, to authorize the Secretary of War to sell, transfer title to, exchange, lease, lend, or otherwise dispose of, to the government of any country whose defense the President deemed vital to the defense of the United States, any defense article procured from funds appropriated for the military establishment prior to or since March 11, 1941.[21]

In formulating an export policy for the period following World War II era, Congress doubtless has been influenced by the post war inflation. The Export Control Act of 1949, in granting the President power to prohibit or curtail the exportation of certain materials, including technical data,[22] made explicit the Congressional intent to protect the domestic economy from the excessive drain of scarce materials and to reduce the inflationary impact of abnormal foreign demand.[23]

Domestic Conservation: With a view to stabilizing prices and encouraging the conservation of deposits of crude oil situated within the United States Congress in 1935 prohibited the interstate shipment of contraband oil (i.e., oil produced in excess of state imposed quotas).[24] Two different provisions of the Second War Powers Act of 1942 related to conservation of strategic materials. Section 801 empowered the President to direct the Administrator of the Federal Security Agency to assign the manpower of the Civilian Conservation Corps to the extent necessary to protect the munitions, aircraft, and other war industries, municipal water supply, power and other utilities, and to protect resources subject to the hazards of forest fires.[25] Section 1201 permitted the Director of the Mint to vary the metallic composition of five cent pieces to conserve strategic metals.[26]

Priorities and Allocation: In late May 1941, Congress provided that whenever the President was satisfied that the fulfillment of requirements for the defense of the United States would result in a shortage in the supply of any material for defense or for private account or for export, the President could allocate the material in whatever manner he deemed necessary or appropriate in the public interest and to promote the national defense.[27] This provision was retained in the Second War Powers Act of 1942.[28] In a joint resolution of March 1947 declaring the need for maintenance of a technologically advanced and rapidly expandable domestic rubber-producing industry and for a Congressional study of the problem, Congress provided that in the interim, pending the enactment of permanent legislation, the government should continue allocation, specification, and inventory controls of natural and synthetic rubber.[29] A year later this power was continued. The President was authorized to exercise allocation, specification, and inventory controls of natural rubber and synthetic rubber to insure the consumption of general-purpose synthetic rubber as a part of the estimated total annual consumption of natural rubber.[30]

The First Decontrol Act of 1947, providing for the termination of certain of the provisions of the Second War Powers Act, permitted the continued exercise of power to allocate materials which were certified by the Secretaries of State and Commerce as necessary to meet international commitments.[31] Section 101 of the Defense Production Act of 1950 empowered the President to allocate materials in such manner, upon such conditions, and to such extent as he deems necessary or appropriate to promote the national defense.[32] A related section provided that no person should accumulate (1) in excess of the reasonable demands of business, personal, or home consumption, or (2) for the purpose of resale at prices in excess of prevailing market prices, materials which had been designated by the President as scarce materials or materials the supply of which would be threatened by such accumulation.[33] The Atomic Energy Act of 1946, as amended in 1951, expands the allocation power to its logical extreme by allocating all fissionable material to the federal government, making it unlawful for any person to possess or transfer any fissionable material, except as authorized by the Atomic Energy Commission.[34]

CONTROL OF PRODUCTIVE FACILITIES

Priorities: Particularly in the conversion period preceding full-scale defense production it is necessary to compel producers to accord first priority to fulfillment of government contracts. During such interval prior to all-out defense mobilization, when his competitors may be satisfying the demands of consumers, the businessman has ample cause to fear that in giving priority to government orders disgruntled private customers will be permanently lost to competing firms. Accordingly, a June 1940 statute provided that, in the discretion of the President, fulfillment of Army or Navy contracts was to take priority over all deliveries for private account or for export.[1] In a year this was amended to extend the President's power over priorities to include contracts or orders for the Government of any country whose defense the President deemed vital to the defense of the United States and contracts or orders, or subcontracts or sub-orders, which the President deemed necessary or appropriate to promote the defense of the United States.[2] In May 1941 the Maritime Commission was empowered to demand that work on its contracts take priority over the furnishing of materials or performance of work for private account or for export.[3] The Second War Powers Act continued in effect the provision of the June 1940 and May 1941 statutes[4] by providing that all orders for vessels, equipment, and weapons placed by the Army and Navy were, in the discretion of the President, to take priority over all deliveries for private account or for export.

To repair the Spring 1945 flood damages, Congress in June of that year granted the War Production Board, and every other governmental agency which had jurisdiction over allocations and priorities relating to farm machinery and equipment, authorization to take such steps as might be necessary to provide for the necessary allocations and priorities to enable farmers in the areas affected by floods in 1944 and 1945 to replace and repair their farm machinery and equipment which was destroyed or damaged by floods, or windstorms, or fire caused by lightning, and to continue farming operations.[5]

Again, the Defense Production Act of 1950 gave the President virtually plenary power to require that defense orders be given priority by private industry: "The President is hereby authorized. . . to require that performance under contracts or orders (other than contracts of employment) which he deems necessary or appropriate to promote the national defense shall take priority over performance under any other contract or order."[6] Perhaps not classifiable as examples of an assertion of governmental priority in the use of productive facilities are three enactments under which the Federal Government has exercised the right to withhold issuance of patents and to reserve certain inventions for its exclusive use whenever the public safety or defense so require.[7]

Compulsory Orders: The establishment of priorities for the fulfillment of contracts presupposses voluntary fulfillment of government contracts by private industry. Do the principles of democratic government preclude conscription of industrial plants, regardless of the willingness or unwillingness of owners to execute war contracts? Having conscripted physically eligible young men under the Selective Training and Service Act of 1940 Congress also established therein priority for industrial performance on military orders, and a provision to compel acceptance and priority performance on defense orders.[8] The President was empowered, through the head of the War Department or the Navy Department, to place orders with any individual, firm, association, company, corporation, or organized manufacturing industry for whatever materials might be required, and which were of the nature and kind usually produced or at least capable of being produced by the productive units involved. General Motors produced automobiles, but they could also produce tanks or trucks as the Army required. Compliance with all such orders for products or materials was obligatory and took precedence over all other orders and contracts previously placed.[9] The use of plant seizure by the government as the sanction for infraction of the provision has previously been reviewed in the section on acquisition. In the Second War Powers Act of 1942 the President was given the plenary power to require acceptance of and performance under defense contracts or orders in preference to all other contracts or orders.[10] More recently, the Defense Production Act of 1950 and the 1953 amendment to it authorize the President to require acceptance and performance of such contracts or orders as he deems necessary or appropriate to promote the national defense.[11]

Protection of Quality: Only one example in this category has been discovered. In 1940 Congress amended an old World War I law, vintage 1918, that provided punishment for the willful injury or destruction of war materials or war premises used in connection with war material.[12] Sections 5 and 6 of this Act imposed maximum penalties of $10,000 fine and ten years imprisonment for willfully injuring or destroying national defense materials, whatever they might be, premises or utilities, or willfully making defective defense material or equipment utilized for the production of defense material. An important element of the offense was existence of an intent to injure, interfere with, or obstruct the national defense of the United States.[13] While laws against sabotage have been enforced vigorously, this 1918 law was designed to protect the Government against shoddy workmanship and poor equipment.

Controlling Labor Relations: Emergency provisions regulating labor relations in private enterprise appear to have four different motivations. First, wide scale control of the relations between employers and employees may constitute an integral part of a total program aimed at countering an economic depression. Second, it may be aimed at preventing unethical practices. Third, the purpose may be to avoid interruption of vital production. And, fourth, the control may be designed as a precaution against espionage, sabotage, or other violation of the national security.

The National Industrial Recovery Act obviously conceived as

emergency legislation which it indubitably was, is the outstanding example of an endeavor in part through the regulation of employer-employee relations, to overcome an economic depression.[14] The objective of course was to increase consumer income and purchasing power, which in turn was to stimulate production, with related chain effects. Section 7 (a) required that every code of fair competition established under the Act guaranteed employees the right to bargain collectively, and to join or refrain from joining a union. Company unions were outlawed. Employers were to comply with the maximum hours or labor, minimum rates of pay, and other conditions of employment, approved or prescribed by the President. In Section 4 (b) the President was granted the unprecedented power whenever he found "that destructive wage or price cutting or other activities contrary to the policy of this title were being practiced in any trade or industry or any subdivision thereof," to license business enterprises in order to make effective a code of fair competition or an agreement that would carry out the policy of the Act. Once a finding had been made, and publicly announced, no one could carry on any business, if in interstate commerce, unless a license had been obtained. Any order of the President suspending or revoking any such license was to be final if in accordance with law.

Title II of the Act, pertaining to public works projects, closely regulated employment practices on projects contracted under the Act: Convict labor was prohibited; no one, except in an administrative or executive position could work more than thirty hours a week; all employees were to be paid just and reasonable wages sufficient to provide a standard of living in decency and comfort; wherever possible ex-servicemen with dependents were to be given preference in employment; and human labor in preference to machinery was to be used wherever practicable and consistent with sound economy and public advantage.[15] In June 1934 Congress authorized the establishment of labor boards to enforce the labor relations provisions of the N.I.R.A.[16] As is well known these sweeping provisions were later swept aside in the famed case of *Schechter Poultry Corporation* v. *United States*,[17] wherein Mr. Justice Cardozo, speaking for a unanimous Court, said "this is delegation run rampant."

Next to be considered are controls designed to forestall interruption of vital production. Section 8 of the War Labor Disputes Act required 30 days notice of a prospective strike and secret balloting of the union members concerned.[18] Other sections of the Act authorized government seizure of struck plants, and made it unlawful to interfere with government operation of plants.[19] The Labor Management Relations Act of 1947 set forth procedure whereby the President may secure injunctions postponing strikes or lockouts which will, if permitted to occur or to continue, imperil the national health or safety.[20]

Controlling Profits: The campaign of the 1930's to take the profits out of war is well known. Correlative to the deeply felt aspiration in time of peace to end the resort to war as an instrument of policy, is the popular thesis that war and the profitability of war production have a causal connection. In time of war, the public, on the other hand, is receptive to the proposal that command of the services and lives of mature young human beings warrants conscription of capital at least to the extent necessary to avoid profiteering, or to the extent such conscription facilitates the attainment of other worthy defense goals. In harmony with these beliefs the Vinson-Trammell Act of 1934 authorizing naval construction within the limits of the Washington and London treaties of 1922 and 1930 instructed the Secretary of the Navy to make no contract for the construction and/ or manufacture of any complete naval vessel or aircraft, or any portion thereof unless the contractor agreed to certain conditions: (1) he had to agree to pay any profit in excess of ten percent of the total contract price to the United States Treasury (twelve percent was allowed as the profit margin on aircraft); and (2) he could make no subdivisions of any contract or subcontract for the same article or articles for the purpose of evading the provisions of the Act.[21]

In 1938 provisions for close supervision of the leasing of naval petroleum reserves also were imposed upon the Navy Department, obviously directed in part at precluding extortionate profit-making from such leases.[22]

In permitting emergency negotiation of contracts for the acquisition of construction of war vessels or material with or without competitive bidding, upon determination that the price was fair and reasonable the Act of June 28, 1940 to expedite national defense afforded the Secretaries of War and Treasury authority to modify existing contracts, including Coast Guard contracts, as the Secretary concerned believed necessary.[23] Presumably upon a later finding that an agreed price was not fair and reasonable, profits could be revised downward through resort to Section 9 permitting contract modification at the discretion of the Secretary. Again, the Second War Powers Act of 1942, in permitting the Secretary of the Navy, when authorized by the President, to negotiate contracts for the acquisition, construction, repair, or alteration of complete naval vessels or aircraft, or any portion thereof,[24] stipulated that the cost-plus-a-percentage-of-cost system of contracting should not be used unless considered necessary by the Secretary of the Navy, in which case the percentage was not to exceed seven percent.[25] By way of enforcement the government reserved the right to inspect the plants and audit the books of contractors.[26]

Authority to award contracts without competitive bidding was not freely granted. A Supplemental Defense Appropriations Act of 1942 required the Secretaries of War and Navy to report to the Congress all defense contracts in excess of $150,000 and to justify those awarded without competitive bidding.[27] The Secretaries were authorized and directed to insert in any contract for an amount in excess of $100,000 a provision for the renegotiation of the contract price.[28] In 1951, declaring that sound execution of the national defense program requires the elimination of excessive profits from contracts made with the United States, and from related subcontracts, in the course of such program, Congress enacted the Renegotiation Act of 1951 providing for the renegotiation of defense contracts netting contractors more than a reasonable profit.[29]

CONTROL OF CREDIT, EXCHANGE, PRICES

Credit: The major purpose of the Defense Production Act of 1950 was to place the national economy on a war production footing with minimal posible effect upon civilian production and consumption. An effort was made to expand the total productive facilities of the nation beyond the levels needed to meet the civilian demand, thus reducing the need to curtail civilian consumption. To some extent, however, it was anticipated that normal civilian production and purchases would have to be curtailed and redirected.[1] In this connection the Federal Reserve Board by law was empowered to impose consumer credit controls pursuant to an Executive Order[2] until such time as the President determined that the exercise of such controls were no longer necessary. The controls, of course, were to be directed at carrying out the objectives of the Defense Production Act.[3] In addition, the President was authorized from time to time to prescribe regulations for regulating real estate construction credit as he believed necessary to prevent or reduce excessive fluctuations in such credit. He was empowered to prescribe maximum loan or credit values, minimum down payments, trade-in or exchange values, maximum maturities and maximum amounts of credit.[4] These, of course, were direct controls, as distinguished from inducements or incentives designed to reduce civilian demand for materials and productive facilities needed by the military establishment.

Opposite to the use of credit controls as a means of reducing effective consumer demand is direct intervention to insure that adequate credit is available to finance business activities declared by the Government to be essential to national defense. Conceivably the government could require that lending institutions, under certain conditions, make such grants. In lieu thereof it sought to provide incentives to lending institutions to make loans to defense producers, and avoided compelling extension of such credit. In fact, credit was made available through the Reconstruction Finance Corporation, the Smaller War Industries Administration and most recently the Small Business Administration. As a *quid pro quo* the government compels the recipient of such aid to submit to supervision.[5] Equally effective as loans in financing needed defense construction or production are advances to contractors. In providing for the construction of pipe-lines for the transportation of petroleum products, Congress in 1941 permitted the President to make such advances as he deemed advisable, through such departments as he might designate to the contractors.[6] It also authorized the Secretary of Navy to advance to private salvage companies such funds as the Secretary thought necessary to provide for the immediate financing of salvage operations.[7]

Exchange: The May 1937 amendment to the Neutrality Act made it unlawful, when the President had issued a proclamation that a state of war between two or more states or a state of civil war in a foreign state existed for any person in the United States to purchase, sell, or exchange bonds, securities or other obligations of the governments of any belligerent states or to loan, or to collect contributions.[8] The First War Powers Act of 1941 echoed this provision, providing in Title III, Trading with the Enemy, that the President in time of national emergency declared by him might investigate, regulate, or prohibit any transactions in foreign exchange, transfers of credit or payments.[9] The Export Control Act of 1949 permitted the President to stipulate the rules which should apply to the financing, transporting, and other servicing of exports.[10]

Price Control: In time of war the capitalist economy is transformed into a closely administered economy regulated in an effort to maximize war production and minimize dislocation of the civilian economy. To prevent speculation and dissipation of tax and consumer dollars through continuous and unchecked price increases, it becomes neces-

sary that prices be subjected to government control. This was
the aim of the Emergency Price Control Act of 1942. Whenever
in the judgment of the Price Administrator the price or prices of
a commodity or commodities threatened to rise to an extent inconsistent with the purposes of the Act, the Price Administrator could
establish whatever maximum price or prices he thought equitable
and fair. The only guide lines for "fair and equitable" in establishing
a maximum price were the prices prevailing between October 1 and
October 15, 1941.[11] He was further empowered to recommend stabilization or reduction of rents in defense-rental areas. Where state
or local boards failed to heed the recommendation the Administrator
could by regulation or order establish maximum rents for such
accomodations as in his judgment would be generally fair and equitable and would effectuate the purposes of the Act. Rent levels
were established on the basis of those prevailing on April 1, 1941.
The Act was amended in October 1942 when Congress authorized
and directed the President on or before November 1, 1942, to issue a
general order stabilizing prices, wages, and salaries affecting the cost
of living. Stabilization was so far as practicable, to be on the basis
of the levels which existed on September 15, 1942.[12] The President
was also given power by regulation to limit or prohibit the payment
of double time except when, because of emergency conditions, an
employee is required to work for seven consecutive days in any
regularly scheduled work week.[13]

In an effort to adapt the price control program to postwar re-
conversion and prepare for its eventual termination Congress in
July 1946 extended the life of the Price Control Act of 1942 to
June 30, 1947, admonishing the Office of Price Administration and
other agencies to use their price powers to promote the earliest
practicable balance between production and demand: Congress
wanted the control of prices and the use of subsidy powers to be
terminated as rapidly as possible.[14] The President was directed to
recommend to the Congress legislation needed to establish monetary,
fiscal, and other policies adequate to supplement the control of
prices and wages during the balance of the fiscal year 1947. A Joint
Resolution of March 1947 continued the price control program with
regard to sugar until October 31, 1947.[15] Rent control as well as
other war production controls continued in effect by the Defense
Production Act of 1950 which authorized the President to establish
a ceiling or ceilings on the price, rental, commission, rate, fee, charge
or allowance paid or received on the sale or delivery, or the purchase or

receipt, by or to any person, of any material or service. And the same Act required that the President issue regulations and orders stabilizing wages, salaries, and other compensation.[16] Once the Korean War ended, all controls, price, rent and credit were swept off the statute books.

CONTROL OF COMMON CARRIERS

Congressional enactments under this head generally fall into three major categories: control of domestic transportation, control of carriage by American ships, and control of foreign vessels in American ports. Our interest is confined exclusively to emergency controls exercisable by the Interstate Commerce Commission and similar federal regulatory agencies.

Control of Domestic Common Carriers: The Emergency Railroad Transportation Act of 1933 was designed to facilitate rehabilitation of the depression ridden American railroads. An Act addressed to economic rather than military emergency, it had nonetheless military overtones. The maintenance of an efficiently functioning railroad system capable of meeting potential American defense needs was an objective that could not be overlooked in the formulation of a successful railroad policy. The Act set up a Coordinator of Transportation who was to divide the railroad lines into three groups: eastern, southern, and western.[1] A number of railroad coordinating committees were created to carry out the purposes of the Act—i.e., elimination of unnecessary duplication of services and facilities, control of allowances, etc., and avoidance of undue impairment of net earnings, and other wastes and preventable expense, and promotion of financial reorganization.[2] Whenever unable to carry out these reforms the committees were to recommend action to the Coordinator who might, at his discretion, issue an order embodying their recommendations. When the committees failed to act on matters brought to their attention by the Coordinator he was authorized and directed to issue and enforce such order, giving appropriate directions to the carriers and subsidiaries subject to the Interstate Commerce Act as he found to be consistent with the public interest.[3]

Like the N.I.R.A. the Act contained a provision dealing with labor relations. The Railroads were prohibited from reducing the number of their employees below the number as shown by the pay rolls of employees in service during the month of May, 1933, after deducting the number who had been removed from the payrolls after the effective date of the Act by reason of death, normal retirement, or resignation.[4] A regional committee system was established for the representation of employees, and provision made for regional boards of adjustment to settle controversies between carriers and employees. Carriers and employees were to be equally represented on such boards.[5] The Railway Labor Act of 1926, as amended in 1934, attempted to establish a pattern of free union-management negotiation of disputes with ultimate recourse to a National Mediation Board.[6]

Air transportation received the attention of Congress in a June 1934 statute establishing a commission to make a report to the Congress recommending an aviation policy.[7] The Commission was to report its recommendations of a broad policy covering all phases of aviation and the relation of the United States thereto. Subsequently the Civil Aeronautics Act of 1938 was enacted, embodying congressional policy in this field.[8] In 1950 a security provision was added to the Act, permitting the Secretary of Commerce whenever he determined such action to be required in the interest of national security to establish airspace zones in which civilian flights could be restricted or prohibited.[9]

Another original statute in this field was the Communications Act of 1934, whereunder interstate and foreign commerce in communication by wire and radio is regulated. Federal controls were aimed at insuring existence of a rapid, efficient, Nation-wide, and world-wide wire and radio communication service for the convenience of the public and for the purpose of national defense.[10] Created thereunder was the Federal Communications Commission to which elaborate regulatory powers were granted. During the continuance of a war in which the United States was engaged, the Act authorized the President to direct that such communications as in his judgment were deemed to be essential to the national defense and security should have preference or priority with any carrier subject to the Act. He could give these directions at and for such times as he determined and he could modify, change, suspend or annul them.[11] The President also was authorized to prevent any obstructions by physical force or intimidations by threats of physical force of interstate and foreign radio or wire communications.[12]

The pipeline construction provision of July 30, 1941 required that pipe lines constructed with government aid be constructed subject to whatever terms and conditions the President prescribed as necessary for national defense purposes.[13] The second War Powers

Act of 1942 gave the Interstate Commerce Commission wartime
authority with respect to motor carriers, to be exercised under
circumstances and procedure equivalent to the authority it had
with respect to other carriers. It could issue reasonable directives
with respect to equipment, service and facilities of motor carriers
and require the joint use of equipment, terminals, warehouses, garages,
and other facilities. Motor carriers were to be subject to the same
penalties for failure to comply with action taken by the Commission
as any other carriers under its jurisdiction.[14] In June 1953 Congress
continued in effect traffic priority powers of the I.C.C. which had
been granted during the war and continued by the Emergency
Powers Continuation Act.[15]

Control of Carriage by American Vessels: The Neutrality Act of
1935 had provided that, following a presidential finding of the
existence of war between two foreign states, it would be unlawful
for any American vessel to carry any arms to any port of the belligerent or to any neutral port for trans-shipment to, or for the use
of, belligerents.[16] Penalty for violation of this prohibition might
include $10,000 fine, five years imprisonment, and, in addition, the
vessel, her tackle, apparel, furniture, equipment and armaments
would be forfeited to the United States.[17] In addition vessels were
prohibited from carrying war material to belligerent warships which
presumably would effect transfer at sea. If the President or his
delegate had adequate reason to believe a ship about to carry war
material to a belligerent warship, he could prohibit departure; or
if the evidence did not warrant this, the owner or commander
could be required to give a bond to the United States, with sufficient
sureties, in whatever amount the President deemed proper, conditioned so that the vessel would not deliver the men or the cargo, or
any part thereof, to any warship. Evasion of this prohibition subjected a vessel to the possibility of being confined to port for the
duration of the war.[18] Application of this Act to Spain was effected
by a Joint Resolution of January 8, 1937.[19]

The prohibition of American carriage of war material to belligerents in international or civil war was rephrased in the 1937
amendments to the Act but kept essentially intact. Section 10
of the 1937 Act explicitly prohibited the arming of American vessels
engaged in commerce with any belligerent state, or any state wherein
civil strife exists.[20] President Roosevelt immediately issued a Proclamation finding the existence of civil war in Spain, promulgating

a list of articles to be considered material of war, and prohibiting their carriage to Spain by American vessels.[21]

The Neutrality Act was made more stringent in November 1939. While it was unlawful to export or transport war materials from the United States to a belligerent until all right, title, and interest therein had been transferred to some foreign government,[22] it was unlawful for American vessels to carry *any* passengers or *any* articles or materials to *any* belligerent.[23] Furthermore, the President was empowered to define combat areas, from which American vessels were by law excluded. The prohibition against arming American merchant vessels was continued. In August 1940, following the fall of France, and while the British prepared for a German channel invasion, the Act was liberalized to permit American vessels in ballast, unarmed and not under convoy to transport refugee children, under sixteen years of age, from war zones, or combat areas if the vessel were proceeding under safe conduct granted by all of the States named in the proclamations.[24]

In 1953 Congress placed on the statute books a provision suggestive of the old neutrality acts. Under this law the Secretary of the Treasury, or anyone designated by the President, could seize and detain any carrier-vessel, vehicle or aircraft—carrying munitions of war from the United States. The authority to "seize and detain" came into operation whenever an attempt was made to export, ship or take out of the United States any munitions of war or other materials in violation of law. Moreover, the law became operative as long as there was "probable cause to believe" that prohibited items were being removed from the United States in violation of the law.[25]

The Merchant Marine Act of 1936 is, of course, another of those organic statutes designed to promote, rehabilitate, and regulate in the interest of the trade and of the public, a segment of the American transportation system. We have already seen that in this Act the government secured the right in time of war emergency to requisition American registered vessels. As a condition of the grant of subsidies toward the construction of vessels in American yards, the Maritime Commission reserved a power of final approval of the design of such vessels. This power was of course shared with the Navy Department which had to approve all defense features in the proposed vessel.[26] Under the terms of the Act any vessels, the construction of which was subsidized, were to be so designed as to be readily and quickly convertible into transport and supply vessels in a time of national emergency.[27] By permitting it to subsidize operation on approved routes, Title VI of the Act in effect enabled the Commission to control also the allocation of American shipping on the various world trade routes.

In July 1941 the President was given power, during the emergency which he had declared on May 27 of that year, to authorize the Maritime Commission to issue warrants entitling vessels to priority over merchant vessels not holding such warrants, in the use of facilities for loading, discharging, lighterage or storage of cargoes, the procurement of fuel, towing, overhauling, drydocking or repair of such vessels. Vessels holding warrants had priority among themselves in accordance with the rules of the Maritime Commission.[28] In granting warrants, the Commission was to make fair and reasonable provision for priorities. The criteria for helping the Commission determine priorities were: (1) the importation of substantial quantities of strategic and critical materials, (2) the transportation of substantial quantities of materials when such transportation was requested by any defense agency, and (3) the transportation in the foreign or domestic commerce of the United States of substantial quantities of materials deemed by the Commission to be essential to the defense of the United States.[29]

Certain controls were imposed on the staffing of American vessels. A statute of December 17, 1941 made it unlawful to employ any person or to permit any person to serve as radio operator abroad any vessel (other than a vessel of foreign registry) if the Secretary of the Navy disapproved the employment for any specified voyage, route, or area of operation and had notified the master of the vessel of the disapproval prior to the vessel's departure.[30] In 1934 a new stipulation permitted the Commission to suspend the rule requiring radio operators to have at least six months service before being qualified as a radio operator. However, suspension of this qualification could not be retained once the emergency had been terminated.[31]

Control of Foreign Vessels in American Waters: The Neutrality Act of 1935, as amended in May 1937, empowered the President to place special restrictions on the use of the ports and territorial waters of the United States. The restrictions which could be imposed involved limiting access to American ports and territorial waters by the submarines or merchant vessels of a foreign state. Special restrictions could be imposed at the President's discretion once he determined that such restrictions were needed to protect the commercial interests of the United States and its citizens, or to promote the security of the United States. Once limitations on port usage had been imposed, it became unlawful for any foreign submarine or armed merchant vessel to enter a port or territorial water of the United States. Only the President could prescribe the conditions and circumstances which would justify an exception to the rule.[32]

On October 18, 1939, President Roosevelt issued Proclamation No. 2371 declaring it unlawful for belligerent submarines, whether commercial or ships of war, to enter the ports or territorial waters of the United States except when forced into such ports by *force majeure*.[33] The Panama Canal Zone was exempted from this order. Following enactment of the November 4, 1939 amendment to the Neutrality Act,[34] a new proclamation with identical provisions was promulgated in conformity with the revised law.[35]

Chapter VII

CONTROL OF COMMUNICATIONS

A contemporary "revisionist" school of historians devoted to a reappraisal of accepted views of the cause and effect of American participation in the Second World War, attributes significance to the charge that the Roosevelt and Truman Administrations selected, withheld, and released data to historians in a manner calculated to distort the reasons for American involvemnt in that war.[1] Similar charges of selective withholding or release of information, have, of course, been levied against the Eisenhower Administration.

A daily reading of responsible newspapers quickly discloses abundant examples of careful selectivity in the release of information by government officials, can scarcely be denied. Indeed scholars, journalists, and the American public are becoming increasingly dependent upon the release of information by the federal government for their interpretation of recent historical and current events.[2] Whatever the import of this development, however, it is not within the scope of this treatise. The present chapter is limited to a survey and classification of statutory provisions relating to the withholding and release of information by the government. It is accordingly appropriate merely to acknowledge the possibility that intensive research subsequently may disclose to what extent public opinion has been prejudiced, distorted, or confused by the federal government's policies concerning the release of information.

THE RELEASE OF INFORMATION BY THE GOVERNMENT

Statutes concerning the release of information by government agencies appear to have been drafted with a view to accomplishing the following purposes: (a) the convenience of other federal agencies; (b) promotion of program administration or enforcement; (c) to enable public opinion to influence and restrict administrative action. Legislative provisions aimed at disseminating information for the convenience of the public are included with (b) and (c).

The Convenience of Federal Agencies: The Tennesee Valley Authority Act of 1933 contains the only clearcut and noteworthy example of the convenience type of provision thus far ascertained. Section 19 of that Act affords the Tennessee Valley Corporation access to the Patent Office as an instrumentality and agency of the United States Government. The Corporation is authorized to study, ascertain, and copy all methods, formulate any scientific information necessary to enable it to employ the most efficient and economical process for the production of fixed nitrogen.[3]

Publicity as an Instrument or Program Administration: As an instrument of program administration, publicity may be utilized to influence or coerce conformity with a program of control, or to facilitate the servicing of agency clientele. The use of publicity as an integral part of a control program is exemplified by routine publication of that which is prohibited, as well as by disclosure designed to exact compliance with government policy by subjecting those exposed to unfavorable publicity. Section 102 of the Defense Production Act of 1950, for example, prohibits the accumulation of scarce materials in excess of personal or business needs or for purposes of speculation. The President was directed to publish either in the *Federal Register* or elsewhere, a list of materials the accumulation of which would be unlawful.[4] Violators of this section of the law would presumably suffer from publicity about unlawful hoarding, if and when their activities became known to the federal government. More explicit, but indicative of the same intent, was an Act of July 1940 permitting the President to publish a list of persons designated as collaborators with the Axis powers. Any person so designated was prohibited from receiving military equipment or munitions for export.[5] In a proclamation of July 1941, President Roosevelt authorized compilation and publication in the *Federal Register* of "The Proclaimed List of Certain Blocked Nationals" under the Act.[6]

In statutory provisions for registration of categories of persons, or maintenance of lists of various kinds, it is difficult, if not impossible, to discern the various purposes to be served by such requirements. Thus, if the major objective of the Foreign Agents Registration Act of June 1938 was to secure for the government current information concerning persons represting foreign governments or businesses, and to impose a penalty for failure to register as a foreign agent, certainly a minor purpose was to insure that members of the public also should have this information available to them. Section 4 of the Act required the Secretary of State to retain in permanent form all statements filed under the Act, and to make them available for public examination and inspection at all reasonable hours.[7] One can hazard a guess as to what extent this publicity provision was designed to intimidate so-called foreign agents.

For a precise illustration of an attempt to utilize public opinion as a sanction, we need only look to the Labor-Management Relations Act of 1947, which, in specifying the procedures to be followed in settling national emergency strikes, obviously contemplated the marshalling of public opinion, at a strategic point, through publication of the second report of the President's board of inquiry, describing the current position of the parties and the efforts made for settlement.[8] The report is releasable after expiration of a sixty-day suspension of the strike, as ordered by a Federal district court on petition of the Attorney General.[9]

In the Armed Services Procurement Act of 1947, Congress announced its intention that a fair proportion of the total purchases and contracts for supplies and services for the government should be placed with small business concerns, and provided with certain exceptions for suitable advance publicity to achieve this end.[10]

In setting up the Small Business Adminstration in July 1953, Congress directed it to provide technical and managerial aids to small-business concerns, by advising and counselling on matters in connection with government procurement and on policies, principles, and practices of good management. Part of this responsibility would be met by maintaining a clearing house for information concerning the managing, financing, and operation of small business enterprises, by disseminating such information, and by such other activities as were deemed appropriate.[11] Designed to achieve a similar result is the provision of the Federal Defense Act of 1950 enumerating among the functions of the Federal Civil Defense Agency that of publicly disseminating appropriate civil defense information.[12]

To protect private enterprise the Defense Housing and Community Facilities and Services Act of 1951 requires that private enterprise be afforded full opportunity to provide the defense housing needed wherever possible and that, among other things, the number of permanent dwelling units needed shall be publicly announced and printed in the Federal Register.[13] The Domestic Minerals Program Extension Act of 1953 provides that the responsible agencies controlling such strategic or critical minerals and metals purchase programs publish the amounts of each of the ores and concentrates purchased at the end of each calendar quarter under the program.[14]

Publicity Designed to Enable Public Opinion to Influence and

Restrict Administrative Action: Characteristic provisions in this
category range from the requirement of publicity prior to taking action,
sometimes with the explicit provision for outside approval or disapproval of proposed agency action, to the simple publication of action taken
by the agency, and sometimes to an explanation thereof.   The Bank
Conservation Act of 1933 stated that before returning to private management a bank for which he had appointed a "conservator" (receiver),
the Comptroller of the Currency publicize his intentions and obtain
permission of the depositors and stockholders.[15]

A steadily increasing number of statutory provisions require
an agency to report in advance to Congress, the substance of contemplated agency action, which action cannot be implemented unless
approved by the Congress.[16]   One example will suffice as an illustration.   The Alien Registration Act of 1940 entrusted the Attorney
General with a limited power to suspend deportation of certain
aliens upon his finding that such deportation would result in serious
economic detriment to a citizen or legally resident alien who is the
spouse, parent, or minor child of the deportable alien.[17]   Whenever
deportation is suspended for more than six months, however, the
Attorney General must furnish Congress the name of the person
involved and all of the facts and pertinent provisions of law in the
case.   The information sent to the Congress is printed as a public
document.   If during the time Congress is in session the two houses
pass a concurrent resolution stating in substance that the Congress
does not favor the suspension of such deportation, the Attorney
General is obligated to deport the alien in the manner provided
by law.[18]

The Reciprocal Tariff Act of 1934 provides that prior to conclusion
of a foreign trade agreement reducing tariffs, reasonable public notice
of the intention to negotiate an agreement should be given in order
that any interested person might have an opportunity to communicate
his views to the President.[19]   A similar provision in the Emergency
Price Control Act of 1942 required, so far as practicable, consultation
by the President with members of affected industries prior to
establishment of maximum prices, and publication of such regulations or orders acompanied by a statement of the considerations
involved in the issuance thereof.[20]

The remaining statutes simply provide for publication of agency
action, although in a context which indicates that publication could
be viewed as a check upon the agency's discretion.   The Coordinator
of Transportation, an office created by the Emergency Railroad

Transportation Act of 1933, was required to make public in such reasonable manner as he might determine orders which he issued under the Act.[21] The orders were to become effective not less than twenty days from the date of publication[22] and in the interim interested parties might file petitions asking that the order be reviewed and suspended pending review.[23] The Chairman of the War Production Board, acting with the Attorney General, was given the power with regard to the antitrust laws and the Federal Trade Commission Act to temporarily suspend action against violators. The Attorney General was required to order published in the *Federal Register* every instance of the exercise of this power.[24] The Japanese Evacuation Claims Act of July 1948 provided that written records of hearings, open to public inspection, be maintained.[25] In formulating new criteria for identification of a critical defense housing area Congress, in the Housing and Rent Act of 1953, required publication in the *Federal Register* of notices that before applying the new criteria, a determination had been made to the effect that a specified area constituted a critical defense housing area.[26]

Suppression of Information by Government

Statutory provisions falling within this category may be subdivided into four groupings: (a) exceptions to statutory reporting requirement; (b) suspension of the requirement that contracts be let only after public bidding; (c) suppression of information concerning patent applications of military significance; (d) maintenance of secrecy of testimony under certain conditions at the request of the person testifying.

Exceptions to Statutory Reporting Requirements: As chief recipient of agency reports, Congress very obviously suffers the maximum loss when it sanctions suppression of reporting requirements in the interest of national security. Indicative of its sacrifice are provisions in the Communications Act of 1934 authorizing the Federal Communications Commission "to withhold publication of records or proceedings containing secret information effecting the national defense."[27] Of like import is the requirement in a statute delegating to the President power to authorize production, transfer or export of war material by federal agencies. The Chief Executive had to notify Congress at least every 90 days regarding war material exports. He could withold, however, whatever information disclosure of which he deemed incompatible with the public interest[28]

In the month following Pearl Harbor the Secretary of State was authorized during the existence of a state of war to omit or dispense with reports required by the Neutrality Act of 1939.[29] In extending the effect of certain emergency statutes Congress, in the Mutual Security Act of 1951, permitted the President to submit biannual reports on operations under the Act. He was privileged to exclude from his report information, the disclosure of which he deemed incompatible with the security of the United States.[30]

To prevent information of value to the enemy from being disclosed in litigation during World War II, Congress provided for staying of judicial proceedings against the U.S. in time of war on claims for damages caused by Navy vessels, or for towage or salvage services to such vessels, when the Secretary of the Navy certified that the prosecution of such proceedings would endanger the security of naval operations or interfere therewith.[31] Upon receipt of certification courts were required to stay all further proceedings in a suit until six months after the cessation of hostilities or until an approved earlier date as stated in the certificate. The claimant could petition the Secretary of the Navy to reconsider the stay, but his petition was not to contain any recital of the facts or circumstances involved. Identification of a petitioner's case was to be solely by reference to the Secretary's certificate.[32]

Suspension of Financial Controls: In a partially regulated economy, advertising and competitive bidding on public contracts benefit producer and taxpayer. These requirements insure relatively equal access to public contracts by private enterpreneurs, minimize nepotism or favoritism, and protect the public from extravagance. In a controlled war economy advertising and public bidding very probably would frustrate efforts to rationalize the productive facilities of the nation, and certainly would present the enemy with valuable intelligence. Indeed, intelligence considerations may lead to provision for the secret letting of certain contracts, even in time of peace.

The chief of the supply service of the War Department was authorized in 1936 to purchase materials for the Chemical Warfare Service or the Signal Corps in whatever manner he deemed most economical. This authority was delegated to the chief of the supply service in order to prevent secret military information from being divulged to the public.[33] A 1939 Act to authorize the procurement, without advertising, of certain aircraft parts and instruments or aeronautical accessories, contained a similar provision.[34] If a secret order was necessary, the Secretary of War, after certification to that effect, could submit the proposed purchase to three reputable concerns for their respective bids.[85]

After the fall of France, an act of June 28, 1940 to expedite national defense authorized the Secretary of the Navy, whenever deemed necessary by the President during the existing emergency, to negotiate contracts with or without advertising or competitive bidding upon determination that the price was fair and reasonable.[86] A few days later a more general statute gave the President plenary power to authorize the War Department to purchase urgently needed military hardware during the great national defense revival of 1940-41, with or without reference to advertised bids.[87] As long as the President could justify his actions as necessary "to provide for emergencies affecting the national security and defense," (and who, within the Congress or among the public, had access to the information essential to challenge the military necessity for given presidential action), he had virtually a *carte blanche* authority to write his own ticket. The great atomic bomb project, involving the ultimate in secrecy, was carried forward without the Congress being aware that the two billion dollars subsequently appropriated for the Manhattan Project were being expended for development of a weapon that might never work.[38]

Title II of the First War Powers Act, enacted shortly after Pearl Harbor, permitted the President to "authorize any department or agency of the Government exercising functions in connection with the prosecution of the war effort, . . . to enter into contracts and into amendments or modifications of contracts . . . without regard to the provisions of law".[39]

Appropriation measures, as for example the Independent Offices Appropriation Act of 1948, included funds to be expended for objects of a confidential nature and required auditing officials to accept the certificate of the expending agency as to the amount of the expenditure and that it was deemed inadvisable to specify the nature thereof.[40] Similarly, the National Military Establishment Appropriation Act of 1950 stipulated that the determination of the propriety of expenditure of the funds by the Secretaries of the military departments should be final and conclusive upon the accounting officers of the government. Payments from this appropriation might in the discretion of the Secretary, be made on his certificate that the expenditures were necessary for confidential military purposes.[41] The Central Intelligence Agency Act of 1949 granted the Central Intelligence Agency a sweeping exemption "from the provisions of any law which requires the publication or disclosure of the organization, functions, names, official titles, salaries, or numbers of personnel employed by it," and provided further that "the Director of the Bureau of the Budget shall make no reports to the Congress in connection with the Agency."[42]

Suppression of Information Concerning Inventions of Military Significance: Here an abridgment of a private economic right which is quasi-constitutional in character is justified on grounds of security. The Government appears to be concerned not so much with gaining access to inventions as with suppression of the publication, particularly abroad, of inventions of military value.[43]

A Congressional Act of July 1, 1940 states in part: "Whenever the publication or disclosure of an invention by the granting of a patent might, in the opinion of the Commissioner of Patents, be detrimental to the public safety or defense he may order that the invention be kept secret and withhold the grant of a patent for such period or periods as in his opinion the national interest requires."[44]

Like provisions are contained in the Invention Secrecy Act of 1951. When the head of a government agency holding a property interest in an invention deems publication or disclosure by the grant of a patent detrimental to the national security, the Secretary of Commerce, as soon as notified, is required to order that the invention be kept secret and withhold the patent therefore.[45] When the Secretary of Commerce believes that publication or disclosure of an invention by the granting of a patent, in which the government does not have a property interest, might be detrimental to the national security, he must make the application for patent in which such invention is disclosed available for inspection to the Atomic Energy Commission, the Secretary of Defense, and the chief officer of any other department or agency of the government designated by the President as a defense agency of the United States. He must also issue a secrecy order at the request of any of the defense agencies. Moreover, if there is a proper showing by the head of the department or agency who caused the secrecy order to be issued that the examination of the application might jeopardize the national interest, the Secretary of Commerce must maintain the application in a sealed condition and notify the applicant accordingly.

Secrecy of Testimony: Two statutes examined contained provisions requiring or approving the suppression of information at the request of persons who had provided it to emergency agencies. In Sction 202 thereof the Emergency Price Control Act of 1942 authorized the Price Administrator to make investigations, subpoena witnesses, and compel testimony upon the grant of immunity from prosecution. The same Act also provided that the Administrator should not publish or disclose any information obtained under the Act that the Administrator deemed confidential or with reference to which a request for confidential treatment had been made by the person furnishing such information, unless he determined that the withholding thereof was contrary to the interest of the national defense and security.[46] This, of course, is the reverse of the usual requirement that information be made public unless contrary to the interest of the national defense and security. The Export Control Act of 1949 also contained a compulsory testimony provision, with the requirement that, except as necessary to the national interest, information given in such testimony be kept confidential upon request of the witness.[47]

REGULATION OF PROPAGANDA ACTIVITIES

The Foreign Agents Registration Act of 1938, provided for public disclosure by persons engaging in propaganda activities and other activities for or on behalf of foreign governments, foreign political parties, and other foreign principals so that the government and the public could be informed of the identity of such persons and could thereby appraise their statements and actions in the light of their associations and activities.[1] By virtue of a 1942 amendment the necessity for foreign agents to register with the Attorney General was waived for agents of allied and friendly nations and thus propaganda efforts encouraged.[2] These agents could escape the registration requirement provided they engaged only in activities which were in furtherance of the policies, public interest, and national defense, of their own government and the American government, and were not not intended to conflict with any of the domestic or foreign policies of the United States. However, the agent had to be convinced of the truth and accuracy of each communication or expression which he made in this country.

Under the same Act persons required to register as foreign agents also had to furnish the Library of Congress with two copies of any political propaganda intended for dissemination to two or more persons. This material had to be transmitted within forty-eight hours after dissemination had begun and it had to be accompanied by a statement, duly signed by or on behalf of the agent, setting forth full information as to the places, times, and extent of actual transmittal.[3] In addition, the Act made it unlawful to disseminate the matter unless the political propaganda was conspicuously marked at its beginning with, or prefaced or accompanied by, a true and accurate statement, in the language or languages used in the political propaganda. The Act further required that the person transmitting political propaganda be registered under the Act with the Department of Justice "as an agent of a foreign principal, together with the name and address of the agent and of each of his foreign principals."[4]

The Internal Security Act of 1950 applied a similar requirement to any organization registered as a Communist organization, or ordered to register by the Subversive Activities Control Board.[5] Such an organization is guilty of a crime if it transmits through the United States mails or by any means or instrumentality of interstate or foreign commerce, any publication which is intended to be, or which it is reasonably believed will be, circulated or disseminated among at least two or more persons, unless the container in which the publication is mailed contains this statement: "Disseminated by ————, a Communist organization." Programs sponsored by Communist organizations on radio or television, in order to comply with the Internal Security Act, must be preceded by the statement, "the following program is sponsored by ————————, a Communist organization."

CENSORSHIP AND OTHER RESTRICTIONS

Thus far we have surveyed the discretionary power granted government agencies, consistently with national defense to withhold information from the public, the courts or the legislature, and those powers accorded the executive branch to regulate or conditionally promote propaganda activities of foreign nations. The following section pertaining to censorship and other restrictions may be differentiated from the foregoing as follows. Whereas the first section dealt with government agencies as custodians of information, here we are concerned with limitations imposed upon the efforts of individuals and groups to secure information or to disseminate specified kinds of information which they may possess.

The relevant statutes are reviewed under three headings. Certain statutes prohibit the acquisition or attempted acquisition of specified types of defense data. Others prohibit the dissemination of specified kinds of information, or the communication of prescribed opinions. A third group of statutes reflect the disposition of Congress to empower the government to review and edit personal communications media.

Illegal Acquisition of Defense Information: In January 1938 the President was authorized to define certain vital military and naval installations or equipment requiring protection against the general dissemination of information about them. It became unlawful thereafter to make any photograph, sketch, picture, drawing, map, or graphical representation of these vital military and naval installations or equipment without first obtaining the permission of the commanding officer of the installation concerned. If permission were granted to anyone seeking information, it was necessary to submit to censorship whatever information had been obtained.[1]

Dissemination of Information and Proscribed Opinions: The same 1938 statute also made it illegal to reproduce, publish, sell, or give away data without first obtaining official permission.[2] The Alien Registration Act of 1940 proscribed the advocacy of certain opinions. It is unlawful for any person, with intent to interfere with, impair, or influence the loyalty, morale, or discipline of the military or naval forces of the United States by seeking to advise, counsel, urge, or in any manner cause insubordination, disloyalty, mutiny, or refusal of duty by any member of the military or naval forces of the United States. And it is unlawful for any person to distribute any written or printed matter which advises, counsels, or urges insubordination, disloyalty or mutiny.[3] This Act also makes it unlawful to knowingly or willfully seek the overthrow of any government in the United States by direct or indirect action. Equally proscribed is any effort which has as its goal the assassination of any governmental official.[4] Conspiracy to commit any of the acts enumerated in the statute is also unlawful.[5]

The Export Control Act of 1949 gave the President power to prohibit or curtail the export of technical data.[6] Also pertinent is the stipulation in an August 1953 statute permitting the government to lend certain vessels to Italy, which prohibited the transmission to Italy of information, plans, advise, material, documents, blueprints, or other papers bearing a secret or top secret classification.[7]

In 1951 legislation was enacted prohibiting disclosure of classified information. It is unlawful knowingly and willingly to communicate, furnish or transmit to an unauthorized person the following categories of classified information: (1) codes, cipher or the cryptographic system of the United States or any foreign government; (2) the design, construction, use, maintenance, or repair of any device, apparatus, or appliance used or prepared or planned for use by the United States or any government for cryptographic or communication

intelligence purposes; (3) the communication intelligence activities
of the United States or any foreign government; or (4) obtained by
the processes of communication intelligence from the communications of any foreign government knowing the same to have been
obtained by such processes.[8] Violators of this law can be fined up
to $10,000, be imprisoned for ten years, or suffer the imposition of
both penalties.[9]

The Communist Organization Registration Act of July 1954 requires
organizations found by the Subversive Activities Control Board to
be Communist-action or Communist-front organizations to provide
the Attorney General a listing of all printing presses and machines.[10]
The list of different kinds of presses is very extensive.[11]

Censorship of Communications Media: The War Powers Act
of December 1941 specifically empowered the President to establish
censorship of communications between the United States and
foreign countries. During the existence of the war, the President,
at his discretion, established rules and regulations for the censorship
of communications by mail, cable, radio, or other means of transmission passing between the United States and any foreign country.
The authority to prescribe the rule by which censorship would be
applied, extended to communications carried by any vessel or other
means of transportation touching at any port, place, or territory
of the United States and bound to or from any foreign country.[12]

A month later the Communications Act of 1934 was amended
to enable the President during time of war or threat of war to regulate
or close any or all facilities or stations for wire communication within
the jurisdiction of the United States.[13] Nearly ten years later this
power was extended to any or all stations or devices capable of
emitting electromagnetic radiations within the jurisdiction of the
United States.[14] The power to close stations for radio communication
within the jurisdiction of the United States included those suitable
as navigational aids beyond five miles of the United States.[15]

ACQUISITION OF INFORMATION BY THE GOVERNMENT

Examined herein are statutes requiring private persons or groups
to report their activities to government agencies, or compelling them
to testify before such agencies; and providing for the conduct or study
of experiments by government agencies, including congressional
committees, for the purpose of obtaining certain information. Other
measures provide for a variety of investigations, inventories, audits,

etc., to be conducted by government agencies and congressional committees, and intelligence.

Compulsory Reporting:[1] Compulsory reporting on an occasional or periodic basis, it is generally assumed, constitutes an effective enforcement device. Thus to aid the President in effectively exercising the powers granted therein, the Bank Conservation Act of 1933[2] provided that he might require specific, detailed, and confidential information to be given under oath by any person then engaged in the banking business. The President could require the production of private papers, letters, contracts, books of account or other papers in the custody of the person required to produce them. Not until a very detailed and thorough examination of the information sought had been completed, could an accurate report be prepared in compliance with the Act.[3] The National Industrial Recovery Act permitted the President to impose such conditions (including requirements for the making of reports, the keeping of records and the keeping of accounts) for the protection of consumers, competitors, employees, and others, and in furtherance of the public interest as he saw fit, as a condition of approval of codes of fair competition.[4] Another section of the Act required trade or industrial associations, if they were to receive the benefit of exemption from antitrust prosecution, to file a statement with the President in accordance with regulations promulgated by the Chief Executive.[5] The Securities Exchange Act of 1934 similarly required periodical reporting[6] as did the 1935 enactment directed at preventing the interstate shipment of contraband oil.[7]

The first Neutrality Act imposed upon all persons required to register with the National Munitions Control Board an obligation to maintain permanent records of all arms, ammunition and implements of war manufactured for importation and exportation under the rules prescribed by the Board.[8] The requirement was continued in the 1937 Amendment which designated the Secretary of State (Chairman of the N.M.C.B. under the old and the amended Act) as recipient of the information to be submitted.[9] The Foreign Agents Registration Act of 1938 (as amended in April 1942) not only required the filing of registration statements by agents of foreign powers, but compelled each registered agent to keep and preserve books of account and other records which he was required to disclose under regulations prescribed by the Attorney General.[10]

As to procurement statutes, Congress, in connection with a 1934 enactment directed against excessive profit-making or collusive bidding in connection with naval construction contracts, required contractors to agree, as a condition of receiving a navy contract, to submit reports which would show conformance or non-conformance with the provisions of the Act.[11] The Second War Powers Act of 1942 followed up the grant of power to exact priorities with a section entitling the President to obtain a wide variety of information from any persons holding defense contracts. Contractors were required to keep accurate records in readiness for whatever accounting the President might eventually request.[12]

Authorization for the Conduct or Study of Experiments: The Tennessee Valley Authority Act authorized the T.V.A. to establish .the physical plants necessary to undertake experiments for the production of nitrogen products for military and agricultural uses. Such experiments were to emphasize both economy and high standards of efficiency.[13] A 1938 statute authorizing the construction of naval vessels included provision for the construction of experimental vessels and the construction of a rigid airship of American design and American construction.[14] Implementing the latter, appropriations were authorized for the purpose of rotary-wing and other aircraft research, development, procurement, experimentation, and operation for service testing.[15]

The National Science Foundation was established in 1950 as an independent agency, but within the executive branch of government.[16] Functions of this Foundation include promotion of basic research and education in the sciences, initiation and support of basic scientific research, initiation and support at the request of the Secretary of Defense of specific scientific research activities in connection with matters relating to the national defense, evaluation of scientific research programs undertaken by agencies of the federal government, and correlation of the Foundation's work with that of private and public research groups or individuals.[17] The functions enumerated do not exhaust the total of those assigned to the above mentioned agency.

In 1952 Congress authorized construction of aeronautical research facilities by the National Advisory Committee for Aeronautics. These facilities were to be used for the effective prosecution of aeronautical research. The Committee could expand certain of its experimental facilities especially since one of the purposes of the Act was to promote the national defense.[18] A similar kind of statute enacted in 1953 created an Advisory Committee on Weather Control. The function of this Committee was to make a complete study and evaluation of public and private experiments in weather control for the purpose of determinig the extent to which the United States should experiment with, or engage in, or regulate activities designed to control weather conditions.[19] It was to correlate and evaluate the information derived from experimental activity and to cooperate with the several States in encouraging the intelligent experimentation and the beneficial development of weather modification and control. In carrying out these objectives, the Committee was also required to keep a "weather eye" on seeing to it that harmful and indiscriminate techniques for weather control were not fostered.[20]

GOVERNMENT INVESTIGATIONS, INVENTORIES, AUDITS

Statutory provisions in this category are classifiable as follows: investigations, inventories, audits, etc., (a) incidental to program development or enforcement; (b) precedent to the establishment of policy in certain fields; (c) designed to aid specified agency clientele (private groups); (d) accusatory in nature; (e) military intelligence.

Investigations Incidental to Program Development or Enforcement: The Economy Act passed in the first month of the Roosevelt administration effected reductions in government pensions and salaries with a view to reducing the cost of Federal operations. Salary reductions were to vary with fluctuations in a cost of living index to be ascertained through investigation by government agencies.[21] The Agricultural Adjustment Act of 1933, in setting up an emergency program for the rehabilitation of growers of certain commodities directed the Secretary of Agriculture to make investigations and such reports to the President concerning the program as appeared necessary to its execution. In conjunction with the National Industrial Recovery Act of June 1933 was a 1934 amendment which authorized the President to establish a board or boards to investigate issues, facts, practices, or activities of employers or employees in any controversies arising under section 7 (a) of the statute which were burdening, obstructing, or threatening to burden or obstruct, the free flow of interstate commerce.[22]

The Second War Powers Act required the Secretary of Commerce, under Presidential direction, to make such special investigations and reports of census or statistical matters as might be needed in connection with conduct of the war. The Act imposed a penalty against anyone who refused to answer questions, gave false statements or deliberately neglected to answer questions asked by Departmental

subordinates in the conduct of investigations.[23] It also accorded
the government the right to inspect the plants and audit the books
of defense contractors.[24]

Before presenting to a court a certificate requesting a stay of judicial proceedings on claims for damages caused by naval vessels
during the War, the Secretary of the Navy had to conduct an investigation of the case in order to satisfy himself that the issuance of
the certificate was necessary.[25] A principal purpose of the Employment Act of 1946 was the establishment of an agency to investigate
and report upon the current state of the national economy.[26] The
Housing and Rent Act of 1948 specified that the Housing Expediter
should make surveys from time to time with a view to decontrolling
housing accommodations at the earliest practicable date.[27] The
Federal Civil Defense Administrator is charged by the statute creating the Federal Civil Defense Administration with responsibility
to prepare national plans and programs, and to request reports on
state plans directed at fulfillment of the objectives of the Act.[28]

Policy Development: A number of statutes contain provisions
designed to satisfy congressional need for information as an aid in
policy-making. A joint resolution of April 1934 directed the Federal
Power Commission to investigate the rates charged by private
and municipal corporations, prepare a compilation of the respective
rate structures and submit the information requested to the Congress
as quickly as possible. In making its compilation, the Commission
was requested to submit any analysis it had made of the difference
in rates charged between the privately owned and publicly owned
utilities.[29] The Commission might require reports and testimony
from private power officials and was given the right to examine and
copy any documentary evidence relative to the sale of electrical
energy or its service to consumers by any corporation engaged in
the sale of electricity.[30] Collecting accurate and comprehensive
information regarding the rates charged for electrical energy and its
service to residential, rural, commercial and industrial consumers
throughout the United States[31] was directed toward satisfying needs
of both the agency and the Congress.

Again in 1934, Congress established a Commission to make an
immediate study and survey of aviation and its relation to the United
States and to report to Congress its recommendations of a broad
policy covering all phases of aviation and its significance to the
United States.[32] The Railroad Retirement Board was directed to make
specific recommendations for such changes in the retirement system

created by the Railroad Retirement Act of 1934 as would assure the adequacy and permanency of the retirement system on the basis of its experience and all information and experience then available. For this purpose the Board was directed from time to time to make investigations and actuarial studies necessary to provide the fullest information practicable for the Board's report and recommendation.[33] In the third year of World War II a Joint Committee on Organization of Congress was established. The Joint Committee was given the responsibility of preparing a full and complete study of the organization and operation of the Congress together with recommendations for improvement in its organizaton and operation. Congress sought from the study and report the means for strengthening the Legislative branch of the government by simplifying its operation, improving relations between the Congress and other branches of government, and enabling it to better meet its responsibilities under the Constitution.[34] While some of the more archaic rules under which the Congress operated, indeed to some extent still does operate, were long overdue for a complete overhaul, the more immediate stimulus to action arose from a candid and searching appraisal of Congress' inability to stem the rising tide of government by the executive. The demands of emergency government of all kinds even before the Japanese attack on Pearl Harbor, tended to reduce the role of the Congress to that of mere ratification of executive action, the latter usually taken without regard to possible Congressional objections. Reorganization of the Congress resulting from the Joint Committee study and report was in response to a growing awareness of the need to improve the functioning of Congress as an organ for control of a wartime executive.

An important recent statute within this category is the Civil Rights Act of 1957.[35] This Act created a Commission on Civil Rights, empowered only to investigate, to study, to appraise and make findings and recommendations. It was not to be a Commission for the enforcement of civil rights. Specifically, the Civil Rights Act of 1957 directed the Commission to:

"(1) investigate allegations in writing under oath or affirmation that certain citizens of the United States are being deprived of their right to vote and have that vote counted by reason of their color, race, religion, or national origin, which writing, under oath or affirmation, shall set forth the facts upon which such belief or beliefs are based;

"(2) study and collect information concerning legal developments constituting a denial of equal protection of the laws under the Constitution; and

"(3) appraise the laws and policies of the Federal Government with respect to equal protection of the laws under the Constitution."[36]

The Commission was instructed to submit to the President and Congress a comprehensive report of its activities, findings, and recommendations not later than two years from the enactment of the Act. The Commission's report was submitted to the Congress on September 9, 1959,[37] just in time to win the Commission a two year lease on life.

Many of the statutes in this category are directed at securing information on which to base natural resources or scarce materials policy. In 1947 the President was requested to prepare, through the appropriate departments of the Government, a comprehensive plan for the development of the resources of Alaska, and the expansion and development of the facilities of commerce between the United States and Alaska and within the Territory. The President was requested to have the report ready for the consideration of the second session of the Seventy-fifth Congress thirty-five days after Congress reconvened.[38]

A strategic materials stockpiling statute of 1939 directed the Secretary of the Interior through the Director of the Bureau of Mines and the Director of the Geological Survey to make scientific, technological, and economic investigations concerning the extent and mode of occurrence, the development, mining, of ores and other mineral substances found in the United States which were considered essential to the common defense or the industrial needs of the United States.[39] Preparatory to enacting definitive post-war legislation establishing United States policy with regard to the domestic rubber-producing industry, Congress in 1947 provided for the conduct of a thorough study of the field.[40] Under the Ruber Producing Facilities Disposal Act of 1953 the Rubber Producing Facilities Disposal Commission was created and granted access to all available information concerning the Government-owned rubber-producing facilities in the possession of any department, agency, officer, Government corporation, or instrumentality of the United States concerned with Government-owned rubber-producing facilities.[41] Included in the data it was required to furnish the Congress was an inventory report concerning the Government's current stocks of synthetic rubber and its component materials.[42]

Endeavoring to expand production of abaca within the Western Hemisphere, Congress in 1950 authorized such surveys and research as were necessary or desirable to obtain the best available land in the Western Hemisphere for abaca production.[43]

Information-Gathering For the Aid of Agency Clientele: In 1938 Congress set up the Mediterranean Fruit Fly Board to conduct a complete investigation and survey of all losses sustained by growers and farmers in the State of Florida resulting from the campaign to eradicate the Mediterranean fruit fly within the State.[44] It carefully stipulated that the Board's report did not bind Congress legally or morally to grant relief to the affected farmers.[45]

Like the farmer, the small businessman receives his full share of congressional consideration. For the sake of the nation and the small businessman, the Small Business Concerns Mobilization Act of June 1942 sought to integrate him into the war effort.[46] It created the Smaller War Plants Corporation and included among its functions that of making studies with respect to the means by which small business concerns may be supplied with essential raw materials and receive fair and reasonable treatment from all Government departments without interfering with the efficiency of the war-production program.[47] In liquidating the Reconstruction Finance Corporation in July 1953, Congress substituted for it the Small Business Administration, which, among other things, was to obtain information as to methods and practices which Government prime contractors utilize in letting subcontracts and to take action to encourage the letting of subcontracts by prime contractors to small-business concerns.[48] It was also to make a complete inventory of all productive facilities of small-business concerns which could be used for war or defense production, or to arrange for the inventory to be made by any other governmental agency which has the facilities.[49] Further, it could obtain from suppliers of materials information pertaining to the method of filling orders and the bases for allocating their supply, whenever it appeared that any small business is unable to obtain materials from its normal sources for war or defense production. And it was directed to make studies and recommendations to the appropriate federal agencies to insure a fair and equitable share of materials, supplies, and equipment to small-business concerns in order to effectuate war or defense programs.[50] On the other hand, as a condition to securing loans from the Administration, small business concerns must certify to it the names of any attorneys, agents, or other persons engaged by or on behalf of such business enterprise for the purpose of expediting applications made to the Administration for assistance of any sort, and the fees paid or to be paid to any such persons.[51]

Accusatory Action: The two items of legislation involved here— one a joint resolution, the other a concurrent resolution—extended the staute of limitations as it affected "the possible prosecution of any person or persons, military or civilian, connected with the Pearl Harbor catastrophe of December 7, 1941"[52] and created a joint congressional committee to make a full and complete investigation of the facts relating to the events and circumstances leading up to or following the attack made by Japanese armed forces upon Pearl Harbor on December 7, 1941.[53]

Intelligence: The obvious example here is the statute setting up the Central Intelligence Agency in 1947. Its Director was intrusted with responsibility for protecting intelligence sources and methods from unauthorized disclosure and for operating an American intelligence network.[54]

PROTECTING FREEDOM OF COMMUNICATION

It would be distorting the picture not to take into account those instances in which Congress displayed concern lest the control programs it enacted would constrict freedom of communication. Thus while the Price administrator had the power to require licenses of anybody selling commodities regulated by his office, his power did not extend to various media of communication. The selling or distributing of newspapers, periodicals, books or printed or written material, motion pictures or radio time were exempted from the license requirement.[1] The Universal Military Training and Service Act of 1951 permits any member of the Armed Forces to communicate directly or indirectly with any Member of Congress. The statute expressly forbids any one from restricting or preventing a serviceman from writing to his Congressman or Senator. The only limitation placed on such communication is that the subject matter does not violate the law or the regulations necessary to the security and safety of the United States.[2]

Chapter VIII

LEGISLATIVE RESTRAINTS ON THE
ADMINISTRATION OF EMERGENCY POWERS

It is generally conceded that the problem of the responsibility of administrative officials in a democracy is the very crux of the problem of the maintenance of the democratic system,[1] and that we must look chiefly to the Congress for performance of the task of happily combining administrative responsibility with the administrative discretion so vital to the maintenance of the democratic government in time of peace or war. Members and critics of the federal legislature, particularly since the 77th or first wartime Congress (1941-1942), have acknowledged and responded to the need to equip it more effectively to formulate basic policy as well as to scrutinize administrative execution of the legislative mandate.[2] As appraised by these critics the problem is one of adequately and accurately informing the Congress,[3] of concentrating congressional checks upon essentials rather than trivia,[4] and, in contradiction of those who seek an unchecked executive discretion in time of emergency, of "including closer, stronger, steadier cooperation between the President and the Congress."[5]

Among recent innovations which may be viewed as the product of this movement to perfect administrative accountability to Congress are the requirements of executive reporting to the Legislative Branch and the "legislative veto." Whether statutes embodying these devices provide Congress with a check on the Executive Branch in excess of that deemed essential, and in effect, accord to the Legislative Branch an actual participation in the administration of the laws is the major issue to which this chapter is devoted.

Accounting to Committees

In the course of signing H. R. 6042, a defense appropriations bill, on July 15, 1955, President Eisenhower rebuked Congress for including therein Section 638 requiring the Secretary of Defense to secure prior consent of the House and Senate Appropriations Committees before separating from his Department functions which he thinks could better be performed by private industry. The President alleged that the Congress has no right to confer upon its committees the power to veto Executive action or to prevent Executive action from becoming effective. Invoking the constitutional principle of the separation of powers, he declared his intention to ignore this provision.[1]

While the bill which President Eisenhower reluctantly signed represented an effort to delegate a share in the executive function to committees of the Congress, such legislative action is not wholly without precedent. A survey of legislation in the fields of foreign affairs and economic or military emergency since 1933 indicates not infrequent attempts by Congress to secure for its committees some measure of continuing influence over the exercise of powers delegated to the executive. This may take the form of requiring periodic or special reports to policy committees instead of the full houses, it may take the form of compulsory consultation with committees—and whatever this entails by way of consequent committee influence on administrative action, or the committee may be secured a suspensive, enabling, or veto power over administrative action. It would be rash to construct, on the basis of our study, a judgment of the potential good or evil attending the increasing effort of Congress to share the detailed burdens of administration. The trend, it seems clear, exists, however.

Reporting to Committees: The requirement that administrative units report to superiors, to Congress, or to units of the latter, may be designed to achieve many purposes. The requirement may be devoid of any overtone of control—e.g., its aim may be limited solely to providing of technical information or advice as an aid to policy formulation, or it may be utilized to promote maximum scrutiny and control of executive action. For when one must report in detail and frequently on the discharge of delegated functions, it is necessary either to attempt to mislead the Congress—a dangerous pastime—or to toe the line and act as a meticulous surrogate of the legislature, in anticipation of an imminent accounting with it.

Thus it would be difficult to distinguish the informative and conrol purposes of the provision of the Supplemental National Defense Appropriations Act of 1948 requiring that the Secretary of Defense report quarterly "to the Committees on Appropriations and Armed Services of the Congress . . . the amounts obligated" for "the construction of aircraft and equipment."

The Secretary's reports were to include a statement of finding by the President that the contracts let were necessary in the interest of the national defense and that the contract specifications insured the maximum utilization of improvements in aircraft and equipment consistent with the defense needs of the United States.[2] The Mutual Defense Assistance Act of 1949 permitted the President, upon his own determination of the need therefore, to transfer funds from one project to another provided for in the Act. The amounts transferred could not exceed five percent of the total funds appropriated.[3] Whenever he made such a determination, however, he was required forthwith to notify the Committee on Foreign Relations of the Senate, the Committees on Armed Services of the Senate and of the House of Representatives, and the Committee on Foreign Affairs own determination of the need therefore, to transfer funds from one to report to the Congress biannually on the administration of the Act. The Mutual Security Act of 1951 contained a similar provision.[5]

Similar to the above is the 1950 requirement that the Secretary of the Navy annually file with the Committees on Armed Services in the Congress information as to the proceeds of all sales of condemned naval material and the expenses connected with such sales.[6] The 1950 statute permitting the summary suspension of civilian officers and employees of specified departments and agencies (State, Commerce, Justice, Defense, Treasury, Atomic Energy Commisssion, National Security Resources Board, National Advisory Committee for Aeronautics) gave the President authority to extend the list of agencies to which the Act applied. Any additions to the list, however, had to be based upon the best interests of national security and communicated to the Committees on the Armed Services of the Congress.[7]

In the Mutual Defense Assistance Act of 1951, which established an embargo on the shipment of arms, ammunition, and implements of war to any nation or combination of nations threatening the security of the United States, Congress gave the Administration the power to determine what items constituted arms, ammunition, and implements of war and items should be embargoed.[8] Aid to any nation knowingly permitting shipment of such materials or equipment to the U.S.S.R. and its satellites was to be suspended, unless the President found that unusual circumstances indicated that the cessation of aid would clearly be detrimental to the security of the United States. Upon making such a decision, the President was to report his decision and the reasons for it to the Appropriations and Armed Services Committees of the Senate and House of Representatives, the Committee on Foreign Relations of the Senate, and the

Committee on Foreign Affairs of the House of Representatives. Moreover, the President was required to review, at least once each quarter, all determinations made previously and report his conclusions to the foregoing committees.[9]

A postwar statute of limited dimensions was enacted in August 1953, enabling the President to lend to Italy, France, and any friendly foreign nation in the Far Eastern area, on terms satisfactory to him, naval vessels of stated categories.[10] This legislation charged the Secretary of Defense with the duty to keep the respective Committees on Armed Service of the Senate and the House of Representatives advised of all transfers or other dispositions of naval vessels.[11] The Defense Cataloguing and Standardization Act of 1952 established within the Department of Defense a Defense Supply Management Agency which was to develop a single catalogue system and related supply standardization program.[12] The Director of the Agency was required to transmit to the Committees on Armed Services of the Senate and House of Representatives on January 31 and July 31 of each year, progress reports on the cataloguing and standardization programs.[13] Similarly, in authorizing the Secretaries of the Army, Navy, and Air Force to acquire or develop industrial plants as needed for defense mobilization Congress required the Secretary of Defense to report semi-annually to the Committees on Armed Services of the Senate and of the House of Representatives with respect to those activities authorized by statute which were not otherwise the subject of reporting under law.[14]

The foregoing can perhaps best be characterized as legislative adaptations of Carl J. Friedrich's so-called "rule of anticipated reaction."[15] In context the rule implies that administrative officers, aware of the imminent necessity of reporting to the legislature the details of exercise of discretion under delegatory statutes, will attempt so to pattern their action as to maximize the likelihood of legislative approval.

Consultation with Committees: Legislative restraint is less obvious —though nonetheless present—in statutes which, instead of requiring detailed reporting of administrative discharge of delegated functions, provide for periodic or continuous administrative consultation with congressional committees. The Economic Co-operation Act of 1948 created a Joint Committee on Foreign Economic Co-operation, consisting of ten members from the Foreign Relations and Appropriations Committees of the Senate, and the Foreign Affairs and Appropriations Committees of the House. The Economic Co-operation Administrator was to consult with the committee from time to time as the Committee might request.[16] In 1950 the Secretary of Defense was empowered after consultation with the respective Armed Services Committees of the Congress to provide the facilities necessary or the administration and training of the Reserve components of the Armed Forces.[17] The Defense Production Act of 1950 established a Joint Committee of Defense Production to make a continuous study of the programs authorized by the Act, and to review the progress achieved in the execution and administration of such programs. It required all agencies and officials administering programs authorized by the Act, at the request of the committee, to consult with the committee, from time to time, with respect to their activities under this Act.[18] A Joint Committee on Immigration and Nationality Policy was created to make a continuous study of the administration of the Immigration and Nationality Act of 1952.[19] The Act instructed the Attorney General and the Secretary of State to submit to the Committee all regulations, instructions, and all other information as requested by the Committee relative to the administration of the Act. The Secretary of State and the Attorney General were required to consult with the Committee from time to time with respect to their activities under this Act.[20]

Committee Participation in Administrative Decision-Making: The history of recent use of the "legislative veto" might lead one to expect that, in those instance in which it seeks to retain a power of continuous oversight of administraton action, Congress would be prone to locate this function in either or both houses rather than to delegate it to committees. However, the fiscal 1956 Defense Appropriations Act, earlier mentioned, is by no means the first instance in which committees have been assigned the function of participating in administrative decision-making. In fact, careful study of the functioning of Congressional Committees might reveal that compulsory consultation and joint committee-agency decision-making are more the rule than the exception.[21]

Certainly Congress, in requiring the Atomic Energy Commission to report to the Joint Committee on Atomic Energy any instances in which it imparted atomic secrets to other nations, contemplated committee control of such action. Arrangements with other nations were not to be consummated until the Joint Committee on Atomic Energy had been fully informed for a period of thirty days in which the Congress was in session.[22] If the Committee disapproved the arrangement and found the Commission unresponsive to its influence, the former would have time in which to report this fact to Congress.

When it authorized the establishment of a long-range proving ground for guided missiles in 1949, Congress stipulated that prior to the acquiring of lands under this law the Secretary of the Air Force had to come "into agreement with the Armed Services Committees of the Senate and the House of Representatives with respect to the acquisition of such lands."[23] This clearly established a joint committee-agency decision-making arrangement. A 1951 statute required the Secretaries of the Army, Air Force, and Navy, and the Federal Civil Defense Administrator, to come into agreement with the two Armed Services Committees whenever real estate actions by or for the use of the military departments or the Federal Civil Defense Administration were involved.[24] The Emergency Powers Interim Continuation Act of July 1952, continued this provision in force.[25]

In conclusion we mention a device for securing to congressional committees a form of suspensive power over administrative action. This is the familiar provision for suspension of deportation orders where either the Immigration and Naturalization Committee of the House or of the Senate Committee on Immigration has favorably acted on a bill for the relief of the alien in question. The Act cited here was restricted in effect to the Seventy-fifth Congress, and stays of deportation under it were to be terminated at least by the date of adjournment of the first regular session of the Seventy-sixth Congress.[26]

ACCOUNTING TO CONGRESS

The preponderance of relevant data collected under this particular head consists of routine requirements, inserted in delegatory statutes, that administrators periodically report to the Congress on the discharge of their functions. It need hardly be stressed that by this method of acquiring information Congress not only equips itself with data vitally prerequisite to its exercise of the function of oversight, but that its demand for such information in itself represents a form of control. The necessity of periodic reporting interposes an effective psychological hurdle between the administrator and intentional malfeasance. Certain reporting provisions clearly reflect a desire to maintain a continuous check upon the administration; others appear directed more at securing information and advice as an aid to policy-making.

Reporting Administrative Activity: In delegating powers in the areas of defense, foreign affairs or in time of emergency, Congress is

inclined to insist upon frequent reporting, and to specify carefully
the kind of information and supporting documentation it expects
to receive. It may stipulate, as in the Japanese Evacuation Claims
Act of 1948 and the Mutual Defense Assistance Act of 1949, the
subjects on which it wishes reports, and refrain from imposing an
obligation to report at specified calendar intervals. The Japanese
Claims Act instructed the Attorney General to submit to Congress
a full and complete statement of all adjudications, name and address
of each claimant, the amount of the settlement and a brief synopsis
of the facts of each claim case and the reasons for each adjudication.[27]
A 1935 statute required that the Secretary of the Navy report to
Congress at the next regular session thereof all expenditures on
ship repairs in excess of the amounts specified by appropriations
legislation.[28] In April, 1937 the Secretary of Agriculture was granted
one million dollars to "be expended for the control of grasshoppers,
Mormon crickets or cinch bugs," and required to report to Congress
on his handling of the fund.[29] Similarly, in establishing an emergency
fund for the President in 1940, to enable him to furnish government-
owned facilities to privately owned plants and procure and train
civilian personnel in the production of critical materials, Congress
stipulated that an account be kept of all expenditures made from the
fund and required that a report on the condition of the fund be submitted to the Congress on or before June 30, 1942.[30]

The Federal Emergency Relief Act of 1933 went so far as to require
the Federal Emergency Relief Administrator to print a report of
his activities and expenditures monthly, and submit them to the
President and the Congress.[31] The foregoing, like the statute of
June 1942, mobilizing small business concerns for war production,
which provided for reports to Congress by the Attorney General
at least once every quarter ("not less frequently than once every
one hundred and twenty days"[32]) is somewhat unusual. Standard
practice requires quarterly,[33] biannual,[34] or annual reporting. Annual
reporting may be in terms of a report to be submitted to both houses
of Congress "on the first day of"[35] or "at the beginning of"[36] each
regular session of Congress. However, it more likely will be phrased
an "annual report."[37]

Congress sometimes requires great specificity in administrative
reporting. Exemplifying such demands are the following statutes.
A 1950 statute limited the number of Army officers who might be
assigned to permanent duty in the Department of the Army and
the number who could be assigned to the Army General Staff at any

one time. The Secretary of the Army is required to report quarterly to the Congress the number of officers and the justification therefor.[38] This is a simple but extremely precise reporting requirement. The May, 1937 amendment to the Neutrality Act more generally defined and described the various topics to be covered in the annual report of the National Munitions Control Board, but stipulated that the report contain a list of all persons required to register under the provisions of the Act, and full information concerning the licenses which had been issued thereunder.[39] A like blend of liberality and rigidity in stipulating the content of reports was manifested in a 1937 Act designed to establish a government monopoly of the production of helium gas.[40] The National Munitions Control Board was to include in its Annual Report to the Congress full information concerning the export licenses issued thereunder and whatever additional information and data the Board considered of value in the determination of questions related to the exportation of helium gas.[41]

The Secretary of the Navy was directed in 1938 to report annually to the Congress all agreements entered into for leasing naval petroleum reserves;[42] and a 1939 statute to facilitate certain construction work for the Army required the Secretary of War to report annually to the Congress all contracts entered into under authority of the Act, including the names of the contractors and copies of the contracts concerned, together with the amounts involved.[43] The Sixth Supplemental National Defense Appropriation Act of 1942 established the duty of the Secretary of War and Secretary of the Navy to submit a complete list of all contracts awarded in excess of $150,000 together with the names of the contractors, and the subject matter of each contract. If the contract had been awarded without competitive bidding, the Secretaries had to supply Congress with a statement of the principal or controlling reason for selection of the contractors. Reports had to be submitted within sixty days after the end of the fiscal year.[44]

In the main the congressional requirement of reporting is cast in general terms, permitting the administrator considerable discretion as to content and precise date (if not periodicity) of submission. On occasion, however, Congress is disposed to insist upon specificity in exacting reports from agencies, particularly agencies assigned such tasks as the registering of individuals, licensing, letting contracts, and the like.

Informing and Advising the Congress: A large number of statutes require reports which appear not so much directed at enforcing responsibility on the part of executive agencies as eliciting information and specialized advice for policy-making. In 1934 Congress required the Federal Power Commission to submit a report and analysis of rate schedules charged by private and municipal utility companies at the earliest practicable date.[45] The Tennessee Valley Authority Act[46] contains a reporting requirement commonly found in legislation pertaining to newly established programs. The President was directed to recommend to Congress such legislation as he deemed proper to carry out the general purposes stated in the law.[47] His recommendations were to be made from time to time as work progressed. In 1934 Congress authorized the President "to appoint a Commission composed of five members . . . for the purpose of making an immediate study and survey, and to report to Congress not later than February 1, 1935, its recommendations of a broad policy covering all phases of aviation and the relation of the United States thereto."[48] In setting up the Federal Communications Commission in 1934 Congress indicated that it expected the Commission's annual reports to contain information and advice facilitating further congressional policy-making in the communications field. The Commission was directed to prepare an annual report for the Congress which would contain information and data collected by the Commission considered to be of value in the determination of questions connected with the Commission's regulatory responsibilities involving wire and radio communication and radio transmission of energy. The Commission was also required to submit recommendations for additional legislation in the report if the Commission believed it necessary.   And on February 1, 1935 the Commission was specifically directed to make a special report to the Congress recommending amendments to the F.C.C. Act.[49]

In the Price Control Act of 1946 Congress indicated its desire that the control of prices be terminated as rapidly as possible, and directed the President to recommend to the Congress whatever was judged by him as needed to supplement the control of prices and wages during the remainder of 1947.[50] The national emergency provisions of the Labor Management Relations Act provide that upon exhaustion of the procedures for deferring and attempting settlement of national emergency strikes "the President shall submit to the Congress a full and comprehensive report of the proceedings . . . together with such recommendations as he may see fit to make for consideration and appropriate action."[51] A final illustration is drawn from the June, 1951 amendments to the Universal Military Training and Service Act. This measure established a National Security Training Commission of five members which, in addition to generally supervising the training of the National Security Training Corps, was to submit to the Congress certain legislative recommendations. These recommendations were to include, but not be limited to—(a) a broad outline for a program to assure that the training be of a military nature, (b) measures for the personal safety, health, welfare and morals of members of the Corps and (c) a code of conduct.[52]

THE CONCURRENT RESOLUTION

The suggestion has been made that Congress would be better informed and could exercise a more adequate check upon the administration of delegated powers "if the major rules and regulations of the agencies were submitted to Congress under a provisional order system. Under this system they would become effective after a certain time, unless negatived by Congress."[1] This would in effect adapt to American purposes the provisions of the British Statutory Instrument Act of 1946, requiring that important administrative rules and regulations issued under delegatory statutes be submitted to the Parliament, where they would be reviewed by a "Scrutiny Committee" of the Commons.

The resultant veto power might be exercised in a number of ways. A congressional committee might be given power to scrutinize and report on such rules and regulations, or delegated a final power to approve or disapprove. We have earlier noted the extent to which Congress has equipped committees with a power to review and approve or disapprove administrative action.

Were Congress to utilize the Joint Resolution as an instrument for approving or disapproving administrative action, no innovation would be involved. The Joint Resolution requires presidential signature to become effective. This legislative instrument traditionally has been relied upon to clarify congressional intent in delegatory statutes which it thought had been misinterpreted by administrative agencies or the courts. However, if in delegating powers to the executive, Congress conditioned the grant by reserving power to itself by concurrent resolution or by simple resolution of one house to define the terms under which the executive was to act and to review, approve or disapprove such administrative action, a signal departure from established practice would be recorded. In effect, the Congress would have retained the power to curb administration through legislative procedures which do not require Presidential signature to be effective, and which traditionally do not have the force of law, serving simply to express the intent of the Congress.[2]

While the Constitution provides that "every order, resolution, or vote to which the concurrence of the Senate and House of Representatives may be necessary . . . shall be presented to the President . . . and before (they) take effect shall be approved by him," concurrent resolutions have not for over a century and a quarter been submitted for presidential approval.[3] Apparently the earliest use of the concurrent resolution as a device for enhancing the ability of Congress to control administrative action is to be found in the Reorganization Act of 1932, followed by the Reorganization Act of 1939.[4] These statutes empowered the President to submit reorganization plans to Congress, the plans to have legal effect unless disapproved by concurrent resolution adopted within a prescribed period.

Within the past two decades all three instruments—the joint resolution, the concurrent resolution, and the simple resolution passed by one house—have been used by Congress in an attempt to retain influence and control over the administration of emergency programs. Whether for good or for bad, in statutes delegating emergency authority the present trend is pointed toward inclusion of congressional power to review administrative action by concurrent resolution.

DELEGATORY LEGISLATION INCORPORATING POWER
TO CHECK BY CONCURRENT RESOLUTION

Congress appears to have pursued a variety of objectives in incorporating within delegatory statutes a power to influence or control administration through concurrent or simple resolution. (a) In some instances it has reserved power to terminate a statute or program by concurrent resolution. (b) It has asserted power to enable or require executive action by concurrent resolution. (c) Finally, it has made administrative execise of delegated power subject to congressional approval or disapproval by concurrent or simple resolution. The forty odd delegatory statutes noted in the course of this study, which reserve to Congress the right to influence or limit administrative action by simple or concurrent resolution, will be discussed in this order.

Terminating Programs: Use of the concurrent resolution for the express purpose of terminating legislative delegations of power to the executive branch may take two forms: (a) congressional reservation of a power to repeal the authorizing statute, or (b) congressional reservation of the right, by concurrent resolution, to declare an end to the particular conditions under which the President is empowered to take action. Exercise of congressional power to repeal by concurrent resolution generally has been expressed as follows: "The provisions of this Act, . . . shall terminate on June 30, 1943, or upon the date of a proclamation by the President, or upon the date specified in a concurrent resolution . . ."[5] A similar provision is contained in at least twenty-three emergency statutes enacted since 1941 and listed below.[6] The Mutual Defense Assistance Act of 1949 secured to the Congress a form of item veto through reserving to it the power by concurrent resolution to terminate assistance to any nation under the Act.[7]

Instances in which Congress reserves the right by concurrent resolution to declare terminated the conditions authorizing executive action are fewer. In a 1941 statute the Secretary of the Navy was authorized to establish a plant protection force for naval shore establishments and to maintain and operate this force until June 30, 1943, unless Congress at an earlier date, by concurrent resolution, declared such force no longer necessary.[8] A 1942 amendment to the Communications Act of 1934 gave the President certain powers to control wire communication facilities upon proclamation by the President that a state or threat of war exists involving the United States. The President's powers in this respect were to end not later than six months after the termination of such state or threat of war and not later than such earlier date as the Congress by concurrent resolution may designate.[9] In defining national emergency for purposes of the Federal Civil Defense Act of 1950,[10] Congress stipulated that "the provisions of this title shall be operative only during the existence of a state of civil defense emergency . . . The existence of such emergency may be proclaimed by the President or by concurrent resolution of the Congress if the President in such proclamation, or the Congress in such resolution, finds that an attack upon the United States has occurred or is anticipated and that the national safety therefore requires an invocation of the provisions of this title." Congress also has reserved the right, although not on an exclusive basis, to determine by concurrent resolution the "dates of commencement and termination of an armed conflict."[11]

Enabling or Requiring Executive Action: An example of the use of the concurrent resolution as an enabling device is the provision of the Neutrality Act of 1939,[12] which imposed rigorous limitations upon United States carriage to belligerents "whenever the President, or the Congress by concurrent resolution, shall find that there exists a state of war between foreign states."

The Legislative Veto: The Reorganization Acts of 1939, 1945 and 1949[13] are also illustrations of the use of the simple and concurrent resolution to effect approval or disapproval of administrative action. All three Acts were designed to foster reorganization to enable the government to cope with emergency conditions, and the 1945 Act had the expressed purpose of facilitating orderly transition from war to peace.[14] The 1939 Act stipulated that the President's reorganization plans were to take effect sixty calendar days after the date on which the plan was transmitted to the Congress, but only if during the sixty-day period the two Houses of Congress had not passed a concurrent resolution stating in substance that the Congress did not favor the reorganization plan. A similar provision was contained in the 1945 Act, and on July 15, 1946 Congress, by concurrent resolution, disapproved the President's Reorganization Plan No. 1.[15] The 1949 Act provided for a veto of Reorganization Plans by one house. Under the latter, a reorganization plan becomes operative "upon the expiration of the first period of sixty calendar days, of continuous session of the Congress, following the date on which the plan is transmitted to it; but only if, between the date of transmittal and the expiration of such sixty-day period there has not been passed by either of the two Houses, by the affirmative vote of a majority of the authorized membership of that House, a resolution stating in substance that the House does not favor the reorganization plan."[16]

In a class by itself is the Federal Civil Defense Act of 1950, by the terms of which the concurrent resolution may be employed to veto interstate civil defense compacts.[17] The consent of the Congress would be granted to each compact, after the termination of sixty calendar days of continuous session of the Congress from the time Congress first received notice of the compact. But Congressional consent could be denied anytime during the sixty day period if Congress passed a concurrent resolution stating that it did not approve the compact.

Remaining for consideration is the utilization of the concurrent resolution to enable Congress to achieve a more intimate participation in the administration of selected programs, principally in the field of immigration and naturalization. In the Alien Registration Act of 1940[18] Congress provided for the deportation of additional classes of aliens. Aliens of proved good moral character might have deportation suspended under certain conditions at the discretion of the Attorney General. However, if deportation were suspended for more than six months, all of the facts and pertinent provisions of law in the case must be reported to the Congress within ten days after the beginning of its next regular session, with the reasons for such suspension. If during that session the two Houses pass a concurrent resolution stating in substance that the Congress does not favor the suspension of such deportation, the Attorney General is required to carry out the deportation as provided by law. If, however, during that session the two Houses fail to pass such a resolution, the Attorney General is required to cancel deportation proceedings at the end of the session. In subsequent legislation Congress reserved the right by concurrent resolution to suspend deportation of aliens or to grant permanent residence,[19] and a considerable proportion of the concurrent resolutions enacted each year now constitute directives to the Attorney General in this regard.[20]

The Rubber Producing Facilities Disposal Act of 1953[21] set up a Rubber Producing Facilities Disposal Commission and authorized it to enter into contracts for disposal of federally held rubber producing facilities. The Commission was to report to Congress in considerable detail on the negotiations and the contents of the contracts. The report had to be submitted to both Houses of Congress on the same day. Upon the expiration of sixty days of continuous session of the Congress following the date upon which the report was submitted to it, the Commission was free to proceed to carry out the contracts and proposals as outlined in its report, but only to the extent that such contracts and proposals had not been disapproved by either House of Congress by a resolution during the sixty-day period. Congress in recent years also has asserted the right by concurrent resolution to "declare . . . that the period of active service required of any age group" under the Universal Military Training and Service Act "should be decreased . . . or . . . should be eliminated."[22]

USE OF CONCURRENT RESOLUTION
PROVISIONS TO CHECK ADMINISTRATIVE ACTION

A survey of the statute books from 1939 through 1954 reveals few instances of congressional employment of the device of the concurrent resolution so thoughtfully included in delegatory statutes. However, the *Congressional Record* for the same period bears evidence of repeated effort on the part of members of the legislature to influence the administration of delegatory statutes through concurrent or, in some instances, the simple resolution.

Terminating Powers. Legislative efforts to terminate statutes by concurrent resolution prove anticlimactic in view of the many instances in which the power to accomplish this was included in the delegatory statute. The statute which provoked the most vigorous and persistent effort at termination by concurrent resolution was that of January 20, 1942, establishing daylight saving time.[23] From 1943 through 1945 some twenty-four concurrent resolutions were introduced to terminate the effect of the Daylight Savings Act.[24] None of these concurrent resolutions survived committee screening.

In 1941 a House concurrent resolution abrogating the authority of the President to provide aid to Russia under the Lend-Lease Act died in the Foreign Relations Committee.[25] The appropriate provision of the Lend-Lease Act provided in general terms for termination of the lend-lease authority upon adoption of a concurrent resolution by both Houses.[26] The Act did not provide for suspension by concurrent resolution of authority to aid specified countries and the resolution probably sought to exercise a power which Congress had not reserved to itself in the Act.

Pressure to terminate war controls intensified following the September 2, 1945, signing of the Japanese instrument of surrender. On September 14, House Concurrent Resolution 84 was introduced, "to terminate the effectiveness of certain provisions of the Second War Power Act, 1942." Section 1501 of the Act provided for termination of certain of the Titles of the Act by concurrent resolution.[27] The resolution did not emerge from the Judiciary Committee, to which it was referred. Another unsuccessful effort was made to invoke the concurrent resolution provisions of the Act two years later.[28] The year following termination of hostilities saw a short-lived effort to terminate by concurrent resolution a statute which did not incorporate provision to this effect.[29]

Some ten additional concurrent resolutions were introduced in the two years succeeding 1945, the effect of which would have been formal termination of the state of hostilities to which the lives of various statutes had been hinged.[30] None of the resolutions emerged from committee.

Enabling and Requiring Executive Action. Aside from action on reorganization plans submitted to Congress by the President, the sole striking instance of successful employment of a concurrent resolution provision incorporated in a delegatory statute concerned initiation of a postwar highway construction program, under the Federal-Aid Highway Act of 1944. The Act, it will be recalled, enabled the Congress by concurrent resolution to stipulate the date the program was to go into effect. Senate and House concurrent resolutions were introduced in the Seventy-ninth Congress in 1945 fixing the first post-war fiscal year under the Act as the year ending June 30, 1946.[31] The House resolution passed in that chamber and was agreed to by the Senate.[32]

The Neutrality Act of 1939 is the outstanding, in fact the only, recent instance of congressional effort to exercise power by concurrent resolution to require executive action.[33] The Act drastically curbed American carriage to and trade with belligerents. The President could proclaim the existence of war between two nations; or, upon passage of a concurrent resolution finding that war existed between two countries, the President must issue a proclamation identifying the belligerents.[34] Thereupon the trade restrictions in the Act become effective and criminal penalty attaches to their violation.

On the theory that Section 1 (a) "places on this Congress a responsibility corresponding with that which has been placed on the President in the matter of finding a condition of war to exist,"[35] individual members introduced concurrent resolutions declaring the existence of war between the U.S.S.R. and Finland,[36] Japan and China,[37] and Germany and the U.S.S.R.[38] These were decently interred in committee.

The Legislative Veto. Although the first Reorganization Act containing provision for legislative veto of reorganization plans was enacted in 1939, concurrent resolutions disapproving such plans were introduced in vain until 1946. In July of that year both houses agreed to House Concurrent Resolution 155 disapproving President Truman's Reorganization Plan No. 1.[39] The next May a new Congress disapproved Reorganization Plan No. 2 of 1947.[40] The third and last reorganization plan to be defeated by concurrent resolution was Plan No. 1, 1948, which incurred congressional disapproved in March of that year.[41] The Reorganization Act of 1949 permitted veto of the President's plans by simple resolution of one house.[42] President Truman's efforts to elevate the Federal Security Agency to departmental status were frustrated by Senate Resolution 147 of 1949, which was adopted by that body on August 16, 1949.[43] All of the veto resolutions passed by Congress were favorably reported from committee to the house of origin.

During the period studied three veto resolutions died in committee,[44] three (all favorably reported from committee) passed the House of Representatives only to be rejected by the Senate,[45] and four were adversely reported from committee and defeated in the chamber in which they originated.[46] Only one veto resolution was discharged from committee. It subsequently passed the House but failed in the Senate.[47]

CONCLUSION

In an era in which governmental controls invade every sphere of human activity, from economic to cultural and political, administrative responsibility is essential to the maintenance of the democratic system. Administration which is responsible is lacking in the elements of bad faith, arbitrariness, or capriciousness. It constitutes a reasoned effort, in good faith, to approximate the legislative intent.

Congress is one important source of oversight of administration. Its effectiveness in performing this role is a function of (a) the adequacy of its tools, and the skill, conscience, and sustained interest of the members in wielding them, and (b) the standards it applies in measuring the adequacy of administrative action.

Experience in this area indicates that Congress is more imaginative in fashioning tools for checking and influencing the administration of delegated powers than it is skillful and determined in employing them to hold administrators to clearly defined standards of performance.

The national legislature has attempted to employ reporting devices and the concurrent resolution to influence, enable or require executive action, to terminate or suspend the conditions authorizing it, or to restrict the application of programs to specified groups. Not infrequently it has made the exercise of delegated powers contingent upon prior congresional approval or disapproval.

With the exception of the last category, however, Congress has not effectively wielded the tool it engineered. The veto resolution has received ample use because the executive automatically initiates congressional review when it invokes the delegated power which is subject to veto. Where Congress must initiate review, the concurrent resolution provisions tend to lie dormant, or congressional action tends to be directed at vindicating sectional interests (revocation of daylight saving time), or direct participation in the framing of administrative decisions, case by case (deportation suspensions).

Perhaps the moral of the story is that we must free congressmen from constituency loyalties and subject them to strict party discipline if we wish to insure that available techniques for the legislative control of administration are effectively employed to serve an interest which is broad and public.

CHAPTER IX

INTER-AGENCY RELATIONSHIPS

The study of administration proceeds within the framework of a taxonomy of human relationships, the breadth and content of which remain fluid. In large measure, when we speak of law we refer to a socially prescribed and sanctioned taxonomy of human relations. The analysis offered in this chapter is grounded upon the premise that clarification and refinement of, a taxonomy of administrative relationships may result from the study of legislative enactments prescribing relationships between administrative agencies. It also reflects the supposition that at a time when the behaviorial or human-relations approach to the study of administration is in ascendancy, such a review may provide an essential foundation for the contrasting of formality and actuality which is one of the characteristics of behaviorism.

In the following pages we record and classify various kinds of inter-agency relationship prescribed by statute. We have attempted to employ the inductive approach, permitting the categories and gradations of relationship to emerge from the materials. But we are not unaware of the inevitable intermixture of the *a priori*.

When fashioning economic regulatory legislation, Congress must heed the complexity of the industrial society to which the controls are to be applied, and of the bureaucracy through which regulation is to be accomplished. It will be possible to realize the legislative purpose only if the active co-operation and help of a wide variety of official agencies and private groups can be enlisted. And these must include the groups to be regulated.[1]

Thus it is not surprising to find, upon examining a large number of emergency regulatory statutes enacted during the last twenty-five years, that they contain many provisions detailing the relationships which should prevail between the administering agencies and other groups, official, semiofficial, or private. Such provisions establish a variety of rights and obligations. They may have the effect of enlarging or constricting the discretion of a particular agency to interpret and pursue legislative policy goals. In the pages which follow we attempt to sort out and categorize such provisions.

The confusing medley of statutory provisions for kinds and gradations of inter-agency relationship is perhaps best reduced to order
by invoking the image of three overlapping spheres.

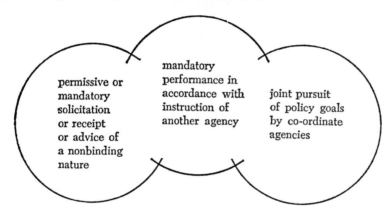

permissive or
mandatory
solicitation
or receipt
or advice of
a nonbinding
nature

mandatory
performance in
accordance with
instruction of
another agency

joint pursuit
of policy goals
by co-ordinate
agencies

The center sphere, into which and from which the others spill,
represents the kind of inter-agency relationship in which one agency
performs a mandatory, nondiscretionary function at the direction or
"request" of another. Flowing into it, from the left, is the sphere
in which agencies are permitted or compelled to receive advice from,
to consult or confer with others, but are under no obligation to follow
the advice received. The third sphere is that in which two or more
co-ordinate agencies share active responsibility and authority for
the pursuit of a common policy goal.

If the interagency relationships provided for by statute are scaled
according to the binding quality of the advice received by one agency
from another or according to the degree to which two or more agencies
share authority and responsibility for program administration subtle
nuances of interagency relationship are revealed. Advice received
may be purely of an informative and nonbinding nature, or the
statute may be so worded as to indicate that "advice" from one
agency to another amounts virtually to direction. In the sharing
of program authority and responsibility, one agency may perform
ministerial functions at the direction or "request" of another, or,
at the opposite extreme, interagency personnel, judgment, and resources may be fused toward the accomplishment of a common goal.

COMMUNICATION

Herbert A. Simon's definition of communication "as any process
whereby decisional premises are transmitted from one member of

an organization to another,"[2] generally describes the kinds of legislative provisions which will be reviewed in this section, with the exception that we are here concerned with the transmission of decisional premises from one agency to another. The transmission may be permissive or mandatory. The information or advice conveyed may or may not be related to the framing of a particular decision; it may or may not be binding upon the recipient agency.

COMMUNICATION UNRELATED TO THE
FRAMING OF A PARTICULAR DECISION

Permissive Consultation: Provisions for communication are perhaps seen in their mildest form in the Foreign Agents Registration Act of 1938, which established the right, although clearly not the duty, of the Secretary of the Treasury and the Postmaster General to accede to the request of the Librarian of Congress that they provide the librarian with copies of foreign printed matter excluded from the United States under congressional statutes.[3]

Must Receive Advice: The 1938 Naval Reserve Act created a Naval Reserve Policy Board, at least half the members of which were to be naval reserve officers called to Board duty from inactive duty status, which was to be convened annually for the purpose of advising the Secretary of the Navy on the formulation of Naval Reserve Policies.[4] Here a definite obligation to communicate, and a special agency for communication are established, and the Secretary of the Navy is by inference required to receive proffered advice, although he is not obligated to act in conformance with it.

Must Confer or Consult: Dictionaries tend to regard the words "advice" and "consult" as synonyms. And it may be that the Congress tends to employ these terms interchangeably. Yet it is reasonable to suppose that the legislature does not regard the transmission of decisional premises as an invariable one-way process. If this be true, it is possible although not demonstrable that "advise" as employed in statutes connotes the offering of counsel or opinion, recommending as wise or prudent—the communications process flowing in one direction; and "consult" implies a two-way communication process, "talking over a situation or a subject with someone to decide points in doubt."[5]

The Emergency Railroad Transportation Act of 1933 is infused with a quality of briskness which is absent from the statutes alluded to above. In this Act Congress created a co-ordinator of transportation and a number of regional railroad co-ordinating committees. It stipulated that the co-ordinator must "confer freely with the committees, and the committees, the carriers, the subsidiaries, and the Interstate Commerce Commission shall furnish him . . . such information and reports as he may desire."[6]

The Defense Production Act of 1950 required the President, in exercising the price and wage stabilization provisions of the Act, "so far as practicable, (to) advise and consult with, and establish and utilize the committees of, representatives of persons substantially affected by regulations or orders issued hereunder."[7]

Must Consider: While not saying that proffered advice must be accepted, Congress indicated in a 1946 statute that the Civil Aeronautics Administrator was to hold himself open to influence. In drawing up his plan for the development of public airports in the United States, he was required as far as possible to consult and give consideration to the views and recommendations of the Civil Aeronautics Board, the States, the Territories, Puerto Rico, and their political subdivisions.[8] He also had to consult and consider to the extent feasible the views and recommendations of the Federal Communications Commission.

The Philippine War Damage Commission was created in 1946 and assigned the task of making compensation for war damage to private property in the Philippines. The Commission was required so far as practicable to give consideration to the recommendations of the Filipino Rehabilitation Commission created in an earlier act. But, said Congress, the Commission was not required to await, or be bound by such recommendations.[9]

COMMUNICATION RELATED TO FRAMING OF A PARTICULAR DECISION

The foregoing advice and consultation provisions fall short of setting the requirement in a specific action context. They seem to have the objective of maximizing the likelihood that interested official and private groups will have the opportunity to influence program content. At the same time they imply or categorically state that the action agency need not be guided by such advice. It is not patently clear in any instance that the administrator must defer action until after consultation; and, of course, in one instance he is specifically advised that he is free of such a requirement.

The statutes referred to below clearly link the prescribed advice or consultation to the taking of specified action by the administrator. In some instances he must advise with others prior to taking action, but is not required to follow the advice. In others he is enabled but not required to act upon receipt of a report or information from another agency. An occasional statute will require not only consultation, but the making of specific findings precedent to exercising powers delegated by Congress. The administrator will sometimes find himself in a position in which he may take certain action only if it is acceptable to, or meets the approval of, other groups. And, carrying us to the end of this progression, we have the statutory requirement that the administrator act in conformance with advice received.

Must Seek Advice Prior to Acting: A June, 1934 amendment to the Tariff Act of 1930 sought to assist recovery from "the present emergency in restoring the American standard of living" by authorizing the President to enter into reciprocal trade agreements for the relaxation of duties and import restrictions.[10] Prior to concluding individual agreements, however, the President had to seek information and advice with respect thereto from the United States Tariff Commission, the Departments of State, Agriculture, and Commerce and from such other sources as he deemed appropriate. The advice need not be followed, but it must be sought precedent to concluding a reciprocal trade agreement. The 1934 grant of power to the President to prohibit the sale of arms to participants in the Chaco War made the exercise of that power contingent upon prior consultation with governments of other American Republics.[11]

Similarly, in granting the President power, in March, 1941 to authorize the transfer of American military equipment to the government of any country whose defense the President considered vital to the defense of the United States, Congress specified that no defense article not manufactured for such a foreign power might be disposed of except after consultation with the Chief of Staff of the Army or the Chief of Naval Operations of the Navy, or both.[12] The War Risk Insurance Act of 1950 permitted the Secretary of Commerce "with the approval of the President, and after such consultation with interested agencies of the Government as the President may require," to "provide insurance and reinsurance against loss or damage" of American merchant vessels "by war risks."[13] In 1950 security provisions were added to the Civil Aeronautics Act of 1938. Among these was an authorization for the Secretary of Commerce to establish zones or areas in the airspace above the United States as he found necessary in the interests of national security. Having established such spaces, he might, "after consultation with the Department of Defense and the Civil Aeronautics Board . . . prohibit or restrict flights of aircraft" within them.[14]

These statutes simply open up the channels of communication and insist that they be used prior to the taking of action. They do not explicitly require the administrator to accept proffered advice, and whatever effect they have upon his freedom of discretion is subtle and impalpable.

May Act on Receipt of Advice or Request: The 1937 statute extending the life of the Reconstruction Finance Corporation permitted the Board of Directors of the Corporation to report to the President that private credit was sufficiently available from private sources to meet legitimate demands of any class of eligible borrowers, whereupon the President might authorize the directors to suspend lending to that class.[15] Here, in effect, the Board of Directors of the RFC was given power to report (recommend) and thereby enable presidential action. The 1947 surplus property act authorized the disposal agency, upon the request of the Administrator of Civil Aeronautics, the Secretary of War, or the Secretary of the Navy to omit any of the terms, or conditions for the transfer of title to such property.[16] The agency granted a dispensing power which it was enabled to exercise upon receipt of a request from specified officials.

The first of these two statutes enabled the President to act after the RFC had made what amounted to a finding. In this, it is similar to the Nationality Act of 1940, which provided that the President might, in his discretion, exempt certain aliens in the United States from the classification of alien enemy, provided the Department of Justice investigated and established the loyalty of the alien.[17] A Department of Justice finding of loyalty enables but does not compel the President to act.

The Secretary of War was granted power in 1941 to remove any officer from the active list of the Regular Army for such causes and under such regulations as he might prescribe. He could not exercise this power in individual cases, however, until the officer had been recommended for removal by a board of not less than five general officers convened for this purpose by the Secretary of War.[18]

Action on Making an Independent Finding: At least two of the statutes covered in this survey required the President not only to consult, or to receive recommendations prior to taking action, but in addition, to make an explicit finding of fact. The India Emergency Food Aid Act of 1951 permitted the President, after consultation with appropriate Government officials and representatives of private shipping, and after finding and proclaiming that private shipping was not available on reasonable terms and conditions for transportation of supplies made available under Act, to provide for carriage in government-owned ships.[29] Four days after signing the Act, the President proclaimed that he had consulted with public officials and private shipping representatives, and had found it necessary to use government ships.[20] The 1951 amendments to the Universal Military Training and Service Act authorized the President "upon finding by him that such action is justified by the strength of the Armed Forces in the light of international conditions," and "upon recommendation of the Secretary of Defense" to decrease or eliminate periods of compulsory military service.[21]

The remaining statutes, in varying degree, subject administrative decision-making to external controls.

Action if Acceptable to Others: Congress in 1935 imposed, for three years, limitations upon imports of Philippine yarns, twines, cables, and other fibers. The limitation was subject to continuance for an additional three years by presidential proclamation, provided such extension was acceptable to the President of the Commonwealth.[22] Such an extension was made by a proclamation of January, 1938, in which the President recited that "the President of the Commonwealth of the Philippnes has indicated to me . . . his acceptance of an extension of the operation of that Act for an additional period of three years."[23] Unlike the earlier statutes which require consultation prior to action, or sometimes permit action only following recommendation and findings, here the substance of the President's action is subject to approval from a source external to the presidency.

Action Upon Receipt of Prior Approval: We have already employed, in another context, the provision of the War Risk Insurance Act of 1950, which hinged action by the Secretary of Commerce to the prior approval of the President.[24] The Defense Production Act of 1950 exempted from anti-trust prosecution business agreements made pursuant to the request of the President. The President was given a limited authority to delegate this power to subordinate officials, but only upon the condition that such officials consult with the Attorney General and with the Chairman of the Federal Trade Commission not less than ten days before making any request or finding thereunder. In addition, the request was to be subject to the prior approval of the Attorney General.[25] In August, 1950, Congress legislated on the matter of termination of government employment for security reasons. Persons whose employment was thus terminated might be employed elsewhere in the government only if the

Civil Service Commission approved a request coming from the individual or the prospective employing agency.[26]

The Rubber Producing Facilities Disposal Commission was directed to "consult and advise with the Attorney General" concerning the disposal of such facilities. The 1953 statute creating the Commission required that its report to Congress, suggesting an appropriate manner of disposing of government-owned producing facilities, be submitted first to the Attorney General who would advise the Commission "whether, in his opinion, the proposed disposition would violate the anti-trust laws." His findings approving the proposed disposals were to be appended to the report which the Commission made to Congress. Thus, in effect, the Commission was gently admonished to bring in a report bearing the Attorney General's approval.[27]

Must Act in Conformance With Request: The next group of statutes compel the administrator to accept and to act in accordance with recommendations or requests coming from a source beyond his agency. The Foreign Agents Registration Act of 1938, as amended in 1942, permitted certain exemptions from its registration provisions. The Attorney General might, after notice to the employing government or the person concerned, and with the approval of the Secretary of State, terminate in whole or in part an exemption from registration granted to United States residents who were employees of a foreign government. When the Secretary of State initiated a request for termination of an exemption, the Attorney General had to comply with the request.[28] The Second War Powers Act of 1942 contained a provision for the waiving of navigation and inspection laws under certain conditions. The head of each department or agency responsible for the administration of the navigation and vessel inspection laws was directed to waive compliance of such laws upon the request of the Secretary of the Navy or the Secretary of War to the extent believed necessary in the conduct of the war by the officer making the request.[29]

The discretion of federal jurists has to some extent been subjected to constriction by the executive. The Secretary of the Navy was given power, in a July, 1944, statute, to certify to federal courts that pending suits arising out of damage caused by naval vessels or towage or salvage services to naval vessels would, if tried, tend to endanger the security of naval operations. Upon receiving such a certification, the federal court having jurisdiction in the case was required to stay further proceedings until six months after the cessation of hostilities or such earlier date as the Secretary of the Navy might set.[30]

Congress, in February, 1952, took emergency action temporarily
suspending the import duty on lead. The Tariff Commission was to
advise the President at the end of any month in which the average
market price of lead delivered at New York had fallen below eighteen
cents per pound, "and the President shall, by proclamation, not later
than twenty days after he has been so advised by the Tariff Commission, revoke such suspension of the duties."[31] In June, 1952, the
President issued a proclamation under this Act, revoking the suspension of the duty.[32]

The converse of these arrangements whereby an administrator is
compelled to take prescribed action upon the request, or upon a
finding of others, is the situation in which he may be barred from
taking contemplated action, in consequence of a request or finding
coming from another agency. Our final illustration falls into this
bracket. The President was permitted by the Export Control Act
of 1949 to "prohibit or curtail the exportation from the United States
. . . of any articles, materials, or supplies, including technical data."
But he could not exercise this power "with respect to any agricultural
commodity, including fats and oils, during any period for which the
supply of such commodity is determined by the Secretary of Agriculture to be in excess of the requirements of the domestic economy."[33]

INTEGRATIVE RELATIONSHIPS

The statutory provisions enumerated above have the apparent
objective of facilitating communication between agencies or introducing checks and balances—contrived frustrations—into the administrative process. At the least intense end of the scale is permissive
interagency communication; gradually the relating of interagency
communication and agency action intensifies until the point is reached
at which an agency may exercise a delegated power only upon clearance with another agency, or is compelled to exercise it upon the
direction of another. However, the relationship between agencies is
communicative, and they do not by statute have joint responsibility
for decision-making or day-to-day program development and
execution.

The broad group of statutes to which we now turn attempts to
distribute among a number of agencies responsibility and authority
for joint decision-making and action. The resources and judgment
of many agencies may be focused on one program, or a system may
be set up for co-ordinating the activities of many agencies toward the
attainment of broad policy goals. The kind of interagency relation-

ship contemplated by Congress appears to be more active and positive, more a harnessing of equals, than those which we have thus far reviewed.

Four principal categories of statutory provisions may be distinguished under this general head. Some aim at joint decision-making by two or more agencies. Others enjoin agencies to "co-operate" in the administration of a given program. A third group establishes mutual assistance arrangements among agencies. Finally, we have those statutory provisions which seek co-ordination of interagency activities.[35]

JOINT DECISION-MAKING

A 1939 stockpiling act required the Secretary of War, the Secretary of the Navy, and the Secretary of the Interior, to determine whether certain materials purchased under the Act were strategic and critical. Once this determination was made, they then were permitted to determine the quality and quantities of materials to be purchased under the Act.[36] The Secretary of War and the Secretary of the Navy, when they considered such action appropriate because the domestic production or supply of certain materials was insufficient to meet the industrial, military, and naval needs of the country, were to direct the Secretary of the Treasury, through the medium of the Procurement Division of his Department to make purchases in accordance with specifications prepared by the Procurement Division of the Treasury Department and approved by the Secretary of War and the Secretary of the Navy. Two months later Congress authorized the Commodity Credit Corporation to accept such strategic and critical materials in exchange for such surplus agricultural commodities; and for the purpose of such exchange it was left to the three Secretaries to determine which materials are strategic and critical and the quantity and quality of such materials needed.[37]

The Central Intelligence Agency Act of 1949 set up procedures for granting asylum to foreign nationals who have performed valuable security services for the United States. Whenever the Director of the CIA, the Attorney General, and the Commissioner of Immigration determines that the entry of a particular alien for permanent residence is in the interest of national security or essential to the furtherance of the national intelligence mission, such alien and his immediate family shall be given entry into the United States for permanent residence without regard to their inadmissibility under the immigration or any other laws and regulations, or to the failure to comply with such laws and regulations pertaining to admissibility.[38] The Immigration and Nationality Act of 1952 assigns to the Secretary of State, the Secretary of Commerce, and the Attorney General jointly the function of determining the annual quota of immigrants for any quota area.[39] On June 30, 1952, the President issued a proclamation reciting that the quotas had been determined, and listing them.[40]

The National Security Act of 1947 recited as one of its purposes the establishment of integrated policies and procedures for the departments, agencies, and functions of the Government relating to the national security.[41]

CO-OPERATION

Joint decision-making shades into co-operative relationships which, if loose and flexible, may be continuing and steady. Such relations may exist with private as well as official groups.

Must Co-operate: The Small Business Concerns Mobilization Act made it the duty of the Chairman of the War Production Board to co-operate to the fullest practicable extent with the Director of Civilian Supply and other appropriate governmental agencies in the issuance of all orders limiting production by business enterprises with a view to insuring that small business concerns would not be bypassed in the production of war materials and goods essential to the civilian population.

In granting the Secretary of the Interior power to construct demonstration plants for production of synthetic and liquid fuels from coal oil shale, and agricultural and forestry products, the Congress specified that "any activities under this Act relating to the production of liquid fuels from agricultural and forestry products should be carried out in co-operation with the Department of Agriculture and subject to the direction of the Secretary of Agriculture."[43] A 1945 flood-control act clearly sought to effect interagency co-operation in facilitating the replacement by farmers of flood-damaged or -destroyed farm equipment. The War Production Board, and every other governmental agency which had jurisdiction over allocations and priorities relating to farm machinery and equipment were authorized and directed immediately to take whatever steps were necessary to provide for the necessary allocations and priorities to enable farmers in the areas affected by floods in 1944 and 1945 to replace and repair their farm machinery and equipment which was destroyed or damaged by such floods, or windstorms, or fire caused by lightning, and to continue farm operations.[44]

The Defense Production Act of 1950 provided that whenever the price and wage stabilization powers contained in the Act were exercised, all agencies of the Government dealing with price and wage stabilization, within the limits of their authority and jurisdiction, should co-operate in carrying out the purposes of the Act.[45]

May Co-operate: The Emergency Price Control Act of 1942 was in part designed "to permit voluntary co-operation between the Government and producers, processors, and others to accomplish the . . . purposes" of stabilizing prices and preventing speculation.[46] "It shall be the policy of those departments and agencies of the Government dealing with wages (including the Department of Labor and its various bureaus, the War Department, the Navy Department, the War Production Board, the National Labor Relations Board, the National Mediation Board, the National War Labor Board, and others heretofore or hereafter created), within the limits of their authority and jurisdiction, to work toward a stabilization of prices, fair and equitable wages, and cost of production."[47]

MUTUAL ASSISTANCE

Congress will not infrequently require or enable one agency, on an interim or continuing basis, to come to the assistance of another in the execution of its program. This may take the form of providing money, material, facilities, or service to the agency. It is a kind of mutual assistance program within the executive branch.

The Reconstruction Finance Corporation, for example, was occasionally treated by Congress as a source of credit to enable agencies to launch authorized programs immediately after enactment, and thus avoid the delays which attend appropriation of funds for authorized programs. The Far Eastern Economic Assistance Act of 1950 authorized the appropriation to the President of sixty million dollars to enable the Economic Co-operation Administration to furnish assistance to the Republic of Korea. As a way of getting the program started at once, the Reconstruction Finance Corporation was authorized and directed to make advances not to exceed thirty million dollars in the aggregate, until the regular appropriation was available.[48] It can readily be seen that this device might be employed not only to avoid the normal delays of the appropriations process, but to circumvent or nullify the obstructive tatics of an unfriendly appropriations subcommittee.

The India Emergency Food Aid Act of 1951 contained a similar provision. If the President, after consultation with public and private shipping officials, found that private shipping was not available to carry American food to India on reasonable terms and conditions, the Reconstruction Finance Corporation was authorized and directed to make advances not to exceed in the aggregate twenty million dollars to the Department of Commerce for activation of vessels for such transportation.[49]

Other mutual assistance provisions enable or require agencies to produce or procure goods or services for other agencies under certain conditions. The Tennessee Valley Authority Act required the Corporation, upon the requisition of the Secretary of War or the Secretary of the Navy to manufacture for and sell at cost to the United States explosives or their nitrogenous content. Upon the requisition of the Secretary of War the Corporation was to allot and deliver without charge to the War Department whatever power was necessary in the judgment of the Department for use in operation of all locks, lifts, and other facilities in aid of navigation.[50] The Helium Gas Act of 1937 permitted the Army, Navy, and other government agencies to requisition helium from the Bureau of Mines, which agency was charged with responsibility for the production of helium.[51]

The Maritime Commission was assigned responsibility, in July, 1941, for meeting the shipping needs of defense agencies.[52] The Secretary of the Air Force was directed to make available to the Civil Air Patrol by gift or by loan, sale or otherwise, with or without charge, obsolete or surplus aircraft and aircraft parts to permit utilization of facilities of the Air Force, and to furnish to Civil Air Patrol the fuel needed to enable it to complete any specifically assigned mission.[53]

CO-ORDINATION

If co-operation involves working together, co-ordination is the process whereby things are placed in position relative to each other and to the system of which they form parts. Administrators may work together, or co-operate, toward the end of co-ordinating their programs. But joint decision-making, or co-operative programming are vitally, if subtly, different from the co-ordination of programs. In the first place, joint decision-making or co-operation have the purpose of focusing the judgment and resources of many agencies upon the execution of one program, whereas co-ordination involves the relating of many similar, or possibly diverse, programs. Secondly, to indulge a tautology, joint-decision-making and co-operation (as provided for in the statutes just reviewed) involve a positive, creative elaboration and execution of programs, whereas co-ordination consists of minimizing conflict of purpose among two or more programs.

The Commissioners of the District of Columbia were authorized in August, 1950, to set up an Office of Civil Defense for the District, which office would, among other things, plan for integration of the District's civil defense effort with that of the federal government and nearby states, and co-operate with governmental and nongovernmental agencies and co-ordinate the activities within the district.[54] The National Science Foundation's functions include that of correlating its scientific research programs with those undertaken by individuals and by public and private research groups.[55] The Immigration and Nationality Act of 1952 authorized the Commissioner of Immigration and the administrator of the Bureau of Security and Consular Affairs of the Department of State to maintain direct and continuous liaison with the Directors of the Federal Bureau of Investigation and the Central Intelligence Agency and with other internal security officers of the Government for the purpose of obtaining and exchanging information for use in enforcing the provisions of this Act in the interest of the internal security of the United States. The Commissioner and the administrator are to maintain direct and continuous liaison with each other with a view to a co-ordinated, uniform, and efficient administration of this law, and all other immigration and nationality laws.[56]

There were some statutes with regard to which it is difficult, if not impossible, upon the basis of reading alone, to determine whether the purpose was to bring the facilities of many agencies to bear upon the administration of one program, or to enhance the prospect that the program would be administered in a manner consistent with the objectives of other related programs. A study of the legislative history and the administration of these provisions would probably disclose that the legislative intent was mixed, or that in the process of administration both objectives were joined.

We might include within this category the Neutrality Act of 1935 which set up the National Munitions Control Board, to be composed of the Secretaries of State, Treasury, War, and Navy. The Board, acting largely through the Secretary of State, was the agency for execution of the neutrality program.[57] The Contract Settlement Act of 1944 set up an Office of Contract Settlement, headed by a Director, and a Contract Settlement Advisory Board, with which the Director was required to advise and consult. The Board was composed of the Director, the Secretaries of War, Navy, and Treasury, the Chairman

of the Maritime Commission, the Administrator of the Foreign
Economic Administration, the Chairman of the Board of Directors
of the Reconstruction Finance Corporation, the Chairman of the War
Production Board, the Chairman of the Board of Directors of the
Smaller War Plants Corporation, and the Attorney General.[58] Any of
these officials might appoint representatives.

The Atomic Energy Act of 1946 contained provision for a Military
Liaison Committee.[59] The National Advisory Committee for Aeronautics, created to supervise the scientific study of the problems of
flight, under a 1948 statute, was to be composed of not more than
seventeen members appointed by the President including two representatives of the Department of the Air Force; two of the Department of the Navy, from the office in charge of naval aeronautics,
two of the Civil Aeronautics Authority; one of the Smithsonian
Institute; one of the United States Weather Bureau; one of the
National Bureau of Standards; the Chairman of the Research and
Development Board of the National Military Establishment; and
others.[60]

Are these representative of congressional efforts to organize co-
operation, or to organize co-ordination? We think the latter, although
it is clear that reasonable men could differ, and a careful legislative
history might prove us wrong.

Conclusions

Our findings appear to suggest that either Congress has a considerable feeling for the subtle nuances of administrative interrelationships,
or that it is loose and inconsistent in the language it employs. The
statutory provisions run a gamut, permitting the exchange of information, providing formally prescribed sources of advice, compelling
agencies to consult, to consult and consider, to consult prior to taking
specific action, hinging action to the receipt of a prior enabling report
or request, requiring prior consultation and fact finding, requiring
clearance or approval from a source external to the agency, and
finally, compelling action in conformance with the request of another
agency. It has harnessed the judgment and resources of many agencies
to the making of particular kinds of decisions, it has provided for
interagency co-operation and assistance in the accomplishment of
policy goals; and it has taken care to assure co-ordination or related
programs.

These are the relationships which Congress has sought to establish
among administrative agencies.

CHAPTER X

JUDICIAL REVIEW

Edward S. Corwin has appraised as a misfortune the fact that "Constitutionalism has worked in this country to impress upon the discussion of public measures a legalistic—not to say theological—mold," and has substituted "for the question of the beneficial *use* of the powers of government . . . the question of their existence."[1]

The United States Supreme Court, rather than the judicial system, is popularly conceived to have a distinctive role to play in checking arbitrary government in time of emergency;[2] and it endeavors to perform that role, albeit none too successfully at times by ruling on the constitutionality of the government power asserted during such period of crisis. However, as the chief appellate body in a judicial system which as a whole "handles a mere trickle of the great issues arising"[3] during an emergency, the Supreme Court cannot reasonably be expected to formulate a coherent theory of democratic response to emergency whereby action designed to meet the exigencies of war can be harmonized with our constitutional system with only minimum risk to the preservation thereof.

THE SUPREME COURT'S APPROACH

In its effort to avoid the Scylla of judicial refusal to review the constitutionality of legislative or executive emergency action, and the Charybdis of declaring unconstitutional emergency action which might be vital to national survival,[4]—i.e., in its efforts to "reconcile the irreconcilables" which Cardozo considered the essence of the judicial function—the Supreme Court has traveled various routes. The majority opinions of the Court, or the concurring or dissenting opinions of individual justices, have at times asserted that (a) the Constitution is a rigorously confining document to be inflexibly applied by the Court in measuring governmental action in war and peace; (b) there exists an emergency power which is above constitutional limitations; (c) the Constitution is a flexible charter permitting government action commensurate with need as measured by the Court.

All three of these approaches are characterized by a preoccupation with the question of the existence of the asserted emergency power. Under the first, the Court is guided by a narrow interpretation of the quantum of constitutional emergency power and appears disposed to appraise the validity of asserted authority independently of any consideration of the indispensability of the power exercised for successful resolution of the crisis. Involving covertly virtual acceptance of the principle, *inter arma selent legis,* the second is extremely dangerous; for if applied extensively, it would erode constitutional balance and restraint and perhaps terminate responsible government in time of peril. Insofar as it chooses to be guided by the third and purports to sanction only that which it concedes to be essential for combating an emergency, the Court not only assumes a task for which it is ill-suited but also frequently shirks its responsibilities in the performance thereof. Too often when it dares to condemn as ultra vires action believed unavoidable in the prosecution of a war, it postpones its invalidation until after hostilities have terminated. Such post mortem judicial observations afford most inadequate guides for ascertaining what will be constitutionally permissible in time of crisis.

Apart from a few brief illustrations of the aforementioned judicial approaches, we have placed major emphasis upon the Steel Seizure Case [Youngstown v. Sawyer, 343 U.S. 579 (1952)], for in that decision are to be found signally important indications of the most effective contribution which the Federal judiciary hereafter may make in sustaining responsible government. The need for a more extensive review of the Supreme Court's appraisal of emergency power has been dispelled by Clinton Rossiter's study of *The Supreme Court and the Commander-in-Chief.*[5]

The Constitution as a Rigidly Restrictive Document: In one of the extremely rare instances in which a Supreme Court Justice has defied the Chief Executive engaged in prosecuting a war, Chief Justice Roger B. Taney in 1861, presiding as Circuit Court Judge at Baltimore, demanded that the military produce in court one John Merryman, who had been arrested. When Merryman's jailers replied to Taney that by virtue of the President's proclamation suspending the writ of habeas corpus, they had been directed not to respond to the writ, the venerable Chief Justice wrote a stinging opinion informing the President that the power to suspend the writ belonged to Congress alone and could not be exercised by the chief executive. Notwithstanding his ruling, Merryman was not released and the President continued his suspension of the writ, although Congress did not validate his action until 1863.[1]

Perhaps a better example of Taney's attitude toward the relaxing of constitutional restraints in wartime is to be found in an earlier, unpublished opinion, quoted by Swisher in his biography of the Chief Justice:

"A civil war or any other war does not enlarge the powers of the federal government over the states or the people beyond what the compact has given to it in time of war. A state of war does not annul the 10th article of the amendments to the Constitution, which declares that 'the powers not delegated to the United States by the Constitution, nor prohibited by it to the states, are reserved to the states respectively or to the people.'

"Nor does a civil war or any other war absolve the judicial department from the duty of maintaining with an even and firm hand the rights and powers of the federal government, and of the states, and of the citizens, as they are written in the Constitution, which every judge is sworn to support." [2]

For the other expressions of this absolutist view, we must look to opinions handed down in the immediate postwar periods of 1866 and 1946. *Ex parte Milligan*[3] involved the incarceration of a northerner suspected of Southern sympathies. Could such an individual be tried, convicted and sentenced to death by a military tribunal, in an area far behind the Northern lines, in fact, in a State which had never been invaded by the Southern armies? Scores of such instances of military trial and conviction of civilians had occurred in Northern states untouched by the war.

The majority opinion for the Supreme Court disposing of this issue was written by Justice Davis and constitutes as rigid a definition of the limits circumscribing the war powers as could possibly be stated:

"The Constitution of the United States is a law for rulers and people, equally in war and in peace, and covers with the shield of its protection all classes of men, at all times, and under all circumstances. No doctrine, involving more pernicious consequences, was ever invented by the wit of man than that any of its provisions can be suspended during any of the great exigencies of government. Such a doctrine leads directly to anarchy or despotism; but the theory of necessity on which it is based is false; for the government, within the constitution, has all the powers granted to it, which are necessary to preserve its existence . . .

". . . It could well be said that a country, preserved at the sacrifice of all the cardinal principles of liberty, is not worth the cost of preservation." [4]

This opinion by a Lincoln appointee to the Court was offset in part by the concurring opinion of Lincoln's former Secretary of the Treasury. Chief Justice Chase could conceive of a situation in which Congress might find such measures "essential to the prosecution of the war with vigor and success," and would therefore be entitled under the Constitution to resort to them. Independent of statutory authorization the President, however, could not employ such power. He was limited to executing the measures adopted by Congress.[5]

Some eighty years later, in 1941, martial law was declared in Hawaii. From that time through the Fall of 1945, the Islands were ruled by the military. After bitter and protracted litigation, in which the federal courts in Honolulu were particularly outspoken against the type of military rule practiced in the Islands, the cases of *Duncan* v. *Kahanamoku* and *White* v. *Steer* managed to surmount the obstacle course to the Supreme Court.[6] Duncan and White were civilians who had been apprehended during the war and tried and convicted by the military, the former for assault against a Marine sentry, and the latter for embezzlement. Both were crimes under the Hawaiian civil code. Challenging the jurisdiction of the military to try these men, a lower federal court ordered their release upon petition for habeas corpus; and on appeal the validity of the District Court order was sustained by the Supreme Court in an opinion written by Justice Black. The case turned upon a narrow interpretation of the meaning of "martial law." The term did not, Black said, embrace trial of civilians by military courts. He did leave the door ajar, however, implying that it is not inconceivable in a situation of dire necessity, that such trial of civilians by the military might be upheld.

In a concurring opinion, however, Justice Murphy restated the principle expressed in the *Milligan* case. Exalting civilian supremacy over the military, he reiterated the *Milligan* rule that civilians may not be tried by the military when the courts are open and functioning. Not only did he agree with Justice Black that the acts of the military contravened statutory law, but he also was of the belief they were proscribed by the due process clause and therefore manifestly unconstitutional. Unlike the Civil War Justices, however, he suggested that until the courts were able to resume their functions the military might retain custody of its prisoners.[7]

Extra-Constitutional Sources of Emergency Power. Perhaps the most expansive argument for a constitutionally sanctioned, unqualified emergency power is that developed and expressed by Justice George Sutherland in a work published in 1919,[8] before his accession to the bench, and restated in his opinion for the Court in *United States* v. *Curtiss-Wright Export Corporation.* In *Constitutional Power and World Affairs,* he asserted:

"As the highest duty of the nation is self-preservation, the rights of peace must then be held in subjection to the necessities of war. This does not result in a suspension of the Constitution, as some have petulantly suggested, but it may result in a suspension of constitutional rights of the individual because they conflict with the paramount powers of war . . .

"This power is tremendous; it is strictly constitutional; but it breaks down every barrier so anxiously erected for the protection of liberty, of property and of life."¹⁰

The later Supreme Court opinion only removes the inconsistencies from these passages, and recognizes the war powers as extra-constitutional in nature:

"It results that the investment of the federal government with the powers of external sovereignty did not depend upon the affirmative grants of the Constitution. The powers to declare and wage war, to conclude peace, to make treaties, to maintain diplomatic relations with other sovereignties, if they had never been mentioned in the Constitution, would have been vested in the federal government as necessary concomitants of nationality."¹¹

Justice Jackson, dissenting in the Japanese relocation case, *Korematsu* v. *United States,*¹² advocated complete judicial abnegation of any pretended power to review the necessity for emergency action. Favoring, however, a reversal of the judgment and a "discharge of the prisoner," Jackson added that he couldn't subscribe to the view that the existence of "reasonable military grounds" for such a wartime program made it constitutionally valid and subject to judicial enforcement.¹³ The Court cannot

". . . require such a commander in such circumstances to act as a reasonable man; he may be unreasonably cautious and exacting. Perhaps he should be . . .

"But if we cannot confine military expedients by the Constitution, neither would I distort the Constitution to approve all that the military may deem expedient . . .

"A military commander may overstep the bounds of constitutionality, and it is an incident. But if we review and approve, that passing incident becomes a doctrine of the Constitution . . . a judicial opinion rationalizes such an order to show that it conforms to the

Constitution, or rather rationalizes the Constitution to show that the Constitution sanctions such an order . . ."[14]

It is true that the existence of this power in the government in wartime, and the admitted inability of the Court to restrict it, is "an inherent threat to liberty."

"But I would not lead people to rely on this Court for a review that seems to me wholly delusive. The military reasonableness of these orders can only be determined by the military superiors. If the people ever let command of the war power fall into irresponsible hands, the courts wield no power equal to its restraint. The chief restraint upon those who command the physical forces of the country, in the future as in the past, must be their responsibilities to the political judgments of their contemporaries and to the moral judgments of history."[15]

Like Machiavelli, Jackson conducts an analysis in simple power terms. But while Machiavelli suggested it was possible to devise ways to circumscribe and check the exercise of emergency power by leaders in a republic, the modern liberal, true to the tradition of Locke, can conceive of no limits upon the actions of a war government but the force of public opinion.

The Constitution as a Flexible Charter: Although as recently as World War II all three strains of thought regarding emergency powers of the Chief Executive during wartime found effective expression in opinions of individual justices on the Court, the most persistent has been the attempt to compromise the range of views by positing a Constitution broad and flexible enough to encompass emergency action responsive to existing need, as measured by the Court. This has been described by Professor Corwin as "constitutional relativity."[16]

The "clear and present danger" doctrine, first enunciated by Justice Holmes in the *Schenck* case[17] is an example of constitutional relativity. Its recent application illustrates what is to be expected when the Court, having accepted the obligation to determine the necessity for emergency action, subsequently is led by doubts as to the adequacy of its tools for measurement to redefine the conditions of an emergency in such a manner as virtually to evade the problem.[18] It also points up some of the difficulties in consistently applying whatever criteria for measurement are developed by the Court.

Schenck had been convicted under the Espionage Act of 1917 for seeking to obstruct the draft. He had circularized a mailing list with literature opposing the World War I draft law. Included on the list were a number of persons in the military service at the time of receipt of the material. Holmes' reasoned as follows:

"The question in every case is whether the words used are used in such circumstances and are of such a nature as to create a clear and present danger that they will bring about the substantive evils that Congress has a right to prevent. It is a question of proximity and degree. . .

"It seems to be admitted that if an actual obstruction of the recruiting service were proved, liability for words that produced that effect might be enforced. . . If the act, . . . its tendency and the intent with which it is done are the same, we perceive no ground for saying that success alone warrants making the act a crime."[19]

Schenck remained in jail.

In a subsequent case under the same Act, involving a group of "radicals" who had disseminated a pamphlet condemning United States intervention in Russia and threatening to thwart that intervention by causing trouble on the home front, calling upon munitions workers to quit their jobs, and advocating revolution, Holmes dissented from a decision upholding their conviction.[20] Rejecting as fallacious the conclusion of his colleagues that the surreptitious publishing of a "silly leaflet by an unknown man, without more, would present any immediate danger that its opinions would hinder the success of the government arms or have any appreciable tendency to do so," Holmes maintained:

"An intent to prevent interference with the revolution in Russia might have been satisfied without any hindrance to carrying on the war in which we were engaged. . .

"Even if I am technically wrong and enough can be squeezed from these poor and puny anonymities to turn the color of legal litmus paper; I will add, even if what I think the necessary intent were shown; the most nominal punishment seems to me all that possibly could be inflicted, unless the defendants are to be made to suffer not for what the indictment alleges but for the creed that they avow. . ."[21]

The significance of this latter opinion would appear to derive from the fact that by employing the descriptive adjectives "silly" and "puny" Holmes transformed his clear and present danger doctrine into a vehicle for opposing conviction of persons for what would seem, on the face of the record, possibly a more aggravated offense than Schenck's. Thus the "clear and present danger" test in application may become entangled with the sentiment of the person applying it. Secondly, it is important to note the appraisal which Holmes made as to the military significance of American intervention in

Russia. In his estimation, had it been thwarted our war effort would not have been effected. As a dessenter Holmes, with the support of Brandeis, persisted in applying the "clear and present danger" test in a number of later decisions, notably the *Gitlow* case and the *Whitney* case.[22]

In the post-World War II era, however, this test definitely appears to have been radically altered, if not conclusively rejected. Thus in *Dennis* v. *United States,* sustaining the conviction under the Smith Act[23] of eleven top Communist Party leaders, Judge Learned Hand, presiding over the U.S. Court of Appeals for the Second Circuit, stated:

"The phrase, 'clear and present danger,' has come to be used as a shorthand statement of those among such mixed or compounded utterances which the Amendment does not protect. . . It is a way to describe a penumbra of occasions, even the outskirts of which are indefinable, but within which, as is so often the case, the courts must find their way as they can. In each case they must ask whether the gravity of the 'evil,' discounted by its improbability, justified such invasion of free speech as is necessary to avoid the danger. . .

". . . When does the conspiracy become a 'present danger'? The jury has found that the conspirators will strike as soon as success seems possible, and obviously, no one in his senses would strike sooner. [Meanwhile, the Communist leaders claim the right to continue their activities.] That position presupposes that the Amendment assures them freedom for all preparatory steps and in the end, the choice of initiative, dependent upon the moment when they believe us, who must wait the blow, to be the worst prepared to receive it."[24]

By substituting "probability" for "imminence" in time, Hand substantially changed the clear and present danger doctrine. On appeal the Supreme Court, with certain modifications, in effect affirmed Hand's redefinition.[25]

In connection with these examples of judicial application of the "clear and present danger" doctrine it is equally pertinent to set forth Chief Justice Hughes' famous dictum that "the war power of the Federal Government. . . is a power to wage war successfully,"[26] and to refer to the decisions arising out of World War II Japanese curfew and relocation[27] and rent control.[28] The Court's approach is epitomized by Black's reasoning in his majority opinion in *Korematsu* v. *United States*:

"But when under conditions of modern warfare our shores are

threatened by hostile forces, the power to protect must be commensurate with the threatened danger. . .

". . . hardships are a part of war, and war is an aggregation of hardships. All citizens alike, both in and out of uniform, feel the impact of war in greater or lesser measure."[29]

Whether the Court is competent to fulfill the role of protector of the Constitution in wartime is highly debatable. Is the Court capable of performing the task, even if time were available? Obviously not. It does not have the information requisite for determination of current needs and the adequacy and appropriateness of government actions to meet them. It cannot be presumed to possess the fund of knowledge essential for appraising issues largely military in nature, and, consequently upon the advent of actual hostilities, it invariably displays a reluctance to countermand the executive and legislative branches, no matter how extreme their action. Furthermore, the judicial process with its haphazard accretion of cases, the manifest capacity of government to make cases moot, or failure to prosecute, frequently makes it impossible for the Court even to review significant controversies produced by action of the political departments. For every Milligan or Duncan who manages to bring his case to the Court (usually for post mortem relief), there are hundreds who submit to abusive governmental action without ever contesting the validity thereof. This alone affords adequate demonstration that the court is ineffective in maintaining constitutionalism in time of war. For fulfillment of this objective vigilance on the part of Congress and the Executive no less than the electorate is imperative.

In a democracy the function of defending liberty cannot safely be relegated to any single institution.

A MORE EFFECTIVE EMERGENCY ROLE FOR THE JUDICIARY

Judicial oversight of government emergency action has suffered from concentration upon the question of the existence of power. In the context of emergency the Court can best preserve for itself and the Federal judicial system a meaningful role in preserving constitutional processes if it is invited to measure the consistency of executive action both to executive standards and congressional grants of power,[1] rather than to rhetorically assert a right to admonish a government— Congress and President, armed, mobilized and engaged in war, that the measures which it employs for protection of the nation are unconstitutional. In testing the vires of administrative action the courts are acting in an area vital to the preservation of responsible

government, and in which cooperative legislative-executive validation of judicially disapproved action represents the essence of constitutionalism rather than constitutional immorality.[2]

THE STEEL SEIZURE CASES[1]

When, on April 8, 1952, President Truman issued Executive Order
10340 directing seizure of the steel industry,[2] he set in motion a train
of events which were to culminate in an historic series of concurring
opinions which may herald a significant change in emphasis on the
part of the Court.   The effect of the majority and concurring opinions
in this case is effectively to curb and subject to Congressional sanction a kind of "homemade prerogative"[3] which the President had
asserted, and to reassert the primacy of the Court's role as a balancing
agent in the constitutional system.   Four days before issuance of the
Executive Order, the C.I.O. United Steelworkers of America had
given notice of a nation-wide strike to begin on April 9.[4]   Alleging in
his Order that such a strike would undermine American attempts
to fulfill international responsibilities, to maintain a steady supply
of war materials to the fighting force in Korea, and to maintain the
domestic economy of the nation, the President invoked "the authority
vested in me by the Constitution and laws of the United States, and
as President of the United States and Commander-in-Chief of the
armed forces of the United States," as his legal justification for directing the Secretary of Commerce "to take possession of" the steel
plants.

On April 9th, Judge Alexander Holtzoff in the United States District Court for the District of Columbia rejected the application of
Youngstown Sheet & Tube Co., *et. al.*, for an injunction and declara-
tory judgment protecting the mills from seizure by the Secretary of
Commerce.[5]   The District Court stated two grounds in support of its
ruling.   (1) While it might technically run against Secretary of
Commerce Sawyer, an injunction "actually and in essence. . . would be
an injunction against the President."   (2) The steel companies had
not shown irreparable harm.[6]

Three weeks later the steel companies instituted new proceedings
before Judge David A. Pine of the District Court, District of Columbia.[7]   Injunctive relief was now sought on grounds that the seizure
of the mills, not having been authorized by statute, was unconstitutional.[8]   The government's presentation was completely prejudiced
by the insistence of the Assistant Attorney General that the President's
actions be upheld on grounds of his "inherent" emergency powers.[9]

The Court: "And is it. . . . your view that the powers of the Government are limited by and enumerated in the Constitution of the United States?"

Mr. Baldridge: "That is true, Your Honor, with respect to legislative powers."

The Court: "But it is not true, you say, as to the Executive?"

Mr. Baldridge: "No."

The Court: "So, when the sovereign people adopted the Constitution, it enumerated the powers set up in the Constitution but limited the powers of the Congress and limited the powers of the judiciary, but it did not limit the powers of the Executive. Is that what you say?"

Mr. Baldridge: "That is the way we read Article II of the Constitution."[10]

Judge Pine ruled that the President's action was unsupported by law and granted the injunction.

While the government's claim to an inherent emergency power may have been extreme, it was a natural culmination of the trend of judicial and scholarly interpretation of emergency powers through the Second World War. Two authoritative sources existed, each providing plausible underpinning for executive assertion of inherent emergency powers—unlimited by Constitution, Congress or Court. The first was judicial language such as the Sutherland dicta in *United States* v. *Curtiss-Wright*.[11] The second embraced commentaries by persons generally considered qualified to write exegeses on the Constitution, wherein the previously unchallenged exercise of emergency power by the President has been viewed as controlling precedent legitimizing the acquisition of such power. Thus, as of 1952, in the minds of many, the President had built up imposing historical precedent for the exercise of executive discretion adequate to accomplsh whatever purposes appeared to him essential to counter an emergency.[12] In many instances, however, such action has frequently violated explicit provisions of the Constitution or of congressional statutes.[13]

Justice Frankfurter indicated his acceptance of the validity of this line of reasoning when in his concurring opnion in the *Steel Seizure* cases he asserted that ". . . a systematic, unbroken, executive practice, long pursued to the knowledge of the Congress and never before questioned, engaged in by Presidents who have also sworn to uphold the Constitution, making as it were such exercise of power part of the structure of our government, may be treated as a gloss on 'executive power' vested in the President by Sec. 1 of Ar. II."[14]

By the ruling sustained, however, the District Court and the majority of the Supreme Court lent color of authority to the steel companies' contention that "There could be no more dangerous principle—nor one more foreign to the Constitution—than a rule that past illegality can through some legerdemain serve as authority to legalize present illegality."[15] Justice Jackson disposed of the Solicitor General's contention that although Congress had not provided for seizure of the steel mills, the practice of past Presidents did authorize it, by stating that while it was not surprising that the Government should seek support for nebulous, inherent powers in the customs and unadjudicated claims of preceding administrations, "a judge cannot accept [executive self-assertions of power] . . . as authority in answering a constitutional question . . . Prudence has counseled that actual reliance on such nebulous claims stop short of provoking a judicial test."[16]

The government went into the Court of Appeals, District of Columbia Circuit, seeking an order staying the injunction pending submission of a petition for *certiorari* to the Supreme Court.[17] The order was granted[18] on May 2, and the following day the Supreme Court granted *certiorari*, staying the District Court order pending final dsposition of the cases.[19]

Avoiding the bold and indiscreet assertion of undefined inherent powers which had so prejudiced the government's case in the District Court, Solicitor General Philip B. Perlman on appeal to the Supreme Court submitted a brief devoted to establishing the existence of an emergency of sufficient magnitude to warrant extraordinary action on the part of the executive.[20] As assurance of the President's willingness to subject himself to the desires of Congress, the brief cited his communication to the Senate of April 21, 1952, offering to adhere to any positive line of action prescribed by Congress.[21] The remainder of the brief enumerates the historical and judicial precedent affording a legal justification of the steel sezure[22] and concludes with an argument to the effect that the proper remedy available to the steel companies was suit for just compensation in the Court of Claims.[23]

In the light of the facts of the case counsel for the steel companies could most efficiently sustain their contentions by emphasizing the impropriety of executive sezure in plain oppostion to the obvious intent of Congress expressed in a statute anticipating such emergency and explicitly providing a different solution. They avoided challenging the constitutionality in the absence of a statute of an emergency power to seize private productive facilities. In fact, the steel companies openly conceded the existence of broad emergency power. They made it clear that their view "does not mean that the Government is powerless to deal with the threat to steel production which arises from the current labor dispute." If necessary ". . . Congress can legislate appropriately and specifically to protect the nation from threatened disaster."[24] The determining factor in assessing the legitimacy of government action in this case, however, was the nature of the legislative-executive relationship involved. Presidential action, the companies argued, could be arranged on a "spectrum" of legitimacy[25]—at one end, cooperative executive-legislative action. Congress and President might unite in the execution of a program or Congress subsequently might ratify a prior exercise of power by the executive.[26] At the other end, as in this case, the presidential action violates a clear congressional intent.[27]

Here ". . . the statutory processes have been ignored . . .,"[28] and an early but eminent constitutional precedent was cited as squarely meeting the instant situation. An Act passed by Congress in 1799 suspended commercial intercourse between the United States and France during the undeclared naval war between the two nations. The act provided that no American vessel should be permitted to proceed to any French port under penalty of forfeiture, and authorized the seizure of all American ships bound *to* any French ports. President Adams instructed commanders of United States armed vessels to seize all American ships bound *to* or *from* French ports. Acting under these presidential instructions, Captain Little stopped and seized on the high seas a vessel bound *from* a French port. The Court through Chief Justice John Marshall held that Congress had prescribed by its legislation the manner of which seizures were to be carried into execution and had excluded the seizure of any vessel bound *from* rather than *to* a French port. And even though the executive construction was calculated to increase the effectiveness of the legislation, the executive had no right to expand the law as enacted.[29]

Justice Black for the majority of the Court rejected the notion that unchallenged emergency action by former Presidents provided any solid legal precedent for Truman's seizure of the steel mills.[30] "The President's power to issue the order must stem either from an act of Congress or from the Constitution itself."[31] The seizure order could not be sustained by any of the constitutional grants of executive power to the President.[32] The President, rather than basing his order upon a specific statute, had chosen to direct "that a presidential policy be executed in a manner prescribed by the President."[33] Black did not question "the power of Congress to adopt such public policies as those proclaimed by the order." The action of the President in initiating such a policy was, however, an unconstitutional arrogation of "lawmaking power" to the executve.[34]

Justice Black avoided citation of judicial precedent in that portion of his opinion which invalidated the President's action. The reason for this is clear, and has been stated succinctly by Professor Edward S. Corwin in comments upon the *Steel Seizure* cases:

"The doctrine of the case, as stated in Justice Black's opinion of the Court, while purporting to stem from the principle of separation of powers, is a purely arbitrary construction created out of hand for the purpose of disposing of this particular case, and is altogether devoid of historical verification."[35]

Each of the six justices who concurred in Black's majority opinion in the *Steel Seizure* cases stated his reasons in full.[36] By far the most lucid, best reasoned, and most adequate of any of the opinions appears to be that of Justice Jackson. He avoided the oversimplification of issues which weakens Black's opinion. Filling the theoretical lacunae which Black in his hasty advance to the target (invalidation of Truman's action) left in his wake, Jackson recognized that the real issue of the case was not that the President had taken emergency action unsupported by a declaration of legislative policy, but that his measures had been "incompatible with the expressed or implied will of Congress."[37] Justice Jackson founded his opinion upon the concept of our government as a "balanced power structure."[38] Th Constitution disperses power among the branches of government, but contemplates that practice will achieve the integration essential to effective government. "Interdependence" rather than "separateness" is the relationship that must exist. The powers of a President in time of emergency are not, as the Government had argued, comprehensive and undefined; neither are they fixed, "but fluctuate, depending upon their disjunction or conjunction with those of Congress."[39] Jackson enumerates alternatives of Presidential-Congressional relationships which may determine the extent of executive power:

"1. When the President acts pursuant to an express or implied authorization of Congress, his authority is at its maximum, for it includes all that he possesses in his own right plus all that Congress can delegate. . .

"2. When the President acts in absence of either a congressional grant or denial of authority, he can only rely upon his own independent powers. . .

"3. When the President takes measures incompatible with the expressed or implied will of Congress, his power is at its lowest ebb, for then he can rely only upon his own constitutional powers minus any constitutional powers of Congress over the matter. . ."[40]

The seizure of the steel mills by President Truman in face of a contrary congressional policy fell into the third of these categories and left presidential power "most vulnerable to attack and in the least favorable of possible constitutional postures." The Court could sustain the President's action "only by holding that seizure of such strike-bound industries is within his domain and beyond control by Congress."[41]

Also concurring, Mr. Justice Clark relied on the precedent of *Little v. Barreme*.[42] Although "the Constitution does grant to the President extensive authority in times of grave and imperative emergency"[43] and in the absence of Congressional action "the President's independent power to act depends upon the gravity of the situation confronting the nation,"[44] the lesson of *Little v. Barreme* and sound constitutional exposition demand that "where Congress has laid down specific procedures to deal with the type of crisis confronting the President, he must follow those procedures in meeting the crisis. . ."[45]

In his dissenting opinion Chief Justice Vinson maintained that the majority justices had each assumed the unarticulated major premise" that the emergency was not of sufficient gravity to warrant the mode of action adopted by the President. The Chief Justice chided his colleagues for not weighing the magnitude of the emergency accurately.[46] But this seems hardly a warrantable criticism of a group of opinions which manifested little concern with substantive constitutional limitations upon executive emergency action, but rather emphasized the necessity for compliance with a congressional program anticipating such an emergency and prescribing the mode of response to it.

THE STEEL STRIKE OF 1959

In 1959 the nation's great steel industry once again occupied the center of a dispute which had far reaching consequences.

The dispute was that between representatives of the twelve largest steel producers in the United States and representatives of the United Steelworkers of America, the union representing most of the non-supervisory employees employed in the steel industry.

As the time for negotiating new contracts between the union and the steel companies drew near the deadline date of June 30, 1959, it became evident to representatives of both labor and management that no agreement for new contracts would be reached. Shortly before the June 30th deadline the parties agreed at the request of President Eisenhower, to extend the old agreements for two weeks. By July 15, there was still no settlement, and a strike by 500,000 steelworkers began immediately.

From July until early November the steelworkers refused to return to their jobs. Although negotiations continued between union and management representatives no settlement of the dispute was reached. The President sought during the 116 day old strike to have the strike settled without recourse to the Labor-Management Relations Act (Taft-Hartley) of 1947. On September 8, President Eisenhower wrote a letter to the United Steelworkers of America and to the steel companies in which he expressed disappointment that so little progress toward settlement of the steel dispute had been made, and he urged the parties to act expeditiously to reach agreement.[1]

As the impact of the strike was felt in an ever-widening sector of the American economy, the President of the United States took the first step under the Labor Management Relations Act of 1947[2] by issuing Executive Order No. 10843 pursuant to section 206 of the Act.[3] He appointed a board of inquiry to inquire into the issues involved in the dispute and to make a written report to him. In the Executive Order, the President expressed the opinion that the strike, if permitted to continue would imperil the national health and safety. In his statement explaining his issuance of the Executive Order, the President pointed to the "shutting off" of practically all new supplies of steel, the unemployment of hundreds of thousands of employees in steel and related industries, and the imminent threat to the economic health of the nation if production was not quickly resumed.

The Board of Inquiry submitted its written report to the President on October 19,[4] setting forth a summary of the negotiations up to October 19 and the issues in dispute between the parties.[5] The Board concluded that "we see no prospects for an early cessation of the strike. The Board cannot point to any single issue of any consequence whatsoever upon which the parties are in agreement."[6]

Upon receiving the report, the President directed the Attorney General to petition any district court having jurisdiction over the parties to enjoin the continuance of the strike and to order such other relief as might be necessary or appropriate.

On October 20, 1959, the Attorney General filed a petition in the United States District Court for the Western District of Pennsylvania, seeking an injunction against the union and the steel companies pursuant to section 208 of the Taft-Hartley Act.[7] The Government's petition described the requisite statutory steps which had been taken by the President, and alleged that prolongation of the widespread strike in the steel industry would imperil the health and safety of the country. In summary form the petition stated some of the consequences of the strike on employment, both in the steel industry and many other areas of the economy, on the availability of essential steel products, and on vital national defense projects.[8] The strike had shut down approximately 85 percent of the steel producing capacity of the United States. More than 765,000 persons had been made idle by the strike. If it were allowed to continue, strike-caused unemployment would have reached three million by January 1, 1960.

A considerable amount of evidence was presented concerning the effect of the strike on the national defense program. The District Court found that certain steel products needed in connection with some aspects of the defense program were unavailable because of the steel strike.

Particular stress was put on the impact of the tie-up on the output of missiles, nuclear submarines and advanced types of rocket engines. The Defense Department reported that two plants supplying component's for the polaris missile had been forced to stop production for lack of alloy steel and four others had given notice of the need to do the same within a few days.[9] Moreover, the top priority Project Mercury, an essential part of the nation's space program was being injured. Exported steel products, vital to the support of the nation's overseas bases, for NATO, and similar collective security groups would be cut off; continuance of the strike would impair these programs, thus imperiling the national safety.

On these facts, the District Court made the conclusory finding that the strike imperiled the national health and safety and issued an injunction. The court rejected the union's argument that the statute is unconstitutional because it authorizes the court to issue an injunction which does not enforce a pre-existing legal obligation, but merely creates such an obligation. The court did not pass on the union's further argument that it should, in the exercise of its equitable discretion, refuse to issue an injunction in this case.

The union promptly filed an appeal and moved the District Court for a brief stay to enable the Union to apply to Judge Staley of the Court of Appeals for the Third Circuit for a stay pending appeal.

The Court of Appeals affirmed the judgment of the District Court. Chief Judge Biggs, writing for the majority, analyzed and rejected the union's contention that there was no "case or controversy" before the federal court which it could adjudicate in the sense required by the Constitution. Turning to the critical findings of the District Court dealing with the impact of the steel strike, the majority concluded, after a detailed review of the entire record, that the findings of the lower court were not clearly erroneous. Significantly, the majority noted that:

"We cannot accept the Union's argument in this respect. If our conclusion is correct that there is sufficent evidence in the record of the present or future danger to national health or safety, we conclude that the danger is great enough and calls for a remedy as sweeping as the law will permit. Whether the remedy provided by the Labor-Management Relations Act is sufficient to accomplish a cessation of labor strife is a question not for this court but for Congress. We conclude, therefore, that the court below did not abuse its discretion in granting the relief which the United States prayed for." [10]

The Supreme Court acted with unusual speed. The Court set Tuesday, November 3, 1959 at 11 a.m. as the time for oral argument. All briefs had to be on file by noon, Monday, November 2, 1959. The injunction issued by the U. S. District Court for the Western District of Pennsylvania on October 21, 1959 as modified by the United States Court of Appeals for the Third Circuit on October 22, 1959, was stayed pending the issuance of the judgment of Supreme Court. The petition for *certiorari*, was filed by the union counsel at 1 p.m. The Government's response, asking the court to deny review and thus let the injunction stand, arrived about 4 p.m.

Half an hour later the nine Justices met in conference, the session lasting 40 minutes. Reporters learned of the unscheduled meeting from the ringing of gongs that call the Justices to all formal conferences. Out of the session came an order in the case entitled *United Steel Workers of America*, Petitioner v. *United States, et. al.* [11]

The Supreme Court's opinion was brief. In the *Per Curiam* Opinion, the Court stated its acceptance of, and concurrence in, the findings of the lower Federal Courts which had adjudicated the case:

". . . Petitioner here contests the findings that the continuation of the strike would imperil the national health and safety. The parties dispute the meaning of the statutory term 'national health'; the Government insists that the term comprehends the country's general well-being, its economic health; petitioner urges that simply the physical health of the citizenry is meant. We need not resolve this question, for we think the judgment . . . is amply supported on the ground that the strike imperils the national safety. Here we rely upon the evidence of the strike's effect on specific defense projects; we need not pass on the Government's contention that 'national safety' in this context should be given a broader construction and application.

". . . The statute was designed to provide a public remedy in times of emergency; we cannot construe it to require that the United States either formulate a reorganization of the affected industry to satisfy its defense needs without the complete reopening of closed facilities, or demonstrate in court the unfeasibility of such a reorganization. There is no room in the statute for this requirement which the petitioner seeks to impose on the Government." [12]

The steel strike was finally settled on January 4, 1960, following all-night negotiations between the Vice-President, the Secretary of Labor, representatives of the steel companies and representatives of the steel companies and representatives of the steelworker's union. Vice-President Nixon and Secretary of Labor Mitchell, acting under instructions from President Eisenhower, had been conducting negotiations for several weeks with the parties to the dipute.

While all parties involved were gratified to have this long and costly strike ended, the method of settlement does not confirm the efficacy of the emergency provision of the Taft-Hartley Act. Indeed, it is further confirmation of the fact that the American approach to emergency powers has imposed upon successive executives, not only the incentive, but the absolute need to resort to extra-statutory means for settling emergencies.

CHAPTER XI

CONCLUSIONS

The doctrine of constitutional distatorship is inappropriate for analysis of the problem of democratic response to emergency.

Judicial review of a chief executive's finding that an emergency exists amounts to involvement of Supreme Court Justices in a genre of decision-making which should more properly be performed by the President and Congress, although the 1959 Steel Seizure decision reveals the effective role which the Supreme Court may play in holding the President to the forms of emergency action prescribed by the Congress, if the Congress has so prescribed them.

The recurrent trouble which the nation has confronted in taking timely and effective emergency action at the national level stems from the existence on the statute books of a confusing array of provisions for the declaration of various kinds of emergency, and the excessively precise definition of the techniques which must be employed in coping with the emergency. This invites efforts at evasion of statutory limitations as in the instance of the 1952 steel strike, or requires recurrent special legislation dealing with successive particularized emergencies. Also, in forewarning the private parties in dispute, in the case of a strike, of the precise time-table and program of action to which the executive must adhere, it may lessen their incentive to settle the dispute, for the course of action prescribed by statute may, depending upon the situation, strengthen the bargaining position of one of the disputants.

The recent use of the concurrent resolution in Congress provides a key to the means for equipping the President with the broad discretion he should have to identify conditions warranting emergency action, and to select the appropriate tools to deal with an emergency, while simultaneously keeping him under Congressional surveilance and control.

We propose a generic statute to empower the President to proclaim a national or regional emergency. Under such a proclamation the President may issue rules and regulations which have the force of law. A proclamation of emergency would be placed before the Congress within twenty-four hours of its issuance. If Congress were not in session, it would be called into session within five days from the time of the declaration of emergency. The proclamation of emergency would stand unless revoked by concurrent resolution by both Houses of Congress within five days of Congress' coming into special session.

The rules and regulations issued under the proclamation would be similarly subject to revocation by concurrent resolution and Congress should possess the item veto in this respect; i.e., it may revoke one rule, while permitting others to stand. An emergency proclamation and regulations issued under it, would automatically expire after thirty days, but would be subject to reissuance by the President, provided the Congress concurred. Congress, upon the issuance of an emergency proclamation would establish a scrutiny committee on emergency powers, patterned after the Joint Committee on Atomic Energy. Congress would maintain continuous scrutiny of the administration of powers exercised under the proclamation. The Committee's primary responsibility would be to keep Congress sufficiently advised as to whether powers had been responsibly administered.

There is nothing novel about this proposal. The British have operated under similar statutes in peace and war for fifty years with a record of great success in two respects:

(1) They reacted efficiently to emergencies ranging from a dock strike, and a general strike to two world wars;

(2) Powers during an emergency have been responsibly administered under Parliamentary obervation and control.

Under this plan, the Executive can act, fully cloaked with legitimacy to respond to emergencies ranging from a hydrogen attack to a capital transit strike, and might employ techniques ranging from replacement of state and local administrations which have been destroyed by hydrogen bombings, to compelling motor-car men to return to work.

Such a statute exemplifies our commitment to democratic government and democratic theory in a number of ways. It provides legislative sanction for executive action and precludes the coming into being of a situation which in the words of Locke, "the executive has to act in the absence of law," and it gives the President sufficiently broad and generic power. As contrasted with the unrealistically detailed and restrictive emergency provisions of existing statues, the President is empowered to deal with an emergency without the need to resort to the use of Locke's prerogative: to act under the law, in the absence of the law, or even contrary to the law. In effect it renders unnecessary and unlikely that a future President will define the alternatives which

Lincoln once perceived: to act under the Constitution and lose the Union, or to save the Union by transgressing against the Constitution.

Some persons will fear that a President might take action unnecessarily under such a proclamation of emergency. The answer to this is three-fold: first, it is in the nature of our political system that we must repose a certain amount of faith in the basic integrity and wisdom of the Chief Executive; secondly, the President must operate within carefully prescribed procedural limitations; and third, the President has only today to declare a nation-wide state of martial law in order to equip himself with vast power to take emergency action virtually free from concurring legislative participation.

The vital lesson which emerges from this study is that it is possible to equip government to cope with the crises of Twentieth Century existence without surrendering the two vital principles of constitutionalism that have marked the course of American political development: the maintenance of legal limits to arbitrary power, and political responsibility of the government to the governed.

REFERENCES

CHAPTER I

1. Stanford Research Institute, *Impact of Air Attack in World War II; Selected Data for Civil Defense Planning*, especially Division II, vol. 1, "Economic Effects: —Germany" (Federal Civil Defense Administration, 1953).

2. *Id.*, Division III, vols. 1 and 2, "Social Organization, Behavior, and Morale Under Stress of Bombing," and Irving L. Janis, *Air War and Emotional Stress* (McGraw-Hill, 1951, for the Rand Corporation).

3. Robert Connery, *The Navy and Industrial Mobilization in World War II* (Princeton University Press, 1951) p. 6.

4. Exemplified by Justice Davis's decision for the majority of the Court in *Ex parte Milligan*, 4 Wall. 2, 120-21, 126 (1866):
"The Constitution of the United States is a law for rulers and people, equally in war and in peace, and covers with the shield of its protection all classes of men, at all times, and under all circumstances. No doctrine, involving more pernicious consequences was ever invented by the wit of man than that any of its provisions can be suspended during any of the great exigencies of government. Such a doctrine leads directly to anarchy or despotism; but the theory of necessity on which it is based is false; for the government, within the constitution, has all the powers granted to it, which are necessary to preserve its existence. . . .
". . . It could well be said that a country, preserved at the sacrifice of all the cardinal principles of liberty, is not worth the cost of preservation."

5. Justice Sutherland for the Court in the 1936 case of *United States v. Curtiss-Wright Export Corporation*, 299 U. S. 304, 316-18:
"And since the states severally never possessed international powers, such powers could not have been carved from the mass of state powers but obviously were transmitted to the United States from some other source. . . .
"It results that the investment of the federal government with the powers of external sovereignty did not depend upon the affirmative grants of the Constitution. The powers to declare and wage war, to conclude peace, to make treaties, to maintain diplomatic relations with other sovereignties, if they had never been mentioned in the Constitution, would have been vested in the federal government as necessary concomitants of nationality."

6. Justice Jackson, dissenting in the Japanese relocation case, *Korematsu v. United States*, 323 U. S. 214, 248 (1944) admonished the Court as follows:
"But I would not lead people to rely on this Court for a review that seems to me wholly delusive. The military reasonableness of these orders can only be determined by the military superiors. If the people ever let command of the war power fall in irresponsible hands, the courts wield no power equal to its restraint. The chief restraint upon those who command the physical forces of the country in the future, as in the past, must be their responsibilities to the political judgments of their contemporaries and to the moral judgments of history."

7. The words are, of course, those of John Locke, *Of Civil Government*, Bk. II, Ch. XIV.

The studies referred to include: Edward S. Corwin, *The President: Office and Powers* (New York: New York University Press, 3rd ed., 1948); and *Total War and the Constitution* (New York: Knopf, 1947); Clarence Berdahl, *War Powers of the Executive in the United States,* (Urbana: University of Illinois Press, 1921); Clinton L. Rossiter, *Constitutional Dictatorship* (Princeton: Princeton University Press, 1948) and *The Supreme Court and the Commander in Chief* (Ithaca: Cornell University Press, 1951);Wilfred E. Binkley, *President and Congress* (New York: Knopf, 1947); Bennett M. Rich, *The President and Civil Disorder* (Washington, D. C.: Brookings, 1941); Louis W. Koenig, *The Presidency and the Crisis* (New York: King's Crown Press, 1944); John W. Burgess, Ch. XXVIII, vol. 2, *The Civil War and the Constitution* (New York: Scribners, 1901); James Hart, *The Ordinance Making Powers of the President of the United States* (Baltimore: Johns Hopkins Press, 1925); James G. Randall, *Constitutional Problems Under Lincoln*, rev. ed. (Urbana: University of Illinois Press, 1951); and a recent article by Albert L. Sturm, "Emergencies and the President," 11 *Journal of Politics,* 121, 1949, in which he says, "Lincoln's precedents have afforded warrant for his aggressive successors to meet extraordinary needs with extraordinary remedies, despite their doubtful constitutionality."   Perhaps as broad a claim to an executive prerogative as has been made in the United States is that which Lucius Wilmerding, Jr., bases upon his study of *The Spending Power* (New Haven: Yale University Press, 1943): "There are certain circumstances which constitute a law of necessity and self-preservation and which render the *salus populi* supreme over the written law.   The officer who is called to act upon this superior ground does indeed risk himself on the justice of the controlling powers of the Constitution, but his station makes it his duty to incur that risk." p. 12.

8. Edward S. Corwin strongly emphasizes that incident in his *The President: Office and Powers* (New York: New York University Press, 3rd ed., 1948), pp. 303-6.

9. This is the doctrine which would seem to emerge from *Youngstown Sheet and Tube Co. v. Sawyer,* 343 U. S. 579 (1952), in which the Court rejected contentions on behalf of President Truman that he enjoyed an "inherent" emergency power to seize private industry in time of emergency occasioned by work stoppages.

10. This study should not be interpreted as an effort to catalog exhaustively *existing* delegations of emergency powers to the President.   Statutes of the era 1933 to 1955 are analyzed without regard to their present status as expired or in force.

CHAPTER II

1. Suspension of the writ, and declaration of martial law were, of course, as simulated in the raid itself.   The story of the exercise may be traced in the *New York Times,* June 16, 1955, pp. 1, 16; June 17, 1955, pp. 1, 10, 11.   The full text of the proclamation is available in Senate Committee on Armed Forces, Subcommittee on Civil Defense, *Hearings on the Civil Defense Program,* Part II, p. 746 (1955).   Cf. Professor Charles Fairman's remarks in "Government under Law in Time of Crisis," a paper presented at the Marshall Bicentennial Con-

ference, Harvard Law School, September 1955: "Indeed it is rather a matter for shame that we take so little thought for the morrow. More than mere individual self-preservation is at stake. If we believe that the Western Civilization we know is worth maintaining, if we are devoted to the conceptions of law and justice as they have been defined in the course of our history, then surely we should be moved to make them secure."

2. *Id.* It is this idea that emergency may require executive action contrary to the law, *i.e.*, a suspension of law which is most dangerous to constitutional morality. It presents the executive with false alternatives: "Was it possible to lose the nation and yet preserve the Constitution? . . . I felt that measures otherwise unconstitutional might become lawful by becoming indispensable to the preservation of the nation." Abraham Lincoln, letter to A. C. Hodges, April 4, 1864, Henry J. Raymond, *The Life and Public Service of Abraham Lincoln* (New York: Derby & Miller, 1865), p. 767.

DEMOCRATIC POLITICAL THEORISTS

1. Bk. II, Ch. XIV.   2. *Id.*   3. Locke, *op. cit.*, Bk. II, Ch. XIV.
4. *Id.*   5. *The Social Contract* (New York: Dutton, 1950), pp. 123-24.
6. *Id.*, at 125. Cf. Frederick M. Watkins' findings regarding the use of Article 48 of the Weimar Constitution. *The Failure of Constitutional Emergency Powers Under the German Republic.* (Cambridge: Harvard University Press, 1939.)
7. *Id.*, at 124-125.
8. *Representative Government* (New York: Dutton, 1950), pp. 274, 277-78.
9. Edmund Silberner, *The Problem of War in the Nineteenth Century Economic Thought* (Princeton: Princeton University Press, 1946), p. 66ff.
10. *Id.*, at 46.   11. *Id.*, at 62.

MACHIAVELLI

1. *The Discourses*, Bk. 1, Ch. XXXIV.
2. In contrast to Mill, Machiavelli's use of the term "dictator" is loose and misleading. The so-called dictator was really a temporary emergency executive who by no means enjoyed absolute power.
3. *The Discourses*, Bk. 1, Ch. XXXIV.   4. *Id.*, at Ch. XXXV.

CONTEMPORARY THEORISTS

1. *The Failure of Constitutional Emergency Powers Under the German Republic, op. cit.*, p. 148.
2. See his "The Problem of Constitutional Dictatorship," p. 324ff. in Carl J. Friedrich and Edward S. Mason (editors) *Public Policy* (Cambridge: Harvard University Press, 1940).
3. *Id.*, at p. 328.   4. *Id.*, at 353.   5. *Id.*, at 351.   6. *Id.*, at 356-58.
7. *Id.*, at 338-41.   8. *Id.*, at 338.
9. *Constitutional Government and Democracy*, Ch. XXVI, rev. ed. (Boston: Ginn & Co., 1949).
10. *Id.*, at 573.   11. *Id.*, at 580.   12. *Id.*, 574-584.   13. *Id.*, at 584.
14. Clinton L. Rossiter, *Constitutional Dictatorship* (Princeton: Princeton University Press, 1948), p. 288ff.
15. Here, citing Friedrich, he observes "there might well have been no crisis

in 1933 if President Roosevelt had been required to appoint another to wield the abnormal display of power which he seemed to find so necessary at the moment." *Id.*, at 303. But since he later specifically advocates retention of what he describes as "the inherent emergency power of the President" (p. 308), why hobble it by discouraging a presidential finding of the existence of an emergency? Cf. Grier, J., in *Prize Cases,* 2 Black 635, 669-71 (1862), holding that war (emergency) may commence when the Chief Executive takes up a proferred challenge.

16. Rossiter, *op. cit.*, pp. 298-306.   17. *Id.*, at 310-11.   18. *Id.*, at 309.

19. *The Supreme Court and the Commander in Chief* (Ithaca: Cornell University Press, 1951), p. 1, see p. 19 *infra.*

CONTEMPORARY THEORIES IN THE LIGHT OF RECENT EXPERIENCE.

1. *Op. cit.*, p. 573.

2. *Constitutionalism Ancient and Modern* (Ithaca: Cornell University Press, 1940), p. 180.

3. *Id.*, at 246.   4. *Id.*, at 1.   5. *Id.*, at 146.

6. Justice Jackson's concurring opinion in *Youngstown Sheet & Tube Co.* v. *Sawyer,* 343 U. S. 579 at 634-55 (1952), in which he discusses the relative power of the President acting under his executive powers alone, and acting under a marriage of executive and congressional powers, is opposite here.

7. Note William Y. Elliott's theory of the co-organic society, in *The Pragmatic Revolt in Politics,* (New York: Macmillan, 1928), pp. 355-77.

8. See Cecil T. Carr, *Delegated Legislation* (Cambridge: University Press, 1921) p. 72, and *Concerning English Administrative Law* (New York: Columbia University Press, 1941), p. 189; Lord Hewart of Bury, *The New Despotism* (New York: Cosmopolitan Book Corporation, 1929), p. 308; W. A. Robson, *Justice and Administrative Law* (London: Stevens, 1945), p. 385, and Marguerite A. Sieghart, *Government by Decree* (London: Stevens, 1950), p. 343.

CHAPTER III

1. The Emergency Powers (Defense) Act, 1939, 2 & 3 Geo. 6, Ch. 62, Sec. 1.

2. 61 Stat. 136, June 23, 1947, Sec. 206, 29 U.S.C. 176.

EMERGENCIES VARY IN INTENSITY

1. Proclamation No. 2076, 48 Stat. 1734, February 16, 1934.

2. 63 Stat. 208, June 20, 1949, Sec. 10(b).

3. Proclamation No. 2352, 54 Stat. 2643, September 8, 1939.

4. 48 Stat. 354, February 23, 1934, Sec. 2(b).

5. Bank Conservation Act, 48 Stat. 1, March 9, 1933, Preamble.

6. Proclamation No. 2153, 49 Stat. 3489, January 10, 1936.

7. Veterans' Emergency Housing Act, 60 Stat. 207, May 22, 1946, Sec. 1(a).

8. Agricultural Adjustment Act, 48 Stat. 31, May 12, 1933, Sec. 1.

9. Proclamation No. 2487, 55 Stat. 1647, May 27, 1941.

VARIETIES OF EMERGENCY

Economic Emergencies

1. Proclamation No. 2039, 48 Stat. 1689, March 6, 1933.
2. 48 Stat. 1, March 9, 1933. This was the first act of the new Congress, Public Law No. 1.
3. 48 Stat. 20, March 24, 1933.
4. 48 Stat. 55, May 12, 1933, Sec. 1.
5. 48 Stat. 798, May 24, 1934, Sec. 78.
6. 48 Stat. 31, May 12, 1933, Sec. 1, the first Agricultural Adjustment Act.
7. 48 Stat. 337, January 30, 1934, Sec. 10, (c).
8. Proclamation No. 2153, 49 Stat. 3489, January 10, 1936.
9. 55 Stat. 395, June 30, 1941, Sec. 1.
10. 67 Stat. 149, July 14, 1953, Sec. 1A.
11. 48 Stat. 195, June 16, 1933, Sec. 1.
12. 48 Stat. 881, June 6, 1934, Sec. 2 (4).
13. 48 Stat. 943, June 12, 1934, Sec. 1.
14. 56 Stat. 23, January 30, 1942, Sec. 1 (a).
15. Proclamation No. 2487, 55 Stat. 2643, May 27, 1941.
16. 60 Stat. 664, July 25, 1946, Sec. 1A (a).
17. 56 Stat. 226, April 28, 1942, Sec. 403.
18. 48 Stat. 211, June 16, 1933, Sec. 2.
19. 48 Stat. 1185, June 21, 1934, Secs. 3-5.
20. 57 Stat. 163, June 25, 1943, Sec. 3, 5-8.
21. 61 Stat. 136, June 23, 1947, Sec. 206.
22. 60 Stat. 207, 1946, Sec. 1(a).
23. Proclamation No. 2708, 61 Stat. 1944, October 25, 1946; terminated by Proclamation No. 2735, 61 Stat. 1073, June 28, 1947.
24. 63 Stat. 18, March 30, 1949.
25. 48 Stat. 1478, June 16, 1934.
26. 48 Stat. 1275, June 28, 1934, Sec. 2.
27. 50 Stat. 903, September 1, 1937, Sec. 509.
28. Proclamation No. 2361, 54 Stat. 2654, September 11, 1939; Proclamation No. 2551, 56 Stat. 1952, April 13, 1942; Proclamation No. 2757, 61 Stat. 1098, November 28, 1947.
29. Proclamation No. 2545, 56 Stat. 1945, April 1, 1942.
30. 46 Stat. 590, June 17, 1930, Sec. 318.
31. Proclamation No. 2553, 56 Stat. 1954, April 27, 1942.

Emergencies Occasioned by Natural Catastrophies

1. 48 Stat. 354, February 23, 1934, Sec. 1.
2. 48 Stat. 1021, 1056, June 19, 1934.
3. Proclamation No. 2092, 49 Stat. 3404, August 10, 1934.   4. Id.
5. 48 Stat. 1064, June 19, 1934, Sec. 606 (c).
6. 65 Stat. 611, October 24, 1951.
7. 48 Stat. 20, March 23, 1933, earthquake; 48 Stat. 993, June 18, 1934, Sec. 3, floods, hurricanes, earthquakes, landslides; Disaster Loan Corporation Act, 50 Stat. 19, February 11, 1937, "floods or other catastrophes in the year 1937"; amendment to National Housing Act, 50 Stat. 70, April 22, 1937, "earth-

quake, conflagration, tornado, cyclone, hurricane, flood, or other catastrophe";
Emergency Flood Control Act, 59 Stat. 231, June 5, 1945, "floods, or windstorms, or fire caused by lightning"; 61 Stat. 163, June 23, 1947, floods; Interior Department Appropriation Act, 1948, 61 Stat. 460, July 25, 1947, Sec. 3,
"emergency caused by fire, flood, storm, act of God, or sabotage"; Flood Rehabilitation Act, 1952, 65 Stat. 615, October 24, 1951, "excessive rains, runoff,
and flood-waters"; Reconstruction Finance Corporation Liquidation Act, 67 Stat.
230, July 30, 1953, Sec. 202, "floods and other catastrophes"; Presidential Proclamations No. 2222, and 2223, January 23, and February 1, 1937, 50 Stat. 1810,
1811, January 23, 1937 and February 1, 1937, "disastrous floods", "flood conditions."

8. 50 Stat. 57, April 6, 1937.　　　9. 50 Stat. 120, April 27, 1937.
10. 65 Stat. 69, June 15, 1951.
11. Famine Relief Act, 67 Stat. 476, August 7, 1953, Sec. 1.

National Security Emergencies

1. Proclamation No. 2352, September 8, 1959, 54 Stat. 2643.
2. Proclamation No. 2487, 55 Stat. 1647, May 27, 1941.　　　3. *Id.*
4. 54 Stat. 885, September 16, 1940, Sec. 3 (a).
5. 65 Stat. 75, June 19, 1951, Sec. 3.
6. 61 Stat. 460, 491-492, July 25, 1947, Sec. 5.
7. 54 Stat. 1220, November 30, 1940.
8. 64 Stat. 1257, January 12, 1951, Sec. 1.
9. Proclamation No. 2519, 55 Stat. 1693, October 22, 1941.
10. 64 Stat. 1245, January 12, 1951, Sec. 3 (a).　　　11. *Id.*, Sec. 301.
12. 66 Stat. 315, July 1, 1952, Sec. 2 (a).　Section 201 (g) of the Civil Defense
Act, *op. cit.*, had encouraged such compacts and provided for their automatic
approval in the absence of exercise of the congressional veto.　Here, however,
Congress resorted to the traditional machinery, enacting a statute granting its consent.
13. 46 Stat. 696, June 17, 1930, Sec. 318.
14. 48 Stat. 1064, June 19, 1934, Sec. 606 (c); 65 Stat. 611, October 24, 1951,
Sec. 1.
15. 54 Stat. 213, May 14, 1940.　　　16. 59 Stat. 166, May 9, 1945.
17. Proclamation No. 2561, 56 Stat. 1964, July 2, 1942; not dissimilar to the
December 8, 1941 Proclamations No. 2526 and 2527 declaring the existence of a
threatened "invasion or predatory incursion . . . by Germany" and by Italy.　55
Stat. 1705, 1707.
18. Title II of the Internal Security Act of 1950, 64 Stat. 987, 1021, September
22, 1950, Sec. 102.

PERCEIVING THE EXISTENCE OF AN EMERGENCY

1. 61 Stat. 34, March 31, 1947, Sec. 2.

CHAPTER IV

1. Roy Macridis, *The Study of Comparative Government* (New York: Doubleday and Co., 1955), p. 24.

POSITIVE INTEGRATION

1. 53 Stat. 855, June 27, 1939, Sec. 2.
2. 54 Stat. 265, 297, June 11, 1940.
3. 54 Stat. 712, July 2, 1940, Sec. 4.
4. 54 Stat. 1092, October 10, 1940, Sec. 1.
5. 56 Stat. 176, March 27, 1942, Sec. 801.
6. 60 Stat. 31, February 1946.
7. 62 Stat. 604, June 24, 1948, Sec. 6 (h).
8. 64 Stat. 798, September 8, 1950, Title V, Sec. 501-3.
9. *Id.*, Sec. 503.   10. *Id.*, Sec. 503.
11. 64 Stat. 149, May 10, 1950, Sec. 3 (a) (8).
12. *Id.*, Sec. 37.   13. 49 Stat. 391, June 19, 1955, Sec. 1.
14. 49 Stat. 1028, August 30, 1935.
15. 52 Stat. 220, April 22, 1938.
16. 52 Stat. 221, April 25, 1938.   17. *Id.*
18. 52 Stat. 641, June 11, 1938.
19. 52 Stat. 1175, June 25, 1938, Sec. 1.   20. *Id.*, Sec. 2.
21. *Id.*, Sec. 4.   22. 54 Stat. 213, amending the 1916 National Defense
Act, May 15, 1940.
23. 55 Stat. 799, December 13, 1941, Sec. 1.   24. *Id.*, Sec. 1.
25. *Id.*, Sec. 1.   26. 54 Stat. 858, August 27, 1940, Sec. 1.
27. 54 Stat. 1206, October 21, 1940.
28. 64 Stat. 318, June 30, 1950, Sec. 2.
29. 64 Stat. 1072, September 27, 1950.
30. 54 Stat. 885, September 16, 1940.   31. *Id.*, Sec. 2.
32. *Id.*, Sec. 3 (a).   33. *Id.*, Sec. 2 (a), (b).
34. 54 Stat. 2739, 2745, 2747, 2760.
35. 55 Stat. 1644, 56 Stat. 1929, January 5, 1942.
36. 62 Stat. 604, June 1948, The Selective Service Act of 1948.
37. *Id.*, Sec. 3, 4.   38. *Id.*, Sec. 2, 4.
39. 64 Stat. 826, September 9, 1950.
40. 64 Stat. 254, June 23, 1950.   41. 64 Stat. 318, July 9, 1951.
42. 65 Stat. 75, June 19, 1951.
43. 67 Stat. 86, June 29, 1953, all secs.
44. 67 Stat. 174, July 16, 1953.   45. 53 Stat. 854, June 23, 1939, all secs.
46. 55 Stat. 43, March 17, 1941.
47. 56 Stat. 314, June 5, 1942, Sec. 2.
48. 60 Stat. 92, April 18, 1946, Sec. 2.
49. 62 Stat. 274, May 5, 1948.
50. 67 Stat. 178, July 17, 1953, Sec. 1.
51. 62 Stat. 193, June 25, 1948.   52. 66 Stat. 155, June 24, 1952.
53. 64 Stat. 316, June 30, 1950, Sec. 1.

NEGATIVE INTEGRATION

1. Proclamation No. 2525, 55 Stat. 1700, December 7, 1941; the statutes are
found at 1 Stat. 577, 40 Stat. 531, 50 U.S.C. 21, 22, 23, 24 (1951).

2. 66 Stat. 26, March 20, 1952.   3. 66 Stat. 138, June 18, 1952.

4. Executive Order 9066, February 19, 1942.

5. 64 Stat. 987, 1021, September 23, 1950, Sec. 103.

6. 55 Stat. 252, 967, June 20, 1941.   7. 56 Stat. 173, March 21, 1942.

8. Proclamation No. 2655, 2662, 2685, 59 Stat.

9. Title II of the Internal Security Act of 1950, 64 Stat. 987, 1006, September 23, 1950, Sec. 22.

10. 54 Stat. 1137, 1150, October 14, 1940, Sec. 326.

11. Any person who "within three months from the date upon which such organization was so registered or so required to be registered, renounces, withdraws from, and utterly abandons such membership or affiliation, and who thereafter ceases entirely to be affiliated with such organization, is exempted from this provision." (Sec. 25).

12. 58 Stat. 677, July 1, 1944.   13. 58 Stat. 746, September 27, 1944.

14. Proclamation No. 2497, 55 Stat. 1657, July 17, 1941, Sec. 1 (a), (b), issued under authority of Sec. 5 (b) of the Act of October 6, 1917, 40 Stat. 415.

15. Id.   16. 64 Stat. 987, 1013, September 23, 1950, Sec. 25.

17. 68 Stat. 1146, September 3, 1954.

18. 52 Stat. 3, January 12, 1938, all secs.   19. 64 Stat. 825, September 9, 1950

20. 55 Stat. 1700, December 7, 1941.

21. 49 Stat. 1081, May 27, 1935, Sec. 6.   22. 50 Stat. 121, May 1, 1937.

23. 54 Stat. 4, November 4, 1939   24. Id., Sec. 2 (a).

25. Proclamation No. 2348, 54 Stat. 2629, September 5, 1939.

26. 54 Stat. 80, March 28, 1940.   27. 35 Stat. 1097, March 4, 1909.

28. Proclamation No. 2532, 55 Stat. 1713, December 27, 1941.

29. Proclamation No. 2536, 56 Stat. 1932, January 13, 1942.

30. Proclamation No. 2540, 56 Stat. 1936, February 10, 1942.

31. Proclamation No. 2543, 56 Stat. 1941, March 25, 1942; No. 2569, 56 Stat. 1978, October 21, 1942; No. 2573, 56 Stat. 1985, November 17, 1942.

32. 56 Stat. 173, May 21, 1942.

33. Proclamation No. 2348, 54 Stat. 2629, September 5, 1939.

34. Proclamation No. 2523, 55 Stat. 1696, November 14, 1941.

35. 66 Stat. 163, June 27, 1952.

36. 49 Stat. 1081, May 27, 1935.

37. Id., Sec. 2.   In return for the $500 fee one received a registration certificate valid for five years and renewable.   Exports and imports were subject to licensing by the Board.

38. 50 Stat. 121, May 1937.   Registration fees reduced to $100 for those whose annual sales were less than $50,000. Sec. 5 (c).

39. 52 Stat. 631, June 1938.   40. Id., Sec. 2.

41. Id., Secs. 3, 5.   42. Id.   43. 54 Stat. 670, June 28, 1940.

44. Id., Sec. 35.   45. 56 Stat. 1933, January 14, 1942.

46. 56 Stat. 248, April 29, 1942, Sec. 1.   47. Id., Sec. 3.

48. 54 Stat. 1201, October 17, 1940.   49. Id., Sec. 2.

50. Id., Sec. 1 (c).   51. Id., Sec. 1 (d).

52. 64 Stat. 987, September 23, 1950, Sec. 3.   53. Id., Sec. 7.

54. P. L. 557, 68 Stat. 586, July 29, 1954.   55. Id., Secs. 13, 14.

56. P. L. 637, 68 Stat. 586, August 24, 1954, Sec. 3.   57. *Id.*, Sec. 7.
58. *Id.*, Sec. 10.   59. *Id.*   60. *Id.*, Sec. 6.
61. 50 Stat. 211, May 28, 1937.   62. 54 Stat. 676, June 21, 1940, Sec. 11.
63. 54 Stat. 885, September 16, 1940, Sec. 8 (i). Contrast the relatively simple and clear-cut reference to the two groups with the variety of "Communist organizations" defined in the Internal Security and Communist Control Acts mentioned above.
64. 55 Stat. 808, December 17, 1941, Secs. 1, 3.
65. *Id.*   66. 67 Stat. 408, August 7, 1953, Sec. 7 (a).
67. 57 Stat. 163, June 25, 1943, Sec. 8.
68. *Id.*, Sec. 3, 5. President Roosevelt, in the absence of enabling legislation, had previously resorted to plant seizure in such cases.
69. *Id.*, Sec. 4.   70. *Id.*, Sec. 206.   71. *Id.*
72. *Id.*, Sec. 208.   73. *Id.*, Sec. 8 (d).
74. 54 Stat. 712, July 2, 1940, Sec. 4.   75. *Id.*
76. 55 Stat. 606, July 29, 1941, Sec. 2.   77. *Id.*
78. 61 Stat. 551, July 30, 1947, Sec. 1.
79. See 64 Stat. 595, September 6, 1950, Sec. 1209.
80. 64 Stat. 798, September 8, 1950, Sec. 715.   81. *Id.*
82. 64 Stat. 476, August 26, 1950.   83. P. L. 600, 68 Stat. 745, August 20, 1954
84. 335 U.S. 1, 1948.

CHAPTER V

STOCKPILING

1. 53 Stat. 811, June 7, 1939, Sec. 2-3, 7.
2. 53 Stat. 1407, August 11, 1939.
3. 54 Stat. 265, 297, June 11, 1940.
4. *Id.*, and 54 Stat. 712, July 2, 1940, Sec. 5.
5. 64 Stat. 798, September 8, 1950, Sec. 303.
6. 66 Stat. 141, June 20, 1952, Sec. 514.
7. 65 Stat. 131, July 31, 1951, Title I, Sec. 102.
8. 67 Stat. 417, August 7, 1953, Sec. 2.   9. *Id.*
10. *Id.*, Sec. 3.

MILITARY SITES AND PRODUCTIVE FACILITIES

1. 53 Stat. 1123, July 26, 1939.
2. 63 Stat. 66, May 11, 1949, Secs. 1-2.
3. 65 Stat. 404, October 11, 1951, Secs. 1, 3 (5).
4. 56 Stat. 176, March 27, 1942, Title II, Sec. 201.
5. *Id.*
6. 64 Stat. 1245, January 12, 1951, Title II, Sec. 201.
7. 48 Stat. 58, May 18, 1933.
8. *Id.*, Sec. 3 (h).
9. *Id.*, Sec. 5.
10. *Id.*, Sec. 5 (1).
11. *Id.*, Sec. 20.
12. 56 Stat. 126, March 5, 1942.

13. 61 Stat. 24, March 29, 1947, Sec. 2.

14. 62 Stat. 101, March 31, 1948, Secs. 2-3.

15. 58 Stat. 190, April 5, 1944, Sec. 1.

16. *Id.*, Sec. 1.

17. 64 Stat. 435, August 10, 1950, Sec. 2.

18. *Id.*, Sec. 3.

19. 54 Stat. 396, June 15, 1940.

20. 55 Stat. 31, March 11, 1941, Sec. 3 (a).

21. 54 Stat. 1090, October 10, 1940, Sec. 1.

22. 56 Stat. 467, July 2, 1942, Sec. 2.

23. 54 Stat. 676, June 28, 1940, Sec. 8 (a).

24. 55 Stat. 742, October 16, 1941, Sec. 1.

25. 49 Stat. 1985, June 29, 1936, Sec. 902 (a).

26. 55 Stat. 40, July 30, 1941, Secs. 3-4 (a).   See also 53 Stat. 1254, August 7, 1939, Sec. 3.

27. 55 Stat. 745, October 24, 1941, Sec. (b).

28. 64 Stat. 798, September 8, 1950, Title II, Sec. 201 (a).

29. 67 Stat. 177, July 17, 1953, Sec. 1.

FACILITATING ACQUISITION BY PRIVATE ENTERPRISES

1. 55 Stat. 610, July 30, 1941, Sec. 3.

2. *Id.*, Secs. 2-3.

3. Plantation Pipe Line System (Proclamation No. 2505, 55 Stat. 1670, August 23, 1941); Southeastern Pipe Line System (Proclamation No. 2508, 55 Stat. 1672, September 3, 1941); Portland Pipe Line (Proclamation No. 2517, 55 Stat. 1691, October 1, 1941); Project Five Pipe Line (El Dorado to Helena, Arkansas, Proclamation No. 2567, 56 Stat. 1975, August 28, 1942); Pipe Line from Cushing, Oklahoma to Heyworth, Illinois (Proclamation No. 2657, 59 Stat. 872, July 20, 1945.

4. 56 Stat. 176, March 27, 1942, Title II, Sec. 201.

5. 56 Stat. 351, June 11, 1942, Sec. 4 (a).

6. *Id.*, Sec. 4 (f).

AVAILABILITY OF FEDERALLY OWNED PROPERTY TO PRIVATE ENTERPRISE

1. 52 Stat. 707, June 16, 1938, Sec. 2.

2. 54 Stat. 265, 295, 297, June 11, 1940.

3. 54 Stat. 712, July 2, 1940, Sec. 5 (2).

4. 64 Stat. 798, September 8, 1950.

ACQUISITIONS INCIDENTAL TO ENFORCEMENT OF A CONTROL PROGRAM.

1. 54 Stat. 676, June 28, 1940, Sec. 8 (b).

2. 54 Stat. 885, September 16, 1940, Sec. 9.

3. 57 Stat. 163, June 25, 1943, Sec. 3. This provision took the form of an amendment to Sec. 9 of the Selective Training and Service Act of 1940, above.

4. 56 Stat. 23, January 30, 1942, Sec. 2 (b).

CHAPTER VI

CONTROL OF GOODS AND MATERIALS.

1. 48 Stat. 58, May 18, 1933, Sec. 5 (1).
2. 48 Stat. 811, May 28, 1934.
3. Proclamation No. 2087, 48 Stat. 1744, May 28, 1934.
4. 49 Stat. 1081, August 31, 1935.
5. Id.   6. Id.
7. 50 Stat. 3, January 8, 1937, Sec. 1.
8. 50 Stat. 121, May 1, 1937, Sec. 1.
9. Proclamation No. 2236, 50 Stat. 1831, May 1, 1937.
10. Proclamation No. 2635. Subsequently, on November 4, the President signed a revision of the Neutrality Act, in which emphasis was shifted from export control to control of American shipping as the device for maintaining neutrality. The shipping control provisions are discussed later in this chapter.
11. 54 Stat. 4, November 4, 1939, Sec. 2 (c).
12. Proclamations No. 2376, 54 Stat. 2673, November 4, 1939; 2394, 54 Stat. 2693, April 10, 1940; 2474, 55 Stat. 1628, April 10, 1941.
13. Proclamation No. 2348, 54 Stat. 2629, September 5, 1939.
14. Proclamation No. 2413, 54 Stat. 2712, July 2, 1940, delegating to an Administrator of Export Control his statutory power to prohibit unlicensed export from the United States of basic materials and products. The list included aluminum, antimony, asbestos, chromium, cotton linters, flax, graphite, hides, industrial diamonds, manganese, magnesium, manila fiber, mercury, mica, molybdenum, optical glass, platinum group metals, quartz crystals, quinine, rubber, silk, tin, tolnol, tungsten, vanadium and wool, in addition to specified chemicals, products, and machine tools.

Proclamation No. 2417, 54 Stat. 2726, July 26, 1940, added petroleum products, tetraethyl lead, and iron and steel scrap to the foregoing.

Proclamations No. 2423, 54 Stat. 2737, September 12, 1940; 2453, 55 Stat. 1607, January 10, 1941; 2428, 54 Stat. 2743, September 30, 1940; 2449, 54 Stat. 2768, December 10, 1940; 2451, 54 Stat. 2770, December 20, 1940; 2456, 55 Stat. 1610, February 4, 1941; 2460, 55 Stat. 1614, February 25, 1941; 2461, 55 Stat. 1615, February 25, 1941; 2463, 55 Stat. 1617, March 4, 1941; 2464, 55 Stat. 1618, March 4, 1941; 2465, 55 Stat. 1619, March 4, 1941; 2468, 55 Stat. 1622, March 27, 1941; 2475, 55 Stat. 1629, April 14, 1941; 2476, 55 Stat. 1630, April 4, 1941; 2482, 55 Stat. 1639, May 10, 1941; 2497, 55 Stat. 1657, July 17, 1941, considerably extended the list of materials and products which might not be exported without license.

All of the foregoing Proclamations were issued under the Act to expedite the strengthening of the national defense of the United States.
15. Id.
16. 56 Stat. 463, June 30, 1942, Sec. 6 (a).
17. Id., Sec. 6 (b).
18. 63 Stat.   19. Id., Sec. 2.
20. 65 Stat. 692, October 30, 1951.
21. 55 Stat. 810, December 17, 1941.

22. 63 Stat. 7, 1949, Sec. 3 (a).
23. *Id.*, Sec. 2 (a).
24. 49 Stat. 30, February 22, 1935, Sec. 1, 3.
25. 56 Stat. 176, March 27, 1942.
26. *Id.*   27. 55 Stat. 236, May 31, 1941.
28. 56 Stat. 176, March 27, 1942.
29. 61 Stat. 24, March 29, 1947.
30. 62 Stat. 101, March 31, 1948.
31. 61 Stat. 34, March 31, 1947, Sec. 1501.
32. 64 Stat. 798, September 8, 1950, Sec. 101.
33. *Id.*, Sec. 102.
34. 65 Stat. 692, October 30, 1951, Sec. 1.

CONTROL OF PRODUCTIVE FACILITIES.

2. 55 Stat. 236, May 31, 1941.
3. 55 Stat. 148, May 2, 1941, Sec. 2 (a).
4. 56 Stat. 176, March 27, 1942, Sec. 301.
5. 59 Stat. 231, June 5, 1945, Sec. 3.
6. 64 Stat. 798, September 8, 1950, Sec. 101.
7. 54 Stat. 710, July 1, 1940; 56 Stat. 1013, October 31, 1942; 66 Stat. 3, February 1, 1952.
8. 54 Stat. 885, September 16, 1940, Sec. 9.
9. *Id.*
10. 56 56 Stat. 176, March 27, 1942, Sec. 301, amending Sec. 2 (a) of 54 Stat. 676, June 28, 1940.
11. 64 Stat. 798, September 8, 1950, Sec. 101; 67 Stat. 129, June 30, 1953, Sec. 101.
12. 54 Stat. 1220, November 30, 1940.
13. *Id.*
14. 48 Stat. 195, June 16, 1933.
15. *Id.*, Title II, Sec. 206.
16. 48 Stat. 1183, June 19, 1934.
17. 295 U.S. 495 (1935).
18. 57 Stat. 163, June 25, 1943.
19. *Id.*, Secs. 3, 6.
20. 61 Stat. 136, June 23, 1947, Sec. 206, 208.
21. 48 Stat. 503, March 27, 1934, Sec. 3.
22. 52 Stat. 1252, June 30, 1938, Sec. 1.
23. 54 Stat. 676, Secs. 2 (a), 9, June 28, 1940.
24. 56 Stat. 176, March 27, 1942, Sec. 301, amending 54 Stat. 676, June 28, 1940.
25. *Id.*, Sec. 301.   26. *Id.*
27. 56 Stat. 226, April 28, 1942, Sec. 401.
28. *Id.*, Sec. 403 (b).
29. 65 Stat. 7, March 23, 1951, Sec. 101.

CONTROL OF CREDIT, EXCHANGE, PRICES.

1. 64 Stat. 798, September 8, 1950, Sec. 2.
2. Executive Order No. 8843, August 9, 1941; Fed. Reg. 6:4035.

3. 64 Stat. 798, September 8, 1950, Sec. 601.
4. *Id.*, Sec. 602.
5. 55 Stat. 610, July 30, 1941, Sec. 6.
6. 55 Stat. 745, October 24, 1941, Sec. (c).
7. 48 Stat. 881, June 6, 1934, Sec. 2.
8. 50 Stat. 121, May 1, 1937, Sec. 3 (c).
9. 55 Stat. 838, December 18, 1941, Sec. 301.
10. 63 Stat. 7, February 26, 1949, Sec. 2.
11. 56 Stat. 23, January 20, 1942, Sec. 2 (a).
12. 56 Stat. 765, October 2, 1942, Sec. 2 (d).
13. *Id.*, Sec. 5 (c).
14. 60 Stat. 664, July 25, 1946, Sec. 3.
15. 61 Stat. 35, March 31, 1947, Sec. 1.
16. 64 Stat. 798, September 8, 1950, Sec. 402 (b).

CONTROL OF COMMON CARRIERS.

1. 48 Stat. 211, June 16, 1933, Secs. 2-3.
2. *Id.*, Secs. 3-6.
3. *Id.*, Sec. 5.   4. *Id.*, Sec. 7 (a) (b).   5. *Id.*, Sec. 7 (c).
6. 44 Stat. 577, May 20, 1926, Sec. 2; 48 Stat. 1185, June 21, 1934, Secs. 2-5.
7. 48 Stat. 933, June 12, 1934, Sec. 20.
8. 52 Stat. 973, June 23, 1938.
9. 64 Stat. 825, September 9, 1950, Sec. 1.
10. 48 Stat. 1064, June 19, 1934, Secs. 1-2.
11. *Id.*, Sec. 606 (b).
12. *Id.*   13. 55 Stat. 610, July 30, 1941, Sec. 8 (a).
14. *Id.*, Sec. 101 (e).
15. 67 Stat. 115, June 30, 1953.
16. 49 Stat. 1081, August 31, 1935, Sec. 3.   17. *Id.*
18. *Id.*, Sec. 4.   19. 50 Stat. 3, January 18, 1937
20. 50 Stat. 121, May 1, 1937, Secs. 2 (a), 6-7.
21. Proclamation No. 2236, 50 Stat. 1831, May 1, 1937.
22. 54 Stat. 4, November 4, 1939, Sec. 2 (c).
23. *Id.*, Sec. 2 (a). Emphasis supplied. Note that the effect was to loosen the earlier prohibition upon export of arms to belligerents while simultaneously it more strictly circumscribed the movements of American vessels.
24. 54 Stat. 866, August 27, 1940.
25. Illegal Exportation of War Materials Act, 67 Stat. 577, August 13, 1953, Sec. 1.
26. 49 Stat. 1985, June 29, 1936, Secs. 210, 902 (a).
27. *Id.*, Sec. 610.   28. *Id.*, Sec. 506.
29. 55 Stat. 59, July 14, 1941, Secs. 1, 34.
30. 55 Stat. 808, December 17, 1941.
31. 57 Stat. 161, June 22, 1943.
32. 50 Stat. 121, June 22, 1943, Sec. 8.
33. 54 Stat. 2668.
34. 54 Stat. 4, November 4, 1939, Sec. 11.
35. Proclamation No. 2375, 54 Stat. 2672, November 4, 1939.

CHAPTER VII

GOVERNMENT AS A SOURCE OF INFORMATION

1. See e.g., the collection of essays edited by Harry Elmer Barnes, *Perpetual War For Perpetual Peace* (Caldwell, Idaho: 1952, Caxton Press). In his brilliant history of American naval operations during the Second World War, Professor Samuel Eliot Morison leaves little doubt that President Roosevelt recognized the eventual need to come to military grips with Nazi aggression: "President Roosevelt, considerably in advance of public opinion, apprehended the threat to American security contained in the seizure of the Atlantic Coast of France, and the strong possibility of a German invasion of Great Britain." Samuel Eliot Morison, *The Battle of the Atlantic,* 1939-1943, (Boston: Little, Brown and Company, 1947) p. 27. Chapter III, " 'Short of War' Policy" dramatically describes the efforts of the Administration during the critical months of June 1940-March 1941 to sustain Great Britain by any means at our disposal that did not involve an outright declaration of war by the Germans. In Professor Morison's estimation, Roosevelt guessed right; Hilter could not afford to bring the United States into the war in 1940 or 1941 despite the trade of destroyers for bases with Britain, Lend-Lease, and American aid to British convoys. *Id.,* p. 36.

2. In this regard a group of distinguished American historians wrote to the *New York Times* as follows:

"On May 7 President Eisenhower issued Executive Order 10816 amending an earlier order regarding the treatment of official documents. This order was generally treated in the press as a liberalization of existing procedures, and we have no doubt that this was the intention of its promulgators.

"However, in our view, the order proceeds in the wrong direction. We fear that its consequence will be not to liberate the historian for the writing of independent history but to entangle him in a series of potentially compromising relations with the subject of his researches — in this case, the Government.

"The new Executive Order lays down three prerequisites before a student is permitted to consult classified defense information in the writing of history.

"First, the head of the agency must rule that access to these records is "clearly consistent with the interests of national defense." Second, the historian himself must be determined to be "trustworthy" — a phrase which could be interpreted as requiring security clearance. Third, his manuscript must be cleared.

"The enforcement of these three prerequisites will plainly make it difficult for the most undaunted of historians to exercise the free and unfettered critical judgment which is the heart of the historical enterprise. And, under prejudiced or incompetent administration, this Executive Order could easily result in the restriction of such official records to those historians prepared to accept and defend official views." (*New York Times,* October 25, 1959.)

3. 48 Stat. 58, May 18, 1933.

4. 64 Stat. 798, September 8, 1950, Sec. 102.

5. 54 Stat. 714, July 2, 1940, Sec. 5 (a).

6. Proclamation No. 2497, 55 Stat. 1657, July 17, 1941.

7. 52 Stat. 631, June 8, 1938, Sec. 4.

8. 61 Stat. 136, June 23, 1947, Sec. 208.

9. *Id.*

10. 62 Stat. 21, February 19, 1948, Sec. 2 (b) (c).

11. 67 Stat. 230, July 30, 1953, Sec. 207 (e).

12. 64 Stat. 1245, January 12, 1951, Sec. 201 (f).

13. 65 Stat. 293, September 1, 1951, Sec. 3 (a).

14. 67 Stat. 417, August 7, 1953, Sec. 4.

15. 48 Stat. 1, March 9, 1933, Sec. 203.

16. The trend is discussed at length in the section on the "Legislative Veto," below.

17. 54 Stat. 670, June 28, 1940, Sec. 20.

18. *Id.*   19. 48 Stat. 943, June 12, 1934, Sec. 4.

20. 56 Stat. 23, January 30, 1942, Sec. 2 (a).

21. 48 Stat. 211, June 16, 1933, Sec. 8.

22. *Id.*   23. *Id.*, Sec. 9.

SUPPRESSION OF INFORMATION BY THE GOVERMENT.

24. 56 Stat. 351, June 11, 1942, Sec. 12. See the similar provision in the R.F.C. Liquidation Act, 67 Stat. 230, July 30, 1953, Sec. 217 (b).

25. 62 Stat. 1231, July 2, 1948, Sec. 3 (c).

26. 67 Stat. 23, April 1953, Sec. 5.

27. 48 Stat. 1064, June 19, 1934, Sec. 4 (f).

28. 55 Stat. 31, March 11, 1941, Sec. 5 (a).

29. 56 Stat. 19, January 26, 1942.

30. 65 Stat. 373, October 10, 1951, Section 518.

31. 58 Stat. 723, July 3, 1944.

32. *Id.*   33. 49 Stat. 1277, May 15, 1936.

34. 53 Stat. 1000, July 13, 1939.

35. *Id.*

36. 54 Stat. 676, June 28, 1940, Sec. 2 (a).

37. 54 Stat. 712, July 2, 1940, Sec. 5.

38. James Phinney Baxter 3rd, *Scientists Against Time* (Boston: Little, Brown and Company, 1946), Ch. I.

39. 55 Stat. 838, December 18, 1941, Sec. 201.

40. 61 Stat. 585, July 30, 1947.

41. *Id.*   42. 63 Stat. 208, June 20, 1949, Sec. 7.

43. Cf. Sec. 19 of the T.V.A. Act, 48 Stat. 58, May 18, 1933, discussed above.

44. 54 Stat. 710, July 1, 1940, Sec. 1.

45. 66 Stat. 3, February 1, 1952.

46. 56 Stat. 23, January 30, 1942, Sec. 202 (h).

47. 63 Stat. 1949, February 26, 1949, Sec. 6.

REGULATION OF PRORPAGANDA ACTIVITIES.

1. 52 Stat. 631, June 8, 1938: quotation from 1942 amendment, 56 Stat. 248, April 29, 1942.

2. *Id.*, Sec. 3.   3. *Id.*, Sec. 4 (a).

4. *Id.*, Sec. 4 (b).   5. Sec. 10, September 22, 1950.

CENSORSHIP AND OTHER RESTRICTIONS.

1. 52 Stat. 3, January 12, 1938, Sec. 1.
2. *Id.*, Sec. 3.
3. 54 Stat. 670, June 28, 1940, Sec. 1. (a).
4. *Id.*, Sec. 2 (a), 18 U.S.C. 2385.
5. *Id.*, Sec. 3.   6. 63 Stat. 7, February 26, 1949, Sec. 3 (a).
7. 67 Stat. 363, August 5, 1953, Sec. 4 (b).
8. 65 Stat. 710, 719 ff, October 31, 1951, Sec. 24; 18 U.S.C. 798.   9. *Id.*
10. Public Law 557, 83d Congress, 2d Session, July 29, 1954; amending section 7 (d) of the Internal Security Act of 1950.
11. *Id.*, the list to include, but not limited to rotary presses, flatbed cylinder presses, platen presses, lithographs, offsets, photo-offsets, mimeograph machines, multigraph machines, multilith machines, type machines, monotype machines, and all other types of printing presses, typesetting machines or any mechanical devices used or intended to be used, or capable of being used to produce or publish printed matter or material, which are in the possession, custody, ownership, or control of the organization or its officers, members, affiliates, associates, group, or groups in which the organization, its officers or members have an interest.
12. 55 Stat. 838, December 18, 1941, Sec. 303.
13. 56 Stat. 18, January 26, 1942, Sec. 1.
14. 65 Stat. 611, October 24, 1951, Sec. 1.   15. *Id.*

ACQUISITION OF INFORMATION BY THE GOVERNMENT.

1. The earlier discussion of compulsory testimony should be incorporated by reference into this section, for sake of completeness.
2. 48 Stat. 1, March 9, 1933, Sec. 2.
3. *Id.*   4. 48 Stat. 195, June 16, 1933, Sec. 3 (a).
6. 48 Stat. 881, June 6, 1934, Sec. 4.   5. *Id.*, Sec. 6 (a).
7. 49 Stat. 30, February 22, 1935, Sec. 5 (a).
8. 49 Stat. 1081, August 31, 1935, Sec. 2.
9. 50 Stat. 121, May 1, 1937, Sec. 4 (e).
10. 52 Stat. 631, June 8, 1938, as amended by 56 Stat. 248, April 29, 1942, Sec.5.
11. 48 Stat. 503, March 27, 1934, Sec. (a).
12. 56 Stat. 176, March 27, 1942, Sec. 301.
13. 48 Stat. 58, May 18, 1933, Sec. 5 (h).
14. 52 Stat. 401, May 17, 1938, Sec. 6.
15. 52 Stat. 1255, June 30, 1938.
16. 64 Stat. 149, May 10, 1950, Sec. 2.   17. *Id.*, Sec. 3 (a).
18. 66 Stat. 153, June 23, 1952, Sec. 1.
19. 67 Stat. 559, August 13, 1953, Sec. 2.
20. *Id.*, Sec. 1.
21. 48 Stat. 8, March 20, 1933, Title II, Sec. 3 (a).
22. 48 Stat. 1183, June 19, 1934, Sec. 1.
23. 56 Stat. 176, March 27, 1942, Sec. 1401.
24. *Id.*, Sec. 7307.
25. 58 Stat. 723, July 3, 1944, Sec. 4.

26. 60 Stat. 23, February 20, 1946.
27. 62 Stat. 93, March 30, 1948, Sec. 202.
28. 64 Stat. 1245, January 12, 1951, Sec. 201 (a).
29. 48 Stat. 591, April 14, 1934, Sec. 1.
30. *Id.*, Sec. 2.
31. *Id.*, Sec. 1.   32. 48 Stat. 933, June 12, 1934, Sec. 20.
33. 48 Stat. 1283, June 27, 1934, Sec. 2 (b).
34. 58 Stat. 1120, December 15, 1944, Sec. 2.
35. Civil Rights Act of 1957, Public Law 85-315, 85th Cong., Sept. 9, 1957.
36. *Id.*, Sec. 104 (a) (1)-(3).
37. *Report of the United States Commission on Civil Rights* (Washington: Gov't Printing Office, 1959).
38. House Concurrent Resolution No. 24, August 21, 1937, 50 Stat. 1113.
39. 53 Stat. 811, June 7, 1939, Sec. 7 (a).
40. 61 Stat. 24, March 29, 1947, Sec. 1 (c).
41. 67 Stat. 408, August 7, 1953, Sec. 4.
42. *Id.*, Sec. 9 (a) (6).
43. 64 Stat. 435, August 10, 1950, Sec. 3 (b).
44. 52 Stat. 436, May 23, 1938, Sec. 1, 2.
45. *Id.*   46. 56 Stat. 351, June 11, 1942.
47. *Id.*, Sec. 2.
48. 67 Stat. 230, July 30, 1953, Sec. 212 (b).
49. *Id.*, Sec. 210 (a).   50. *Id.*, Sec. 212 (f) (g).
51. *Id.*, Sec. 219.   52. 58 Stat. 276, June 13, 1944, Sec. 1.
53. 59 Stat. 845, September 11, 1945, Sec. 2.
54. 61 Stat. 495, July 26, 1947, Sec. 102 (d) (3).

PROTECTING FREEDOM OF COMMUNICATION.

1. Emergency Price Control Act of 1942, 56 Stat. 23, 34, January 30, 1942, Sec. 205 (f).
2. 65 Stat. 75, June 19, 1951, Sec. 1 (d).

CHAPTER VIII

ACCOUNTING TO COMMITTEES

1. David M. Levitan, "Responsibility of Administrative Officials in a Democratic Society," 61 *Political Science Quarterly* (December 1946), 562-98.
2. See John A. Perkins, "Congressional Self-Improvement," 38 APSR (June 1944), 499-511; Joint Committee on the Organization of Congress, *Hearings,* 79th Congress, First Session (1945).
3. See Estes Kefauver's plea for a congressional question period in "The Need for Better Executive-Legislative Teamwork in the National Government," 38 APSR (April 1944), 317-25.
4. See Leonard D. White, "Congressional Control of the Public Service," 39 *American Political Science Review,* (February 1945), 1-11.
5. Kefauver, *op. cit.* See Harry A. Foiunlin, Jr., *Dairy of Democracy* (New

York, 1947), the story of the wartime Truman Committee, for examples of such cooperation.

ACCOUNTING TO CONGRESS.

1. *New York Times,* July 14, 1955, pp. 1, 8.
2. 62 Stat. 258, May 21, 1948, Sec. 2.
3. 63 Stat. 714, 720, October 6, 1949, Sec. 408 (c).
4. *Id.*   5. 65 Stat. 373, October 10, 1951.
6. 64 Stat. 10, February 25, 1950, Sec. 2.
7. 64 Stat. 476, August 26, 1950, Sec. 3.
8. 65 Stat. 644, October 26, 1951, Sec. 101, 103 (a).
9. *Id.,* Sec. 103 (b).   10. 67 Stat. 363, August 5, 1953.
11. *Id.,* Sec. 4 (b).
12. 66 Stat. 318, July 1, 1952, Sec. 2.
13. *Id.,* Sec. 9, 10.   14. 67 Stat. 177, July 17, 1953, Sec. 2.
15. *Constitutional Government and Politics* (New York: Harper, 1937), p. 16. Also see Herbert A. Simon's analysis in *Administrative Behavior* (New York: Macmillan, 1954), p. 129f.
16. 62 Stat. 137, April 3, 1948, Sec. 124 (a).
17. 64 Stat. 829, September 11, 1950, Sec. 3.
18. 64 Stat. 798, September 8, 1950, Sec. 712 (b).
19. 66 Stat. 163, June 27, 1952, Sec. 401 (a).
20. *Id.,* Sec. 401 (f).
21. See J. Leiper Freeman, *The Political Process: Executive Bureau-Legislative Committee Relations,* (Garden City: Doubleday, 1955).
22. 65 Stat. 692, October 30, 1951, Sec. 10 (a).
23. 63 Stat. 66, May 11, 1949, Sec. 2.
24. 65 Stat. 365, September 28, 1951, Sec. 601.
25. 66 Stat. 330, 334, July 3, 1952, Sec. 4.
26. 52 Stat. 1249, June 29, 1938.
27. 62 Stat. 1231, July 2, 1948, Sec. 4 (c).
28. 49 Stat. 482, July 18, 1935.
29. 50 Stat. 120, April 27, 1937.
30. 54 Stat. 265, 297, June 11, 1940.
31. 48 Stat. 55, May 2, 1933, Sec. 3 (d).
32. 56 Stat. 351, 357, June 11, 1942, Sec. 12.
33. An Act: To expedite national defense, 54 Stat. 676, June 28, 1940. An Act: Further to promote the defense of the United States, 55 Stat. 31, March 11, 1941. An Act: To make emergency provision for certain activities of the United States Maritime Commission, 55 Stat. 148, May 2, 1941. Emergency Price Control Act of 1942, 56 Stat. 23, January 30, 1942. Contract Settlement Act of 1944, 58 Stat. 649, July 1, 1944. Export Control of 1949, 63 Stat. 7, February 26, 1949. Army Organization Act of 1949, 64 Stat. 1245, January 12, 1951, Sec. 303 (f) (" . . . the Federal Civil Defense Adminstrator to report quarterly during the period of any such emergency.").
34. An Act: To authorize the President to requisition property required for the defense of the United States, 55 Stat. 742, October 16, 1941. Atomic Energy

Act of 1946, 60 Stat. 755, August 1, 1946. Mutual Defense Assistance Act of 1949, 63 Stat. 714, October 6, 1949. Mutual Security Act of 1951, 65 Stat. 373, October 10, 1951. An Act: To liquidate the Reconstruction Finance Corporation and to establish the Small Business Administration, 67 Stat. 230, July 30, 1953.

35. 64 Stat. 438, August 11, 1950, Sec. 6, authorizing the Commissioners of the District of Columbia to establish an office of Civil Defense.

36. Merchant Marine Act, 1936, 49 Stat. 1985, June 29, 1936, Sec. 208.

37. Securities Exchange Act of 1934, 48 Stat. 881, June 6, 1934, Sec. 4. National Housing Act, 48 Stat. 1246, June 27, 1934, Title I, Sec. 5 (". . . and annual report to the congress as soon as practicable after the 1st day of January in each year . . .'). Neutrality Act of 1935, 49 Stat. 1081, August 31, 1935, Sec. 2. 1937 Amendment to Neutrality Act of 1935, 50 Stat. 121, May 1, 1937, Sec. 4 (j). An Act: Authorizing the conservation, production, exploitation, and sale of helium gas . . ., 500 Stat. 885, September 1, 1937. A 1938 Act concerning the leasing of naval petroleum reserves, 52 Stat. 1252, June 30, 1938. An Act: To facilitate certain construction work for the Army, 53 Stat. 1239, August 7, 1939. Second War Powers Act, 1942, 56 Stat. 176, March 27, 1942, Title XI, Acceptance of conditional gifts to further the war program, Sec. 1105. Sixth Supplemental National Defense Appropriation Act, 1942, 56 Stat. 226, April 28, 1942, Sec. 2 (" . . . within sixty days after the end of each fiscal year . . . "). Amend. to Foreign Agents Registration Act of 1938, 56 Stat. 248, April 29, 1942, Sec. 11. Federal Airport Act, 60 Stat. 170, May 13, 1946. Act increasing membership of National Advisory Committee for Aeronautics, 62 Stat. 266, May 25, 1948. Foreign Economic Assistance Act of 1950, 64 Stat. 198, June 5, 1950, Sec. 415. An Act . . . providing for continuation and expansion of Western Hemisphere production of abaca . . . , 64 Stat. 435, August 10, 1950, Sec. 7 (" . . . Within six months after the close of each fiscal year . . . "). Amend. to Merchant Marine Act, 1936, 64 Stat. 773, September 7, 1950, Sec. 1211.

38. 64 Stat. 263, June 28, 1950, Sec. 201 (c).

39. 50 Stat. 121, May 1, 1937, Sec. 4 (j).

40. 50 Stat. 885, September 1, 1937.

41. *Id.*, Sec. 4.   42. 52 Stat. 1252, 1253, June 30, 1938, Sec. 1.

43. 53 Stat. 1239, August 7, 1939, Sec. 1 (d).

44. 56 Stat. 226, 244, April 28, 1942, Sec. 401.

45. 48 Stat. 591, April 14, 1934, Sec. 1.

46. 48 Stat. 58, May 18, 1933.

47. *Id.*, Sec. 23..

48. 48 Stat. 933, June 12, 1934, Sec. 20.

49. 48 Stat. 1064, June 19, 1934, Title I, Sec. 4 (k).

50. 60 Stat. 664, July 25, 1946, Sec. 1A (b) (c).

51. 61 Stat. 136, June 23, 1947, Sec. 210.

52. 65 Stat. 75, June 19, 1951, Sec. 4 (k).

THE CONCURRENT RESOLUTION.

1. Estes Kefauver, "The Challenge to Congress," 6 Fed. Bar J., 325-32, (April 1945).

2. Bertram M. Gross, *The Legislative Struggle* (New York, 1953).

3. Art. I, Sec. 7. See Howard White, "Executive Responsibility to Congress

via Concurrent Resolution," 36 *American Political Science Review* (October 1942), 895-900.

4. White, *op. cit.*

5. Emergency Price Control Act of 1942, 56 Stat. 23, January 30, 1942, Sec. 1 (b).

6. An Act: Further to promote the defense of the United States, 55 Stat. 31, March 11, 1941, Sec. 3.

Second War Powers Act, 56 Stat. 176, March 27, 1942, Sec. 1501.

An Act: To mobilize small business concerns for war production, 56 Stat. 351, June 11, 1942, Sec. 12.

An Act: To further expedite the prosecution of the war by authorizing the control of the exportation of certain commodities, 56 Stat. 463, Jun 30, 1942, Sec. 6 (d).

An Act: To amend the Act which permits the President to requisition certain articles for national defense, 56 Stat. 467, July 2, 1942, Sec. 2.

An Act: To amend the Act authorizing vessels of Canadian registry to transport iron or on the Great Lakes during 1942, 56 Stat. 735, August 1, 1942.

An Act: To suspend temporarily the running of statutes of limitations appicable to certain offenses, 56 Stat. 747, August 24, 1942.

An Act: To amend . . . the Communications Act of 1934, 57 Stat. 161, June 27, 1943.

The War Labor Disputes Act, 57 Stat. 163, June 25, 1943, Sec. 10.

An Act: To extend the Selective Training and Service Act of 1940, 59 Stat. 166, May 9, 1945, Sec. 1.

First Decontrol Act of 1947, 61 Stat. 34, March 31, 1947, Sec. 1501.

Export Control Act of 1949, 63 Stat. 7, February 26, 1949, Sec. 12.

Mutual Defense Assistance Act of 1949, 63 Stat. 714, October 6, 1949, Sec. 405 (d).

Foreign Economic Assistance Act of 1950, 64 Stat. 198, June 5, 1950, Sec. 409 (b).

The Defense Production Act of 1950, 64 Stat. 798, September 8, 1950, Sec. 17, 716.

An Act: To amend the Civil Aeronautics Act of 1938, 64 Stat. 825, September 9, 1950, Sec. 1205.

Federal Civil Defense Act of 1950, 64 Stat. 1245, January 12, 1951, Sec. 307.

Amendment to the First War Powers Act, 1941, 64 Stat. 1257, January 12, 1951, Sec. 12.

Mutual Security Act of 1951, 65 Stat. 373, October 10, 1951, Sec. 530.

67 Stat. 133, June 30, 1953, Sec. 2157.

An Act: To provide certain construction and other authorization for the military departments in time of war or national emergency, 67 Stat. 177, July 17, 1953, Sec. 1.

Military traffic continuance Act, 67 Stat. 244, July 31, 1953.

7. *Op. cit.*, Sec. 405 (d).

8. 55 Stat. 616, August 11, 1941, Sec. 1. See also the Act of June 30, 1953, 67 Stat. 115, continuing certain emergency statutes in effect "until six months after the termination of the national emergency proclaimed by the President on December 16, 1950 . . . or until such earlier date as the Congress by con-

current resolution declares that it is no longer necessary to exercise the powers continued in force and effect by this act."

9. 56 Stat. 18, January 26, 1942.

10. 64 Stat. 1245, January 12, 1951, Sec. 301.

11. E.g., amendment to the Military Personnel Claims Act of 1945, 67 Stat. 317, August 1, 1953. As is usual, the President might establish such dates by proclamation.

12. 54 Stat. 4, November 4, 1939, Sec. 1 (a).

13. 53 Stat. 561, April 3, 1939, Sec. 5; 59 Stat. 613, December 20, 1945, Sec. 6 (a), and 63 Stat. 203, June 20, 1949, Sec. 6.

14. *Op. cit.*, Sec. 2 (a).

15. 60 Stat. 1329. See also 62 Stat. 1428, March 16, 1948, (H. Concurrent Resolution disapproving Reorganization Plan No. 1 of January 19, 1948).

16. Despite this provision, the Congress chose to approve Reorganization Plan No. 1 of 1953 by joint resolution, in order that it might in the course of approving it, also amend it. 67 Stat. 18, April 1, 1953.

17. 64 Stat. 1245, January 12, 1951, Sec. 201 (g).

18. 54 Stat. 670, June 28, 1940, Sec. 20.

19. Concurrent Resolution: Granting of Permanent Residence to Certain Aliens. 65 Stat. B16, April 11, 1951, H. Con. Res. 49.

20. Concurrent Resolution: Deportation Suspensions. 65 Stat. B3, March 6, 1951, S. Con. Res. 7.

Concurrent Resolution: Deportation Suspensions. 65 Stat. B13, March 12, 1951, S. Con. Res. 6.

Concurrent Resolution: Deportation Suspensions. 65 Stat. B18, April 17, 1951, S. Con. Res. 13.

Concurrent Resolution: Deportation Suspensions. 66 Stat. B4, April 1, 1952, S. Con. Res. 58 (over 600).

Concurrent Resolution: Deportation Suspension. 66 Stat. B17, April 9, 1952, S. Con. Res. 63 (over 400).

Concurrent Resolution: Deportation Suspension. 66 Stat. B26, May 20, 1952, S. Con. Res. 67 (over 450).

Concurrent Resolution: Deportation Suspensions. 66 Stat. B40, May 27, 1952, S. Con. Res. 66 (over 250).

Concurrent Resolution: Deportation Suspension. 66 Stat. B36, May 20, 1952, S. Con. Res. 68 (over 200).

Concurrent Resolution: Deportation Suspension. 66 Stat. B65, July 3, 1952, S. Con. Res. 72 (over 300).

Concurrent Resolution: Deportation Suspension. 66 Stat. B72, July 3, 1952, S. Con. Res. 76 (over 400).

Concurrent Resolution: Deportation Suspension. 66 Stat. B81, July 4, 1952, S. Con. Res. 81 (over 600).

Concurrent Resolutions, 1953. The 83rd Congress first session, by concurrent resolution provided for the permanent residence of over 900 aliens in the U.S. and suspended the deportation of over 6,200 aliens. 67 Stat. B5ff.

21. 67 Stat. 408, August 7, 1953, Sec. 3, 9.

22. Amendments to the Universal Military Training and Service Act, 65 Stat. 75, June 19, 1951, Sec. 4.

23. 56 Stat. 9 (1942).

24. H. Con. Res. 9 and 10 (1943; H. Con. Res. 81, 93 (1944); S. Con. Res. 9, 18 and H. Con. Res. 1, 2, 6, 15, 20, 24, 26, 56, 59, 70, 73, 74, 76, 77, 78, 79, 82 (1945).

25. H. Con. Res. 51 (1951).

26. 55 Stat. 31, 32 Sec. 3(c) (1941).

27. 56 Stat. 176, 187 (1942). "Titles I to IX, inclusive, and titles XI and XIV of this Act, and the amendments to existing law made by any such title, shall remain in force only until December 31, 1944, or until such earlier time as the Congress by concurrent resolution, or the President, may designate. . . ."

28. H. Con. Res. 21 (1947).

29. H. Con. Res. 138 (1946), providing for termination of an Act of July 14, 1941, providing for priority in transportation by merchant vessels for national defense purposes. 55 Stat. 591 (1941).

30. H. Con. Res. 85, 86, 91, 98 (1945); H. Con. Res. 132, 133, 156 (1946); H. Con. Res. 5, 9, 25 (1947).

31. S. Con. Res. 31, H. Con. Res. 81 (1945).

32. 91 *Cong. Rec.* 9099, 9217; 59 Stat. 846 (1945).

33. 54 Stat. 4 (1939).

34. *Ibid.*, Sec. 1 (a).

35. The words are those of Senator Gillette at 76 *Cong. Rec.* 355 (1940).

36. S. Con. Res. 35 (1940).

37. S. Con. Res. 36, and H. Con Res. 44 (1940).

38. H. Con. Res. 44 (1941).

39. 92 *Cong. Rec.* 7911, 8994; 60 Stat. Pt. 2 (1946).

40. 93 *Cong. Rec.* 6722, 7857; 60 Stat. Pt. 2, 1023 (1947).

41. H. on C. Res. 131, 80 *Cong. Rec.* 1721, 2921; 62 Stat. Pt. 2, 1428 (1948).

42. 63 Stat. 203, 205 (1949).

43. 95 *Cong. Rec.* 11561 (1949).

44. S. Con. Res. 42 and H. Con. Res. 61 (1940); H. Con. Res. 50 (1947).

45. H. Con. Res. 151, 154 (1946); H. Con. Res. 5 (1947).

46. S. Con. Res. 16, H. Con. Res. 19 (1939); S. Con. Res. 43 (1940); S. Con. Res. 66 (1946).

47. H. Con. Res. 60 (1940).

CHAPTER IX

Communication

1. Chapter IX, on "The Problem of Interest Groups," in Emmett S. Redford's notable study, *Administration of National Economic Control* (New York: Macmillan, 1952), is one of the most complete and valuable reviews of literature on the role of groups in federal regulatory programs.

2. Herbert A. Simon, *Administration Behavior* (New York: Macmillan, 1954), p. 154.

3. 56 Stat. 248, April 29, 1942, Sec. 4 (d).

4. 52 Stat. 1175, June 25, 1938, Sec. 316.

5. *The American College Dictionary.*

6. 48 Stat. 211, June 16, 1933, Sec. 6 (a).
7. 64 Stat. 798, September 8, 1950, Sec. 404.
8. 60 Stat. 798, May 13, 1946, Sec. 3 (a).
9. 60 Stat. 128, April 30, 1946, Sec. 10 (a), 102 (a).
10. 48 Stat. 943, June 12, 1934, Sec. 4.
11. 48 Stat. 811, May 28, 1934.
12. 55 Stat. 31, March 11, 1941, Sec. 3 (a).
13. 64 Stat. 773, September 7, 1950, Sec. 1202 (a).
14. 64 Stat. 825, September 9, 1950, Sec. 1203.
15. 55 Stat. 606, July 29, 1941, Sec. 2.
16. 61 Stat. 678, July 30, 1947, Sec. 3.
17. 54 Stat. 1137, October 14, 1940, Sec. 326 (d).
18. 55 Stat. 606, July 29, 1941, Sec. 2.
19. 65 Stat. 69, June 15, 1951, Sec. 5.
20. 165 Proclamation No. 2931, 65 Stat. 314, June 19, 1951.
21. 65 Stat. 75, June 19, 1951, Sec. 4.
22. 49 Stat. 340, June 14, 1935, Sec. 2.
23. Proclamation No. 2272, 52 Stat. 1534, January, 1938.
24. Note 13, *supra*.
25. 64 Stat. 798, September 8, 1950, Sec. 708 (b), (c).
26. 64 Stat. 476, August 26, 1950.
27. 67 Stat. 408, August 7, 1953, Sec. 3 (c), and (d); 9 (a) (4).
28. 56 Stat. 248, April 29, 1942, Sec. 3.
29. 56 Stat. 176, March 27, 1942, Sec. 501.
30. 58 Stat. 723, July 3, 1944.
31. 66 Stat. 6, February 11, 1952.
32. Proclamation No. 2979, 66 Stat. 35, June, 1952.
33. 63 Stat. 7, February 26, 1949, Sec. (a), (c).
34. James C. Charlesworth, *Government Administration* (New York: Harper, 1951), pp. 252-53, attibutes to the term "integration" the meaning "administrative wholeness, or oneness, or entireness, or-completeness of the elements under control." We would lend the term the same positive tone but use it to indicate tendency or emphasis.
35. The words "co-operation" and "co-ordination" are taken from the texts of statutes, and it is assumed that they have distinctive meanings in the law. "Joint decision-making" and "mutual assistance" are obvious designations for the administrative relationships described in the statutes concerned.

It would be digressive to incorporate any lengthy discussion of the concepts of "co-operation" and "co-ordination" in the text of this book. It should, however, be pointed out that they are fuzzy concepts, indeed, as employed in standard public administration texts, and as defined in standard dictionaries. The indices of Leonard D. White, *Introduction to the Study of Public Administration* (3rd ed.; New York: Macmillan, 1948), John M. Pfiffner and R. Vance Presthus, *Public Administration* (3rd ed.; New York: Ronald Press, 1953), and John D. Millet, *Management in the Public Service* (New York: McGraw-Hill, 1954), do not list "co-operation." Herbert A. Simon, Donald W. Smithburg, and Victor A. Thompson, *Public Administration* (New York: Knopf, 1950), equate administration with co-operation: "When two men co-operate to roll a stone neither could have moved alone, the rudiments of administration have appeared" (p.3). "Any activity involving the conscious co-operation of two or more persons can be called organized activity . . . Thus, by formal organization we mean a planned system of co-operation effort in which each participant has a recognized role to play and duties or tasks to perform" (p.5). ". . . the dignity of the individual can be respected only in an administrative situation in which all partcipants will gan, in one way or another, from the accomplishment of the organization goal. In such a situation, administration can be 'co-operative' in the broadest sense" (p. 23). Charlesworth, *op. cit.*, imputes to co-operation the attributes of "a fast-moving automatic machine, every part (of which) must be positively controlled, so that at any particular phase of the machine's operation, every part is in a precisely predetermined place, and no other place" (p. 220).

Co-ordination, to James D. Mooney and Alan C. Reiley, *Onward Industry* (New York: Harper, 1931), "expresses the principles of organization in toto." All other principles are merely those through which co-ordination acts. And co-ordination means to "act together" (p. 19). White, having criticized Mooney and Reiley for taking the concept of co-ordination to express "the whole of administration," suggests that "to co-ordinate is to bring about the consistent and harmonious action of persons with each other toward a common end" (p. 210). This, some would regard as a shorthand definition of administration.

Charlesworth, *op. cit.*, and Simon, *Administrative Behavior*, attempt to distinguish between co-operation and co-ordination. Charlesworth's effort is perhaps the most elaborate, and Simon's seems, in the context of this study, to have the most operational utility. Charlesworth distinguishes between "vertical and horizontal" co-ordination, and stresses that "co-ordination is promoted both structurally and procedurally" (pp. 245-46). Apparently attributing to the term "integration" the same meaning previously assigned to "co-operation" (Administrative integration means administrative wholeness, or oneness, or entireness, or completeness of the elements of control."), he distinguishes between integration and co-ordination: "Integration is different from co-ordination in that co-ordination relates to causing disjunct elements to work harmoniously together whereas integration relates to the completeness and wholeness of the controls by which the harmony is brought about . . ." (pp. 252-53).

Simon suggests that "Perhaps it would clarify discussion of administrative theory to use the term 'co-ordination' for activity in which the participants share a common goal, and 'co-ordination' for the process of informing each as to the planned behaviors of the others. Hence, co-operation will usually be ineffective—will not reach its goal, whatever the intentions of the participants—in the absence of co-ordination" (p. 72).

These quotations have been placed in juxtaposition to illustrate existing inconsistencies and ambiguities in the use of the terms co-operation and co-ordination in most standard works on public administration in the United States. It would be distortive of the purpose of this study to undertake to refine and relate these concepts. We do suggest, however, that administrative theorists undertaking this task could profitably seek insight in statutory materials and administrative histories—i.e., empirical data.

36. 53 Stat. 811, June 7, 1939, Sec. 2, 3.
37. 53 Stat. 1407, August 11, 1939.

38. 63 Stat. 208, June 20, 1949, Sec. 8.
39. 66 Stat. 163, January 27, 1952, Sec. 201 (b); 202.
40. Proclamation No. 2980, 66 Stat. 136, June 30, 1952.
41. 61 Stat. 495, July 26, 1947, Sec. 2.
42. 56 Stat. 351, June 11, 1942.
43. 58 Stat. 190, April 5, 1944.
44. 59 Stat. 231, June 5, 1945.
45. 64 Stat. 798, September 8, 1950, Sec. 401.
46. 56 Stat. 23, January 30, 1942, Sec. 1 (a).
47. Id.   48. 64 Stat. 5, February 14, 1950, Sec. 3 (d), (e).
49. 65 Stat. 69, June 15, 1951, Sec. 5.
50. 48 Stat. 58, May 18, 1933, Sec. 5 (j), (k).
51. 50 Stat. 885, September 1, 1937, Sec. 3 (a).
52. 55 Stat. 591, July 14, 1941, Sec. 4 (s).
53. 62 Stat. 274, May 26, 1948.
54. 64 Stat. 438, August 11, 1950, Sec. 3 (a), (f).
55. 64 Stat. 149, May 10, 1950, Sec. 3 (a).
56. 66 Stat. 163, June 27, 1952.
57. 49 Stat. 1081, August 31, 1935, Sec. 2 (a).
58. 58 Stat. 649, July 1, 1944, Sec. 4, 5.
59. 60 Stat. 755, August 1, 1946.
60. 62 Stat. 266, May 25, 1948.

CHAPTER X

1."The Constitution as Instrument and as Symbol," 30 *American Political Science Review*, 1936, 1071 at 1077.

2. Yet note Harold D. Lasswell's suggestion: "It is important to view the court system as a whole and not limit ourselves entirely to the words uttered by the Supreme Court. The damage to private rights and civilian principles can be accomplished in the thousands of minor jurisdictions (Federal, State, Local) into which our country is divided. Much of this damage is not brought to the notice of the highest tribunal in the land, if at all, until years have elapsed. In one of our earliest crises of national security, for example, the Alien and Sedition Acts were passed (1798). Thousands of persons were imprisoned, and the Acts were presently repealed. Their constitutionality was never passed upon by the Supreme Sourt." *National Security and Individual Freedom* (New York: McGraw-Hill, 1950), pp. 45-46.

3. Albert L. Sturm. "Emergencies and the President," II *Journal of Politics*, 1949, 121, 141. Sturm said: "Since the judiciary handles a mere trickle of the great issues arising in periods of crisis, it has been unable to retain its traditional potency. When the national security is imperiled, the Supreme Court, along with the other branches of the government, becomes a part of the national mechanism for preserving the existing social order." We doubt that the Supreme Court and the judicial system have adequately been integrated into this effort thus far.

4. Note, c.f., *Duncan v. Kahanamouku*, 327 U.S. 304 (1946), in which Justice Black on behalf of the majority was careful to rest upon statutory interpretation his

1946 (post mortem) invalidation of certain aspects of military rule in the Hawaiian Islands during the War. Dissenting, Burton and Frankfurter asked the Justices in the majority whether the latter, if obliged to dispose of the case during the conduct of the war, would have reached the same conclusion and whether their holding would have been enforced by the Executive.

5. *Op. cit.*, p. 131. Rossiter concludes that "As in the past, so in the future, President and Congress will fight our wars with little or no thought about a reckoning with the Supreme Court . . . This is a sad moral to proclaim after so long a journey, but it is one that we should have firmly fixed in our constitutional understanding."

THE SUPREME COURT'S APPROACH

1. See *Ex parte Merryman*, Fed. Cas. No. 9487 (1861), 17 Fed. Cas., p. 144.
2. Carl B. Swisher, *Roger B. Taney*, New York: Macmillan, 1936, p. 567.
3. 4 Wall. 2 (1866).
4. *Ex parte* Milligan, *op. cit.*, at pp. 120-21, 126.
5. *Id.*, at 139.   6. 327 U. S. 304 (1946).   7. *Id.*, at 328.
8. *Constitutional Power and World Affairs* (New York: Columbia University Press, 1919).
9. 299 U. S. 304 (1936).   10. *Op. cit.*, p. 97.
11. *U. S.* v. *Curtiss-Wright, op cit.*, pp. 316-318.
12. 323 U. S. 214 (1944).   13. *Id.*, at 244.
14. *Id.*, at 246.   15. *Id.*, at 248
16. Edward S. Corwin, *Total War and the Constitution* (New York: Knopf, 1946), p. 80.
17. 249 U. S. 47 (1919). Holmes' reasoning was perhaps based on J. S. Mill's analysis in his essay "On Liberty:" "No one pretends that actions should be as free as opinions. On the contrary, even opinions lose their immunity when the circumstances in which they are expressed are such as to constitute their expression a positive instigation to some mischievous act." *On Liberty* (New York: Dutton, 1950), Ch. III, p. 152.
18. Discussed subsequently in relation to the *Dennis* case.
19. 249 U. S. 47 at p. 52 (1919).
20. *Abrams* v. *United States*, 250 U. S. 616 (1919).
21. *Id.*, at 628-29.
22. *Gitlow* v. *New York*, 268 U.S. 652 (1925); *Whitney* v. *California*, 274 U.S. 357 (1927.   23. 18 USC 2385.
24. 183 F. 2d 201, 212-13 (1950). See, Robert G. McCloskey, "Free Speech, Sedition and the Constitution," 45 APSR, 1951, pp. 662-673.
25. *Dennis* v. *United States*, 341 U.S. 494 (1951). This incidentally is one of many cases in which restrictive measures which doubtless would have been upheld during a wartime emergency, were sustained as a valid exercise of governmental power during peace time. In *American Communications Association* v. *Douds*, 339 U. S. 382 (1949), the Court upheld the Communist oath provision of the Taft-Hartley Act, not as justified in an emergency situation such as we then faced, and confront today, but as a normal power of Congress accruing to it under the Commerce Clause.

26. *Home Bldg. & Loan Ass'n v. Blaisdell,* 290 U.S. 398, 426 (1934). This is a reiteration of a quotation from his "War Powers Under the Constitution," 42 ABA REPORTS, 1917, 238. Also in 8 Doc. 105; 65th Cong., 1st Sess., pp. 7-8.

27. *Hirabayashi* v. *United States,* 320 U.S. 81, esp. 93 (1942); *Korematsu* v. *United States,* 323 U.S. 214 (1944).

28. *Bowles* v. *Willingham,* 321 U.S. 503, esp. 519 (1944).

29. *Op. cit.,* 219. Cf. his narrow view of the meaning of martial law in *Duncan* v. *Kahanamoku, supra,* pp. 22-23.

A MORE EFFECTIVE EMERGENCY ROLE FOR THE JUDICIARY.

1. *Ex parte Endo,* 323 U.S. 283 (1944); *Brannan* v. *Stark,* 342 U.S. 451 (1952), are examples of the Supreme Court performing at this modest but effective level.

2. *The Prize Cases,* 2 Black 635 (1863), and *Hirabayashi* v. *United States, op. cit.,* and *Korematsu* v. *United States, op. cit.,* are examples of the judiciary's willingness to accept *post hoc* Congressional validation of an executive emergency program.

THE STEEL SEIZURE CASES.[1].

1. *Youngstown Sheet & Tube Co.* v. *Sawyer,* 343 U.S. 579.

2. 17 Fed. Reg. 3139.

3. The phrase is that of James Willard Hurst. *The Growth of American Law,* (Boston: Little, Brown and Co., 1950), p. 397.

4. *Youngstown Sheet & Tube Co.* v. *Sawyer, op. cit.,* at 582.

5. *Youngstown Sheet & Tube Co., et. al.,* v. *Sawyer,* 103 F. Supp. 978.

6. *Id.,* at 980, 981.

7. *Youngstown Sheet & Tube Co., et al.,* v. *Sawyer,* 103 F. Supp. 569.

8. *Id.,* at 573.

9. Mr. A. Holmes Baldridge, the Assistant Attorney General, conducting the government's defense, rejected every opportunity offered by the District Court to justify the seizure order under a particular clause of the Constitution, or a specific statute. See *Youngstown Sheet & Tube Co.* v. *Sawyer,* Dockets No. 744 and 745, 1952. Transcript of Record, *passim.* (Washington, 1952). In his brief filed with Judge Pine on April 25, Mr. Baldridge claimed for "The President of the United States of America . . . inherent power in such a situation to take possession of the steel companies in the manner and to the extent which he did by his Executive Order of April 8, 1952. This power is supported by the Constitution, by historical precedent, and by court decisions." *Defendant's Opposition to Plaintiff's Motion for a Preliminary Injunction* — Filed April 25, 1952, p. 113.

10. *Transcript of Record, op. cit.,* p. 377. In addition, the following colloquy is illuminating:

The Court: " . . . As I understand it, you do not assert any statutory power."

Mr. Baldridge: "That is correct."

The Court: "And you do not assert any express constitutional power."

Mr. Baldridge: "Well, Your Honor, we base the President's power on Sections 1, 2 and 3 or Article II of the Constitution, and whatever inherent, implied or residual powers may flow therefrom . . . ."

The Court: "So you contend the Executive has unlimited power in time of emergency."

Mr. Baldridge: "He has the power to take such action as is necessary to meet the emergency."

The Court: "If the emergency is great, it is unlimited, is it?"

Mr. Baldridge: "I suppose if you carry it to its logical conclusion, that is true."
11. 299 U.S. 304, 316-18 (1936).

12. Most of the literature on the subject of emergency power presents an analysis of the range of actual power previously asserted by the President in time of emergency.

13. Scores of examples of such action can be gleaned from the studies cited above, and the dissenting opinion of Chief Justice Vinson in the *Steel Seizure* cases, *op. cit.*, at 667-710. E.g., Lincoln directed the payment of unappropriated funds from the treasury to private individuals, in clear violation of Article I, Sec. 9, Cl. 7 of the Constitution. In patent disregard of Article I, Sec. 8, Cl. 12, delegating to Congress the power "to raise and support armies," he increased the strength of the Army and Navy by presidential proclamation. Binkley, *op. cit.*, pp. 111-14. Corwin has pointed to many administrative agencies established by President Roosevelt without prior legislative sanction (*Total War and the Constitution*, op. cit., pp. 50-52) and has alleged that the transfer of destroyers to Britain directly violated "at least two statutes and represented an exercise by the President of a power which by the Constitution is specifically assigned to Congress." (*The President: Office and Powers, op. cit.*, p. 289; 4th ed., 1957, p. 238).

14. 343 U.S. 579 at 611.   15. *Petitioners' Brief*, p. 66.
16. 343 U.S. 579 at 646.

17. *Sawyer v. United States Steel Co., et. al.*, 197 F. 2d 582 (1952). Both the government and the steel companies petitioned the Supreme Court for *certiorari*.

18. *Id.* Four of the nine judges dissented. The majority, citing *United States* v. *Russell*, 13 Wall. 623 (1871) and *United States* v. *Pee Wee Coal Co., Inc.*, 341 U.S. 114 (1951), found judicial precedent for emergency requisitioning of property by the executive, unsupported by statute, with a concomitant right to compensation on the part of the property owners. Since the government claimed that continued production of steel was vital to the national security, and admitted the right of the companies to compensation, the majority thought the preliminary injunction should be stayed. *Id.*, at 585.

19. 343 U.S. 937. Burton, J., with Frankfurter, J., concurring, noted their belief that *certiorari* should be denied until the cases had been fully heard, on their merits, in the Court of Appeals. *Id.*, at 938-39.

20. *Youngstown Sheet & Tube Co.* v. *Sawyer*, Dockets No. 744 and 745, 1952, *Brief for Petitioner.* Perlman speaks of "inherent constitutional power," however. *Id.*, at 113.

21. *Id.*, at 19-20.

22. *Id.*, at 102-150.   23. *Id.*, at 26.   24. *Id.*, at 73.
25. *Id.*, at 49.   26. *Id.*, at 48.   27. *Id.*, at 49.   28. *Id.*, at 16.

29. *Little* v. *Barreme*, 2 Cranch 170 (1804). (The above discussion of the case closely parallels that in *Petitioner's Brief*, pp. 44-46.

30. *Id.*, at 588.   31. *Id.*, at 585.   32. *Id.*, at 587.
33. *Id.*   34. *Id.*

35. "The Steel Seizure Case: A Judicial Brick Without Straw," 53 *Columbia Law Review*, 53-66, 64-65 (1953).

36. Frankfurter, J., *op. cit.*, 589 and 593-614; Jackson, J., 634-55; Burton, J., 655-60; Clark, J., 660-67; Douglas, J., 629-34.

37. *Id.*, at 637. This identical element is present in Justice Clark's concurring opinion, and perhaps it is more clearly stated. *Id.*, 660-61. Corwin says: "Only Justice Clark, however, guided by Marshall's opinion in the early case of *Little* v. *Barreme*, had the courage to draw the appropriate conclusion: Congress having entered the field, its ascertainable intention supplied the law of the case." *Op. cit.*, at 65.

38. *Id.*, at 634.

39. *Id.*, at 635.   400. *Id.*, at 635-637.   41. *Id.*, at 640.

42. *Op. cit.*   43. *Youngstown Sheet & Tube Co.* v. *Sawyer, op cit.*, at 662.

44. *Id.*   45. *Id.*

46. *Op. cit.*, 667-710, 708. Reed and Minton, JJ. concurred in Vinson's dissent.

The Steel Strike of 1959.

1. Texts of Comments in the Steel Dispute — The President's Letter, *New York Times*, September 9, 1959. The Union reply appears in the same issue; that of the major steel firms appeared in the *New York Times*, September 10, 1959. Reprinted in the *Congressional Record* for September 15, 1959, pp. 18102-18103.

2. 61 Stat. 136, 155 as amended, 29 U.S.C. 176-180.

3. Section 206 states: "Whenever in the opinion of the President of the United States, a threatened or actual strike or lock-out affecting an entire industry or a substantial part thereof engaged in trade, commerce, transportation, transmission, or communication among the several States or with foreign nations, or engaged in the production of goods for commerce, will, if permitted to occur or to continue, imperil the national health or safety, he may appoint a board of inquiry to inquire the issues involved in the dispute and to make a written report to him within such time as he shall prescribe. Such report shall include a statement of the facts with respect to the dispute, including each party's statement of its position but shall not contain any recommendaions. The President shall file a copy of such report with the Service and shall make its contents available to the public."

4. The board was originally directed to make its report on October 16, 1959, but the time was extended until October 19 by Executive Order No. 10848.

5. Report to the President of the Board of Inquiry, Oct. 19, 1959, pp. 11-33.

6. *Id.*, p. 28.

7. *United Steelworkers of America*, Petitioner v. *United States of America*, Brief for the United States in Opposition, p. 5.

8. *Id.*, pp. 11-14. Affidavits of Acting Secretary of Defense Thomas Gates; A. R. Luedecke, General Manager of the Atomic Energy Commission; Hugh L. Dryden, Deputy Administrator of NASA.

9. Government Brief, "The Findings of the District Court," pp. 23-26; 71-81.

10. Govt's brief, p. 26.

11. See Anthony Lewis "Supreme Court Agrees to Rule in Steel Dispute," *New York Times*, Tuesday, October 30, 1959, p. 1, col. 3.

12. United Steelworkers of America v. U.S., 361 U.S. 39 (1959).

INDEX